SERIAL KILLERS

Shocking, Gripping True Crime Stories of the Most Evil Murders

BRIAN INNES

Quercus

First published in Great Britain in 2006 by Quercus Editions Ltd

This updated and revised paperback edition published in 2017 by

Quercus Editions Ltd
Carmelite House
50 Victoria Embankment
London EC4Y 0DZ

An Hachette UK company

A CIP catalogue record for this book is available
from the British Library

PB ISBN 9781786488473

eBook ISBN 9781786488985

Every effort has been made to contact copyright holders.
However, the publishers will be glad to rectify in future editions
any inadvertent omissions brought to their attention.

Quercus Editions Ltd hereby exclude all liability to the extent
permitted by law for any errors or omissions in this book and for
any loss, damage or expense (whether direct or indirect) suffered by
a third party relying on any information contained in this book.

Text by: Brian Innes

2017 text updates by: Nigel Cawthorne

10 9 8 7 6 5 4 3 2 1

Typeset by e-type

Printed and bound in the UK by Clays Ltd. St Ives Plc

CONTENTS

The dates cited below refer to the period from the first known murder to conviction and imprisonment – or year of execution.

INTRODUCTION

History is full of tales of mass murder, both political and domestic. However, what is now called 'serial' killing is something different. Furthermore, it is a disturbing – and increasing – phenomenon of the twentieth century that looks set to continue into the present century. In the past, mass murder was committed either from sheer brutality, for profit, or from some kind of pathological interest in the process of death. Among the brutes, the Harpe brothers, who were only a single instance of the wildness of the 'Wild West' during the eighteenth and nineteenth centuries, are a prime example.

There were many in the past who murdered regularly for profit, most of whom were vagrant thieves of one kind or another. With the establishment of life assurance during the nineteenth century, another motive developed. Taking a policy on the life of someone, and then killing them, was a sure means of profiting. In Britain, for example, the poisoner William Palmer and George Joseph Smith (the 'Brides in the Bath' murderer) are famous instances.

As for those who seem to have killed solely from an obsession with death, Helene Jegado (who poisoned at least 24 people in nineteenth-century France) and nurse Jane Toppan, 'the Angel of Death' (who killed as many as 70 of her patients in late nineteenth-century New England), are notorious examples.

Serial killers, however, can be distinguished from any of the foregoing. Their murders are not political, not domestic and not for profit. Rather, they appear to be motivated by a rage against some specific element or aspect of society. The phenomenon, although it can occur anywhere in the world, is particularly prevalent in the Americas. In fact, serial murder in the United States alone makes up more than three-quarters of the estimated world total.

During the 1950s and 1960s, an average 10,000 homicides per year were committed in the United States. However, nearly all of the cases were solved within twelve months, because most concerned someone close to the victim – a spouse, relative, neighbour or a colleague. However, in 1980 alone 23,000 people were murdered, many for no apparently explicable reason. At this time, the Administration recognized finally that a new category of violent crime existed; and with the election of Ronald Reagan as President, the Task Force on Violent Crime was set up under the new Attorney General, William French Smith. The murder rate has fallen in the United States, to 12,253 murders in 2013.

Foremost among those whom the organization enlisted to this Task Force was, of course, another long-standing law enforcement body – the FBI. In 1982, limited funds were allocated for the establishment of a Violent Criminal Apprehension Program (VICAP), and among those drawn in was Robert Ressler, who had for some ten years been a member of the FBI's Behavioral Science Unit, devoted to the identification of the characteristics of violent criminals.

Ressler and his colleagues have defined a serial killer as follows: '. . . a person who kills more than three victims, during more than three events, at three or more locations, with a cooling-off period in between.'

Micki Pistorius, a psychologist who worked for the South African police on more than thirty cases of serial killing, wrote: 'Serial killers are not monsters: they are human beings with tortured souls . . . The motive is intrinsic, an irresistible compulsion, fuelled by fantasy, which may lead to torture, and/or sexual abuse, mutilation and necrophilia.'

In a single sentence, this describes both what drives the serial killer and the distinctive nature of his – or, in rare cases, her – behaviour.

The principal characteristics of serial murder are as follows:

1 As the FBI definition indicates, the killings are repetitive; and they will usually continue until the perpetrator is identified and apprehended, dies or is killed.

2 In many cases, the period between attacks decreases over time. The accepted explanation for this is that the killer derives great excitement (almost certainly sexual) from the first incident – and the thrill can lie as much in the hunt for a victim, as in the final acts. He (almost always a male) may take a 'trophy' – a purse, jewellery, clothing, or even a body part – from his victim, with which he subsequently relives that excitement in privacy. In due course, this activity palls, and another victim must be found. Each time, the post-killing excitement recedes ever more rapidly.

3 Serial killing, like other forms of homicide, is usually one-on-one. Occasionally, two killers may collaborate. When these are man and woman, the French coined the expression *folie à deux*. The cases of the 'Hillside Stranglers', Kenneth Bianchi and Angelo Buono (pages 171–6), and that of Leonard Lake and Charles Ng (pages 207–11), are unusual in that they involved two killers of the same sex. Group killings, such as those carried out by Charles Manson's 'family', usually claim some kind of 'political' motive, however bizarre.

4 During the course of the murder, or in its aftermath, there is a high degree of disproportionate violence – brutal rape of the most obscene kind, extensive mutilation and even necrophilia.

5 The first evidence that seemingly unrelated murders are serial is the distinguishable pattern of behaviour exhibited by the perpetrator and the absence of any apparent motive, other than the desire to kill.

6 During the course of the twentieth century, the increased mobility afforded by the ownership or use of a car has made serial killing much easier – and more difficult to identify and investigate. As the crime writer Ann Rule pointed out before a Senate sub-committee in 1983: 'The thing that I have found about the serial murderers that I have researched is that they travel constantly: they are 'trollers'. While most of us might put 15,000 to 20,000 miles a year on our cars, several . . . have put 200,000 miles . . . They might drive all night long. They are

always looking for the random victim who may cross their path
. . . The serial killer seldom knows his victims before he seizes
them. They are strangers, targets for his tremendous inner rage.
He is ruthless, conscienceless, and invariably cunning.'

In 1984, following this hearing, sufficient funding was allocated for VICAP to be implemented at the new National Center
for the Analysis of Violent Crime (NCAVC), exploiting the expertise of members of the FBI's Behavioral Science Unit at Quantico.
Since 1972, they had been developing what is now known as
'psychological profiling'. This technique, which employs computerized analysis of the characteristics of any severely violent crime,
has now been adopted by police forces throughout the world.

In Canada, for example, the RCMP have instituted their
Violent Crime Linkage Analysis System (ViCLAS). Dr David
Cavanaugh of Harvard University, who was a consultant on the
FBI system, has praised the Canadians as follows: '. . . [they]
have done to automated case linkage what the Japanese did with
assembly line auto production. They have taken a good American
idea and transformed it into the best in the world.'

Psychologists are generally agreed that the prime cause for
making a serial killer lies in severe childhood neglect and
abuse – whether physical or emotional. It is even claimed that the
newly formed foetus in the womb can be affected by the mother's
alcoholism or drug abuse, or by the psychological trauma of an
unwanted or painful pregnancy.

An unhappy early childhood can result in 'dissociative identity
disorder' (DID). This is described as a 'creative survival technique', which a child will employ to escape physical, sexual or
emotional abuse. One psychologist wrote: 'During dissociation,
one is not able to associate certain information as one normally
could, thus allowing a temporary mental escape from the fear and
pain of experience. This process can, at times, result in a memory
gap concerning the trauma, which may affect the person's sense of
personal history and identity, and may even result in fragmenting
oneself.'

This is evident in the case of many serial killers, who, while not clinically diagnosed as schizophrenic, claim that it is not they who have committed the crimes, but another personality with a different name. Alternatively, they may totally dissociate their crimes from their 'normal' everyday persona, to such an extent that they may become convinced that the killing never took place.

Social scientists have wondered whether it would be possible to identify behavioural traits in a young child, and take steps to treat them before they develop into a pathological condition. Although many psychologists dismiss its significance, what is called the 'Macdonald triad' has certainly been revealed in the history of some of the serial killers considered in this book. This 'triad' is made up of the following factors:

- bedwetting
- fire setting
- cruelty to small animals

The problem is that many children who subsequently develop into perfectly normal adults can also display one or more of these traits at some time. Moreover, treatment would require a wide-ranging and costly agenda, for which neither funding – nor the acceptance of such extensive social intrusion – is likely to be obtained.

So, it is an unhappy truth that the development of a serial killer is impossible to detect until it is revealed in a succession of crimes, as the histories that follow horrifically confirm.

JACK THE RIPPER

THE CLASSIC ENIGMA

The most notorious of all serial killers, without doubt, is the person who became known as 'Jack the Ripper'. More books have been written and more movies made about him than about any other murderer. There are many reasons for this. The case was the first to show all the characteristics of what is now recognized as a classic pattern: the killing of a succession of women of a similar type, with no obvious motive except a sexual element; mutilation of the victims' bodies; the taking of organs as trophies; followed by teasing communications to the investigators; etc. Above all, the case has fascinated professional and amateur investigators alike for more than a century — because no person was ever charged with the crimes.

From August to November, 1888, the Whitechapel district of London's East End experienced a growing wave of panic as, one after another, at least five women were butchered in the night. Although all were prostitutes, this was of little reassurance to other women, as the savagery of the attacks threatened them all.

The first certain victim was Mary Ann Nichols, whose corpse was discovered lying in the gateway to stables in the early hours of August 31. It was only when the body was carried to the local mortuary that the extent of her injuries was revealed. Her throat had been cut twice, the killer's knife having slashed all the way through to the backbone. Yet even more horrifying was the fact that her abdomen had been ripped open, and her intestines partly dragged out. The doctor who carried out the detailed autopsy declared that this murder, in all, had taken no more than four or five minutes, and that the butchery had been carried out 'deftly and skilfully', by someone with 'rough anatomical knowledge'.

The savagery of the killing of Mary Ann Nichols made headlines, and not only in Britain. Even as far away as New York, *The Times* carried the story on September 4. As one newspaper stated: 'No murder was ever more ferociously and more brutally done.' But worse was to follow.

On September 8, around dawn, Annie Chapman's body was found in a small yard at the back of a house that was about a half-mile from where Mary Ann was killed. She had been mutilated with even greater ferocity. Her throat had been slashed so deeply that it seemed possible her killer had tried to decapitate her; and her intestines had been cut free and dumped on her right shoulder. The police surgeon who examined the corpse reported: '. . . the knife used was . . . a small amputating knife, or well-ground slaughterman's knife, narrow and sharp with a blade of six to nine inches in length.'

The police were confident that both murders were by the same hand, and in the following weeks they investigated a number of possible suspects: local slaughtermen, medical students with a record of mental instability, even qualified physicians. But they had no success.

Around September 18–19, the London police received a letter, jeering at their efforts, but which they did not make public. Dated September 17, and apparently smeared with blood, it concluded: 'I love my work an I shan't stop until I get buckled and even then watch out for your old pal Jacky. Catch me if you Can "Jack the Ripper" Sorry about the blood still messy from the last one . . .'

In the early hours of Sunday September 30, the Ripper struck twice, killing Elizabeth Stride and Catherine Eddowes. It seems probable that he was interrupted at his work on Elizabeth, for only her throat was cut and her body left unmutilated; and in a frustrated frenzy he attacked Catherine within half-an-hour, and less than half-a-mile away. She had suffered gross mutilation: she was completely disemboweled, and her uterus and left kidney were missing.

These two new killings fuelled a public panic. Distressed by the failure of the police to find the culprit and prevent further killings, local residents had hastily formed a Whitechapel Vigilance Committee and hired two private detectives to investigate.

It was the chairman of this committee, George Lusk, who received a small parcel at his home on October 16. It contained a gruesome trophy: half a human kidney, which was declared to be, almost certainly, that of Catherine Eddowes. With it was a note in handwriting similar to that of the September 17 letter. Addressed 'From hell', and signed 'Catch me when you can', it read:

> I send you half the Kidne I took from one women prasarved
> it for you tother piece I fried and ate it was very nise I may
> send you the bloody knif that took it out if you only wate a
> whil longer.

The pathologist who had examined the kidney, Dr Thomas Openshaw of the London Hospital, received a letter dated October 19. This, too, was in similar handwriting, and read in its entirety:

> Old boss you was rite it was the left kidny i was goin to hop-
> perate agin close to your ospitle just as i was goin to dror
> me nife along of er bloomin throte them cusses of coppers
> spoilt the game but i guess i wil be on the job soon and will
> send you another bit of innerds

> Jack the Ripper
> O have you seen the devle
> with his mikerscope and scalpul
> a looking at me kidney
> with a slide cocked up

Whether this, so similar to the letters of September 17 and October 16, was nevertheless a hoax is open to debate. There is little doubt that a number of other letters, written during the following weeks by persons with a malicious intention to 'keep the pot a-boiling', were false.

The fifth killing in the series – and the last positively attributed to the Ripper – occurred in the early hours of November 9, and was the most horrific of all. Mary Jane Kelly was only 25 years old and was murdered, not in the street like the other victims, but in her rented room. There, the Ripper had plenty of time to complete his obscene mutilations. The girl's head was almost severed from her body and her facial features hacked beyond recognition. Both breasts, and all the internal organs, were cut away and arranged around the corpse, and much of the flesh was stripped off and piled on a nearby table in a vast puddle of blood. Finally, the autopsy revealed that the killer had cut out Mary Jane's heart – and taken it with him. After this, no more was heard of the Ripper.

Other later deaths were popularly attributed to him, but none of the victims suffered the characteristic mutilations. There are many possibilities, and innumerable theories have been advanced. Could he have been a lunatic who had temporarily absconded from the asylum, and then returned of his own free will? Was he one of those who were committed to a mental institution, for apparently unconnected reasons, by the end of 1888? Perhaps he had died – possibly of syphilis, which would explain his mental state and perverted sexual obsession – or committed suicide. There were even suggestions that he had left Britain, possibly for the United States. All that is certain is that he vanished from the streets of Whitechapel, to survive as no more than a hideous legend.

So, who was the Ripper? There were a number of witnesses who reported having seen a man in company with the later victims on the nights of the murders. Their descriptions had a certain consistency: he was 'shabby-genteel', dark, short in build, and might have been a foreigner. Other details did not match; and the description, such as it was, could have fitted many men to be found in the night-time streets of Whitechapel. The police had very little to go on, and many potential suspects. Over the years, well over one hundred names have been proposed by amateur researchers, but very few suspects stand up to detailed consideration.

One of the first suspects to attract police attention was the self-styled Dr 'Roslyn d'Onston' Stephenson. A practitioner of black magic, he wrote a number of articles about the Ripper case and was twice questioned by the police. His lover was the novelist Mabel Collins, and something that he showed her so horrified her that she became convinced he was the killer. But the authorities, apparently, were unable to establish any connection with the case.

Among those who may be considered a possible Ripper suspect are the following:

William Bury He was in London during the crucial months, and relocated with his wife to Dundee in January 1889. On February 5 he murdered his wife, mutilating her body in a characteristic way. On the walls of the basement in which they lived, police found the chalked messages: 'Jack Ripper is at the back of this door', and 'Jack Ripper is in this seller [sic]'. Bury was hanged for his wife's murder on April 24, 1889.

Aaron Cohen He was brought before the Whitechapel magistrates on December 7, 1888, as 'a lunatic who had been found wandering at large'. He was committed to an asylum where he violently attacked other inmates, refused food, and died on October 20, 1889.

Montague John Druitt A schoolmaster and barrister, he was dismissed from his school, after 'serious trouble', on November 30, 1888, and his drowned body was found in the River Thames on December 31. Sir Melville Macnaghten, who became assistant chief constable of the Metropolitan Police in June 1889, named him as the most likely suspect in a memorandum that came to public attention only in 1959.

Aaron Kosminski A century after the Ripper killings, in October 1988, two FBI psychological profilers – John Douglas and Roy Hazelwood – were invited onto a British TV show to give their opinions on the possible identification of the suspect. They both agreed on Kosminski. He was a Polish Jew, a boot maker who arrived in London in 1882, and was diagnosed as suffering from syphilis six months before the first of the murders. Macnaghten had named him as another suspect, and in 1987 some marginal notes were found in a book that had been written by Sir Robert Anderson, who was for a time in charge of the Ripper investigation.

Anderson wrote: '. . . the only person who ever had a good view of the murderer unhesitatingly identified the suspect the instant he was confronted by him, but he refused to give evidence against him.'

The pencil notes in the margin, written by Chief Inspector Donald Swanson, Anderson's predecessor, confirmed that this was Kosminski, who was committed to a lunatic asylum and died there in 1919.

More recently, the . . . British criminologist Professor David Canter argued that 'to maintain the optimum distance that balances familiarity and risk, you would have to commit your crimes in a circular region around your home'. He drew up a map pinpointing the sites of the Ripper murders: at its centre lay the home of Kosminski's brother, Wolf.

Michael Ostrog Macnaghten described him as: '. . . a mad Russian doctor and convict and unquestionably a homicidal maniac. The man was said to have been habitually cruel to women, and for a long time was known to have carried about with him surgical knives and other instruments; his antecedents were of the very worst, and his whereabouts at the time of the Whitechapel murders could never be satisfactorily accounted for.'

It is recorded that Ostrog was sentenced to two years imprisonment in Paris, France, on November 18, 1888.

Dr John Williams An unlikely suspect, but backed by some persuasive circumstantial evidence. In his book *Uncle Jack*, published in 2006, Tony Williams puts forward the name of his great-uncle as that of the Ripper. Dr Williams was a distinguished Victorian gynaecologist, a consultant to the royal family, and one of the founders of the National Library of Wales. However, his great-nephew received a mysterious box that had been passed down, which yielded a knife, some microscope slides – and a letter from 1888, in which Dr Williams stated that he had to be in Whitechapel that evening. Further research in the National Library archives uncovered a diary entry that appeared to confirm that Dr Williams had performed an abortion on Mary Ann Nichols – one of the Ripper's victims – three years earlier.

Writers of all kinds have claimed to discover evidence that the Ripper was any one of a bizarre gallery of personalities. These include Queen Victoria's grandson, Albert Victor, Duke of Clarence; Dr Thomas Barnardo, famous founder of a home for orphans; Lewis Carroll, author of the 'Alice' books and many more; 'Walter', author of the Victorian pornographic classic *My Secret Life*, who has been identified as William Hayward, engineer to the City of London Commissioner of Sewers; Leopold II, king of Belgium; the poet Algernon Swinburne; Sir William Gull, the Queen's surgeon; and several other medical men.

Recently, two other possibilities have attracted a great deal of interest. In 1991, Michael Barrett, a small-time scrap dealer in Liverpool, England, produced a 63-page diary, written in an old Victorian scrapbook, that he claimed identified James Maybrick, a cotton importer, as the Ripper. On May 11, 1889, Maybrick died of arsenic poisoning and his American-born wife, Florence, was found guilty of his murder. It was known that, discovering her husband had a mistress, Florence herself had taken a lover. She consistently protested her innocence, was released from a term of life imprisonment after fifteen years, and died in the United States in 1941. The sensational claim made by the diary was that Maybrick had expressed his distress, on discovering his wife's infidelity, by murdering prostitutes on his occasional visits to London. His death a few months later would explain why no further Ripper murders occurred.

The *Diary of Jack the Ripper* was published in Britain in 1993. Before its publication in the United States, it was examined by Maureen Casey Owens, who had been the Chicago Police

Department's forensic expert for 25 years. She declared it a fake. In 1994, Michael Barrett confessed to forging the diary, buying the scrapbook at a garage sale and the ink at an art supplies store. Later, he retracted this confession, and the jury is still out.

In 2002, renowned US crime fiction writer Patricia Cornwell published *Portrait of a Killer*, in which she asserted that the distinguished British painter Walter Sickert (1860-1942) was the Ripper. She compared his handwriting with that of certain letters, and also succeeded in having DNA on envelopes possibly matched to Sickert's. The drawback to this theory is that the letters examined by Ms Cornwell were those that nearly every 'Ripperologist' agrees were hoax communications.

Only one thing is certain: the true identity of Jack the Ripper will never be satisfactorily established.

HERMANN WEBSTER MUDGETT

H. H. HOLMES – DEATH IN THE WHITE CITY

Chicago was a booming city in the 1890s, at the time of the World's Fair. Young women flocked there from the farmlands, looking for work as stenographers and garment workers, or perhaps only to see the wonders of the Fair. Many were never heard of again: they died, ill and poverty-stricken, in cheap rooms; they married, and often parted from, men of whom they did not dare tell their family; an untold number disappeared in the sinister labyrinth of 'Holmes Castle'.

'D r H. H. Holmes' was born Hermann Webster Mudgett in Gilmanton, New Hampshire, in May 1860. Unlike his brother and sister, he was, by his own account, a 'mother's boy'. Nevertheless, at age 18 he married – but within the year he had left his wife. He then enrolled in the school of medicine at the University of Vermont in Burlington, but soon found its programme too limited and entered the University of Michigan in Ann Arbor, one of the leading medical schools in the West.

Mudgett graduated in 1884, but he had already embarked on his criminal career, embezzling the proceeds of a book-selling trip through Illinois, and suffering a charge of breach of promise by a widowed hairdresser in Ann Arbor. Desperately needing money to set up a medical practice, he embarked on a series of insurance scams, certifying the death of a cadaver that he had obtained – by who knows what means – as that of the insured.

Wherever Mudgett fetched up – Moores Fork, NY, Philadelphia, and finally Chicago – people died, or simply disappeared. In Springfield, Illinois, he gained a license as a druggist in July 1886; it was the year when Conan Doyle first published the stories of his famous detective, and, inspired, Mudgett took the name of Henry Howard Holmes. He found employment with a drug company in Chicago, but the owner, a widow, mysteriously disappeared soon after, and 'Dr Holmes' took over.

In 1891, Icilius 'Ned' Conner brought his wife Julia and their daughter, Pearl, to Chicago, finding employment in Holmes's jewellery store, on the first floor of the 'Castle'. They took rooms on the second floor, close to Holmes's own suite, and very soon the doctor and Julia embarked upon an affair that caused Conner to divorce his wife.

In November 1891, she announced to Holmes that she was pregnant, and he immediately offered her marriage – and an abortion. The operation was set for the day before Christmas. On Christmas morning there was no sign of Julia or Pearl and Holmes claimed they were visiting family in Davenport, Iowa. They were never seen again.

A few months later, Holmes hired Emeline Cigrand as a stenographer. For some months she seemed deeply in love with him, but by December 1892 her feelings had cooled. She was last seen three weeks before Christmas, and soon afterward Holmes produced a card announcing her marriage, on December 7, to 'Robert E. Phelps'.

The World's Fair, the fabulous 'White City', opened in May 1893. By then, Holmes was a relatively wealthy man. He was part-owner of a company making duplicators; he sold mail-order drugs; and he owned two houses, in one of which he installed his second, bigamously married, wife Myrta Belknap and their daughter. In the district of Englewood he built a luxury hotel, with retail shops on the ground floor, one of which he opened as a drug store. On the first floor, there were six corridors, 35 rooms, and 51 doors. Above, there were a further 36 rooms. All was ready for the crowds of visitors who were flocking to the Fair – many of them single young women. And nobody knows how many of those who entered the hotel lobby never checked out again.

Holmes now began ordering large quantities of chloroform, which he said was for scientific experiments. He bought everything on credit, and seldom paid for anything, relying upon his remarkable charm. One of his managers said: 'Creditors would come here raging and calling him all the names imaginable, and he would smile and talk to them, and set up the cigars and drinks, and send them away seemingly his friends for life. I never saw him angry. You couldn't have trouble with him if you tried.'

It was about this time that employees at the hotel began to leave, 'without notice'. A waitress in the restaurant was at work one day, and gone the next. Jennie Thompson, a stenographer, disappeared, as well as a woman named Evelyn Stewart. Customers and residents complained of strange chemical smells, and Holmes apologized with his usual charm. Occasionally he invited an acquaintance, Charles Chappell, who was skilled in stripping the flesh from bodies in order to reassemble skeletons for doctors' offices and teaching laboratories, to his 'mortuary'. Holmes would explain that the body on the table was one of his patients who had died, and offer Chappell $36 to prepare the skeleton, which he subsequently sold for a profit.

In the weeks before the Fair opened, Holmes went through a fake marriage with a Minnie Williams, who brought her sister Anna to live with them in an apartment that he had temporarily rented. He persuaded Minnie to transfer the deed to land she owned in Fort Worth to himself, and promised the young women a luxurious trip to Europe – but on the night of July 4 they both vanished in the labyrinth of his hotel. Shortly afterward, the wife of Benjamin Pitezel, a carpenter who had worked for Holmes on the hotel's construction, received the gift of a collection of clothing. It had belonged, said Holmes, to his cousin, who had married and moved east, and no longer required it.

Holmes then found a new conquest: Georgiana Yoke, who worked as a saleswoman in a big department store. To her he also offered marriage, and she accepted. But the Fair was already nearing its closing date, and Holmes's creditors were closing in on him. At a meeting with them in the fall of 1893, he was told that his debts totalled at least $50,000. He decided to leave precipitately for Fort Worth, where he owned Minnie's land, and on which he intended to raise money. He took with him Georgiana and Benjamin Pitezel – on whose life he took out an insurance policy for $10,000.

In June 1895, Pinkerton detective Frank Geyer arrived in Philadelphia to investigate an alleged case of insurance fraud. The suspect's name was a physician named Dr Mudgett, otherwise known as H. H. Holmes, who had been in prison for the past seven months. Other Pinkerton agents had tracked Holmes and Pitezel from Fort Worth to St Louis, and then on to Philadelphia, and the case concerned an insurance claim on Pitezel's death in the city in mid-1894. Geyer reported: 'Holmes is greatly given to lying with a sort of florid ornamentation, and all of his stories are decorated with flamboyant draperies, intended by him to strengthen the plausibility of his statements. In talking, he has the appearance of candor, becomes pathetic at times when pathos will serve him best, uttering his words with a quaver in his voice, often accompanied by a moistened eye, then turning quickly with a determined and forceful method of speech, as if indignation or resolution had sprung out of tender memories that had touched his heart.'

Holmes claimed to Geyer that he had obtained a cadaver similar to Pitezel, and rendered it virtually unrecognizable by setting fire to it – but it had become clear that it was indeed Pitezel himself. The Philadelphia coroner had requested that a member of Pitezel's family, now living in St Louis, should identify the body. His wife, Carrie, was too ill to travel, but sent her daughter Alice, aged 15, who agreed that the corpse was that of her father, and the claim had been paid.

Alice was then taken by Holmes back to St Louis, where somehow he persuaded Carrie to let him take her, and two other children – Nellie, 11, and Howard, 8 – on a trip. Alice and her sister wrote regularly to their mother; however, shortly after Holmes was arrested in Philadelphia, the police discovered a deed box containing some dozen letters from the girls that had never been posted.

From the dates on these letters, and various local references, Geyer was able to construct the route the party had taken. 'Alex

E. Cook', with three children, had registered at two hotels in Cincinatti. In Indianapolis, Holmes stayed in one hotel with 'Mrs Georgia Howard' – no doubt Georgiana Yoke – while the children stayed in another hotel. In Detroit, Geyer made a strange discovery. Not only had Holmes and Georgiana checked into one hotel, and the children into another – but Carrie Pitezel and her two other children had stayed in a third, only a few blocks away.

Meanwhile, in his cell in Philadelphia, Holmes insisted that all three children were safe and sound in the company of 'Miss Minnie Williams', and in London.

Geyer's final journey was to Toronto. There, 'G. Howe and wife' had stayed at one hotel, Mrs Pitezel and a daughter at another, and Alice and Nellie at a third. There was no mention of Howard. And in her last letter, dated October 14, Alice had written: 'Howard is not with us now.'

However, a Toronto resident named Thomas Ryves thought that the description of Holmes resembled a man who had rented the house next door to his in October 1894. A quick search led Geyer, accompanied by a police detective, to the cellar, where they found the buried bodies of Alice and Nellie.

Eventually, returning to Indianapolis, Geyer discovered that Holmes had asked for the keys to a house that was for rent. On August 27, 1895, searching the house, he opened a long chimney flue and found a partially-burnt little body. It was Howard's; the hunt was over.

Following the discovery of the bodies of Alice and Nellie, the Chicago police investigated the Holmes hotel. Some of the third floor rooms were furnished as normal hotel bedrooms; others were windowless, and fitted with airtight doors. At least one was fitted with a gas jet, its cut-off valve in Holmes's own apartment. In his office was a bank book belonging to a Lucy Burbank and listing a balance of $23,000. But Lucy Burbank could not be traced.

The police then descended to the cavernous basement. There they found a vat of acid, in which were eight ribs and part of a skull, a large kiln, a dissection table stained with blood and piles of quicklime. Scattered about were the burnt remains of women's shoes, more bones and articles of clothing. Two pits of quicklime contained human remains, possibly those of the Williams sisters. A dumb-waiter descended from the floors above. By this means, Holmes had been able to secretly lower the bodies of his victims to the basement.

It was impossible to establish whether or not Holmes had raped any of the unfortunate women, before or after murdering them. Rumours have persisted that he also possessed a variety of torture implements, but this has never been officially confirmed. Since, with his usual persuasive charm – and the promise of marriage – he was able to develop normal sexual relations with any attractive young woman who took his fancy, more perverted practices seem unlikely.

Holmes stood trial in Philadelphia in the fall of 1895 for the murder of Benjamin Pitezel, the judge ruling that only evidence directly related to the charge could be given. It did not take long to find him guilty. In prison and awaiting execution, he penned a detailed confession to killing 27 people – but this, like his whole life, was a mixture of truth and lies. However, of Pitezel he wrote: 'From the first hour of our acquaintance, even before I knew he had a family who would later afford me additional victims for the gratification of my blood-thirstiness, I intended to kill him.'

On the morning of May 7, 1896, Holmes ate a breakfast of boiled eggs, toast and coffee before being taken to the scaffold. As the rope was put around his neck, he turned to the hangman, smiled, and said: 'Take your time, old man.'

BELA KISS

BARRELS OF BODIES

In the spring of 1916, at the height of World War I, two police officers broke into a barred and padlocked villa on the outskirts of the
Hungarian village of Czinkota in search of much-needed gasoline
for the war effort. In the attic, they found seven large barrels, tightly
sealed. But these barrels contained no hoarded gasoline – in each
was found the putrefying naked body of a woman, immersed in
alcohol and with the marks of strangulation still around her neck.

The house was the home of Bela Kiss, who had been drafted
into the Austro-Hungarian army eighteen months earlier.
When the village constable recalled that Kiss had bought
many more metal drums than these seven, police searched the
surrounding countryside, and unearthed a further 17, each with
a corpse packed inside. One was that of Kiss's wife, who had
disappeared in 1912 – running off, Kiss had told his neighbours,
with her lover Paul Bikari. Bikari's was another of the bodies;
the rest were of women who had been reported missing over the
years from 1912 to 1914.

The villagers of Czinkota went in fear of the 40-year-old man
who had come into their midst in February 1912. A tinsmith by
trade, Kiss was also an amateur practitioner of astrology, and was
regarded by the superstitious locals as a sorcerer in league with
the devil. Few would go near his villa on the edge of the village,
and their fears were fuelled by the gossip of the elderly cleaning
woman, the only person who had been allowed into the house,
whom Kiss had dismissed for peering too closely at the mysterious
sealed barrels in the attic. After he had left for military service,
the locked house stood empty and neglected, shunned by the villagers – until the police arrived.

A thorough search of the villa began. The drawers of Kiss's bureau were found to be full of letters from women who had replied to advertisements in Budapest newspapers, placed by a man calling himself 'Hoffmann', a 'lonely widower seeking female companionship'. There were also many items of women's clothing and jewellery in the house, together with pawn tickets for hundreds more. The implication was clear. Having killed his wife and her lover in a fit of jealous fury, Kiss had spent the next two years inflamed by sexual rage: pursuing lonely women and luring them to his villa, and later strangling them there, and pawning their belongings for profit.

The Budapest police were already investigating the case of two widows who had vanished a couple of years earlier. Both had been seen in the company of a man called Hoffmann, who was said to live near the Margaret Bridge in the capital. Inquiries had yielded no trace of the man, but it seemed very likely that he was Kiss.

The military authorities were contacted in the search for the missing man. They reported that he had been posted to Serbia, where he had been wounded, and died in a military hospital. However, the description of the dead man was not in the least like that of Kiss – apart from anything else, he was far too young. It seemed probable that Kiss had exchanged his paybook and identity disk with the dying patient, and escaped into the chaos of the latter years of the war.

Kiss would have found it difficult to disappear entirely from the army, probably still in uniform and carrying army papers, and may have been among the millions of war casualties. But in 1919, after the war was over, there was a report that he had been seen on Budapest's Margaret Bridge, the former hunting-ground of the mysterious 'Herr Hoffmann'. Then, in 1924, a deserter from the French Foreign Legion informed the police of a fellow legionnaire – intriguingly named Hoffmann – who had often boasted of his abilities as a strangler with a garotte. But, when the matter was pursued, Hoffmann, too, was found to have deserted from the Legion, and vanished without trace.

Much later, in 1932, a New York homicide detective named Henry Oswald was sure that he had spotted Kiss among the crowds emerging from the subway in Times Square, but was unable to force his way through the throng in order to follow him. Four more years passed, and the NYPD then learnt of a rumour that the Hungarian – who would now have been nearing 70 – was working as a janitor in an apartment building on Sixth Avenue. However, once again he could not be found, and his final fate remains a mystery. But who knows how many women, reported as missing, may have fallen victim to his wiles during those previous twenty years?

HENRI LANDRU

THE FRENCH BLUEBEARD

Fortunately, with the social freedom that women now have, 'Lonely Hearts Murders' are relatively rare these days. Yet, the early twentieth century saw a number of cases of poverty-stricken widows and single women attracted by the prospect of domestic security and enticed into the clutches of serial killers. One of the most notorious of these killers was the Frenchman Henri Landru. Ironically, this squat little man, with his bald head, bushy eyebrows – and, above all, big red-brown beard – was dubbed 'the French Bluebeard' by the press. It was the foul-smelling, black smoke that billowed from his chimney that led him eventually to the guillotine.

Henri-Désiré Landru, born in Paris in 1869, was a clever scholar. He took courses at the prestigious School of Mechanical Engineering and, drafted into the army at the age of 18, rose to the rank of sergeant before his discharge. By that time, he had seduced his cousin, who bore him a daughter, and married her on leaving the army.

With his knowledge of engineering, Landru set up as a garage proprietor in Clichy, northern Paris, but also operated as a dealer in second-hand furniture. This business brought newly-widowed women to his door, where he would prey on their concerns and persuade them to invest their meagre pensions in schemes he proposed, which he would promptly embezzle. As a result, in the years 1900–14, he served a succession of prison sentences on no less than seven charges of fraud. Bitterly dishonoured, his father committed suicide.

It was when World War I broke out in 1914 that Landru first embarked upon his career of murder, targeting widows, many of whom had lost their husbands in the trenches of the Western

Front. The details are known because he kept a small notebook in which he meticulously entered the names (sometimes coded) of his victims, their finances, and his own expenses. Like Kiss, he placed advertisements in the matrimonial columns of newspapers: 'Widower with two children, aged 43, with comfortable income, affectionate, serious and moving in good society, desires to meet widow or unattached lady, aged between 35 and 45, with view to matrimony.'

He made no mention that he was already married, and with four children. He kept the replies in a series of folders for further study, at once rejecting many with the note 'SF', to represent *sans fortune* (without resources).

Despite his physical appearance, Landru was a persuasive and romantic talker, telling his potential victims what a comfortable life he could afford them, and his sexual appetite, it has been said, was insatiable. His first conquest, to whom he posed as 'Raymond Diart', was widow Jeanne Cuchet, who had a 16-year-old son and owned a millinery shop. Despite the warnings of her sister and brother-in-law, in December 1914 she helped to furnish a villa at Vernouillet, on the outskirts of the town of Dreux to the west of Paris, and for a short time the three lived there together as a family.

It did not last long: the Cuchets were never seen again after January 4, 1915. Landru gained 5,000 francs, and a gold watch that he presented to his real wife, even though he was separated from her. The police, much reduced in number because the fit and active ones had been drafted, had no time to investigate the circumstances.

On May 1, Landru placed another advertisement in *Le Journal* and attracted the attention of, among others, Thérèse Laborde-Line. On June 21, she sold her furniture, announcing that she was to marry a 'Monsieur Cuchet', and moved into the villa at Vernouillet. She was last seen alive five days later, and Landru immediately sold off her securities and personal belongings.

Another of the women who answered the advertisement in *Le Journal* was Marie-Angélique Guillin. She arrived at Vernouillet on August 2 and disappeared within a few days. Landru at once sold her negotiable securities and by December, using forged papers, he had obtained a further 12,000 francs from her bank account.

He already had another widow waiting in the wings, a Mme Héon. Using the name 'Dupont', he rented the Villa Ermitage at Gambais, a little nearer Paris but in a more secluded location on the edge of the Rambouillet Forest, where he bought a large iron stove for the kitchen. At his eventual trial, he explained: 'The house had stood empty for five years. There was no proper kitchen installation.'

Mme Héon arrived at the house on December 8, and was never seen again.

Entries in the carefully kept notebook of his expenses, such as rail tickets, clearly reveal Landru's murderous intentions.

On December 8, 1915, the day he took Mme Héon to Gambais: 'One return, 3.85 francs. One single, 2.40 francs.'

Another woman who had replied to Landru's advertisements, and to whom he proposed marriage, was Anna Collomb, who gave up her position as a stenographer with the Prudential Insurance Company on December 19, 1916. On December 27 she travelled with Landru, who now called himself Diart, to Gambais – and that was the last seen of her.

On December 27, 1916, when he took Anna Collomb to the villa, and on September 1, 1917, the day Mme Buisson was last seen, there are similar entries. For the latter date, there is also a note that Landru's cash in hand had increased by 1,000 francs.

A few days later, Landru encountered a young servant-girl, Andrée Babelay, in the Paris Metro, and offered to provide her with a place to stay while she looked for work. On March 11 Andrée told her mother she was engaged to be married, and joined Landru in Gambais on March 29. She was very different from his other victims, only 19 years old, and penniless, but by April 12 she too had vanished. Perhaps she had been too inquisitive about his activities.

For more than a year, Landru had been in correspondence with a wealthy widow, Célestine Buisson, under the name of 'Fremiet', and in June he proposed marriage. She bought a wedding dress, and the couple took the train to Gambais on August 19, 1917, where she was last seen on September 1. Much later, after Landru's arrest, a police search uncovered her clothes, hairpiece and papers in his garage.

Landru wasted no time in seeking another victim. Louise Jaume met her supposed husband-to-be through a matrimonial agent, and joined him in Gambais on November 25. But, from there, she wrote to her aunt: 'I don't know what it is about him, but he frightens me. His terrible gaze disturbs me. One might say he is the Devil.' Five days later Landru emptied her bank account, representing himself as her attorney. Anne-Marie Pascal followed her on April 5, 1918, and Maria-Thérèse Marchadier, with her three dogs, on January 13, 1919.

However, time had run out for Landru. He had taken great care to distance his victims from their families and acquaintances, sending them postcards in which he explained that his 'wife' was unwell, and unable to write for a while. But Mme Buisson's sister grew suspicious, and remembered that Celestine had told her she was leaving for Gambais with a 'Monsieur Guillet'. She wrote to the mayor of the village, asking for news of anyone named Buisson or Guillet; he replied that he knew no one of either name, and that the tenant of the Villa Ermitage was a Monsieur Dupont. He proposed that she should meet the family of Anna Collomb, who had also disappeared from Gambais some time before.

The two families approached the police, who went to the villa and could find no trace of its occupant. The house was empty, although there were signs that it had recently been lived in. It was Célestine Buisson's sister who spotted 'Fremiet' in a Paris street, emerging from a dry goods store. She enquired about him in the store and was told that his name was Guillet, and that he lived in the nearby Rue de Rochechouart with his mistress. She immediately informed the police and Landru was arrested on April 12, 1919.

Investigators once more descended upon the Villa Ermitage. They dug in the grounds and searched the ponds surrounding the villa, and also at Vernouillet, but found nothing but the remains of Mme Marchadier's dogs, which had been strangled, in the garden at Gambais. Believing – erroneously – that he could not be found guilty of murder in the absence of any bodies, Landru maintained a confident silence. His cryptic notebook was discovered but provided no more than suggestive evidence.

It was only when locals recalled the clouds of foul-smelling smoke that had on occasion emerged from the kitchen chimney at Gambais that the iron stove was examined. Hundreds of human bone fragments, teeth, hairpins, dress-hooks, pins, and buttons made of mother-of-pearl and metal were discovered. At last it was possible to bring Landru to trial.

The trial was held in November 1921. Landru was accused on eleven counts of murder, to all of which he pleaded 'not guilty'. In court he was arrogant, making witty, dismissive replies to the questions of the prosecution, and denying everything. The evidence mounted, but the sensation of the trial was the testimony of two women who had, miraculously, survived their visits to Gambais. One, a Mme Falque, was in a sanatorium and could only provide an affidavit, but the other was the woman with whom Landru had been living in Paris at the time of his arrest. She was Fernande Segret, 29, a singer.

Mlle Segret described how she had met the accused, under the name Guillet, in May, 1917, when he offered her a seat on a bus. He proposed marriage and she went to live with him in the Rue de Rochechouart. The official betrothal was made in May 1918, the date of the marriage being set for the end of the year, but it never took place. Fernande Segret testified that she had visited the Villa Ermitage seven or eight times, had cooked meals there and had no knowledge of any bones among the cinders. But the forensic evidence was incontrovertible. Landru replied, as arrogant as usual: 'The place is next to the graveyard, and there are not only gossips but practical jokers in the country. The place was left unguarded.'

On November 28, Maître Godefroy began his summing-up for the prosecution. He pointed out that Landru had written to 283 women proposing marriage and went on to say: 'He was admired because, without the physical advances of a seducer, he so readily charmed and conquered women ... Gentlemen, you see before you a cruel, callous and ferocious man. Beside one of his fiancées he kneels devoutly in church. An hour or two later, he is bending over her dead body in the act of cutting it up. Then, quite calmly, he will go and repose on the body of Mlle Fernande Segret. I demand the supreme penalty, death, for Landru, the murderer of Vernouillet and Gambais. He is responsible absolutely and wholly for his deeds, and with no excuse. Death is the sole fitting punishment . . . Gentlemen, I conjure you, do not hesitate, strike without weakness . . .'

For Landru, Maitre de Moro-Giafferi argued that there was no proof of the death of the missing women: 'There wasn't even time for Landru to burn so many bodies . . . Their papers were found. Well, gentlemen, as you know, there is a type of offender in whose possession women's papers are often found. The dealer in women. I do not wish to insult any of the ladies of whom we have heard. Our laws against the white-slave traffic are designed to protect those who set off, as they believe, to an honest trade, only to find out the truth when they reach their destination. There, when it is too late, they are kept by force from returning. One thing is certain. Those women had all broken with their families. All had signified their intention of travelling abroad. Now remember this. In each case, for two months after they disappeared, Landru strove to reassure their friends. It was always two months. That is the length of time it would take to reach Brazil. After that, friends and the law can do nothing. If they left their identity papers behind, it was because they had been told they must change their names. The times shown in the notebook have been said to be times of death. They might equally well have been times of departure.'

Arguing that it was dangerous to find Landru guilty of murder and send him to the guillotine, Moro-Giafferi asked: 'Suppose that tomorrow one of those women returns. What faith would you then have in yourselves strong enough to face the stony gaze of the ghost that came to you in the night and said: "I did not kill! You killed me!"?'

It was to no avail. On the evening of November 29 the jury declared a verdict of guilty. Landru appealed: 'I swear that I never killed anyone.'

His appeal was rejected on February 1, 1922, and he went to the guillotine on February 25. Before his execution, Landru gave his attorneys a drawing that he had made while in prison. Had they taken it out of its frame, they would have found a full written confession behind it. It was not discovered, however, until nearly half a century later.

FRITZ HAARMANN

BUTCHER OF HANNOVER

At the end of World War I, and in the years following its defeat in 1918, Germany was in economic chaos. Soaring inflation reduced many people to poverty; thousands were homeless and starving. Food was very expensive and in short supply, with meat being almost unobtainable. So, when Fritz Haarmann began selling appetizing 'fresh meat' at cut-price on the black market in Hannover, there were many who were only too eager to buy. Little did they know what flesh it really was that they were buying.

Fritz Haarmann was born in Hannover, Germany, on October 25, 1879. The family, in which Fritz was the sixth child, was not a happy one. His father, a morose former railroad fireman, was known as 'Sulky Olle' to his colleagues. His mother was an invalid. Young Fritz was her pet and he grew up estranged from his father, preferring to dress in girls' clothes, playing with dolls and avoiding the company of other boys.

Nevertheless, he was sent off to military school at the age of 16 – probably because his father hoped that it would 'make a man of him'. But, after a few months, Haarmann was sent home to Hannover, having displayed signs of epilepsy. The following year, he was charged with sexually molesting young children. However, at a psychological examination, it was decided that he was unfit to stand trial, and he was committed to a mental institution for observation.

He escaped from the institution after six months and crossed the border into Switzerland. There, he found work and became engaged to a local girl. However, when she became pregnant, he deserted her and returned to Germany, where he enlisted in a crack army regiment. But this attempt at self-rehabilitation eventually came to nothing. After a few months, in 1913, he was honourably discharged on health grounds and granted a full military pension.

Back home, Haarmann successfully avoided his father's efforts to have him declared insane. Instead, he took to a life of petty crime. He spent many spells in jail – ranging from a single night to several months. In 1914, he was convicted of a warehouse burglary, and spent the war years in prison. Released on parole in 1918, he joined a smuggling ring in Hannover, at the same time offering his services to the police as an informer and sometimes identifying himself as 'Detective Haarmann'.

On September 27, 1918, while World War I was still raging, 17-year-old Friedel Rothe ran away from his home in the suburbs of Hannover. Three days later, his father Oswald came home on leave from the front line and began at once to search the streets for his errant son. Among the many young and destitute boys hanging around the city's railroad station he found one who knew Friedel. The youth had become friendly with a police detective, 'a fine man', who often took the boys for rides in the park – or back to his apartment for 'fun'.

Oswald Rothe traced this 'fine man' to his apartment. After suffering several refusals, he finally persuaded the police to accompany him there. To their great discomfort, they found Haarmann, one of their valued informers, in bed with a 13-year-old boy. But of young Friedel there was no sign. (Six years later, Haarmann confessed that, at that time, the boy's head was in a paper bag on the floor behind the stove!)

There was no alternative but to arrest Haarmann on charges of 'indecency with a minor', and he was sentenced to nine months in prison. While in prison, he met up with Hans Gans, 24, a homosexual pimp. On their release, they set up home together as lovers and embarked upon a profitable business.

They lured boys back to their apartment, where Haarmann killed them – by biting them in the throat, he said – and then butchered them. He sold their flesh illegally as 'beef' or 'pork' and dumped the remains in the nearby River Leine. Meanwhile, Gans made a handsome profit disposing of their clothing as secondhand items.

For six years the Hannover police seemed to turn a blind eye to Haarmann's questionable activities. He remained a valuable informant – and was an amusing character – who regularly found them contraband cigarettes and black-market meat. Even when a doubtful customer submitted some of this meat for official analysis, it was pronounced to be 'pork' by the experts.

However, by May 17, 1924, the Hamburg police were forced to open an investigation that was to end Haarmann's gruesome career. That day, a group of children playing on the banks of the Leine found a human skull. Two weeks later, a skull of a young boy was discovered several hundred yards further down the bank. Then, on June 13, two more were pulled from the mud. Even then, at first, the authorities dismissed the discoveries as a practical joke – perhaps by medical students, or remains washed downriver from a higher, ancient cemetery.

Their attitude was dramatically changed on July 24, when some other children found a sack filled with human bones – including a skull – in the river.

The River Leine was dragged and more than 500 skeletal remains were found in a single day. According to the medical examiner, they belonged to at least 22 individuals, boys or young men. There was panic in the city: newspapers remarked on the fact that the disappearance of more than 600 teenage boys had been reported in recent years.

Although suspicion fell on Haarmann, the authorities decided that the local police were unfit to conduct the initial investigation because of their close relations with him. So, two detectives were sent from Berlin.

The detectives mounted a night-time surveillance on the railway station, and soon found Haarmann in violent altercation with one of the youths, who accused him of sexual interference. At once, the yelling couple were arrested, taken to police headquarters and charged with public indecency. Haarmann's apartment was searched, more thoroughly than before, and a wealth of incriminating evidence was discovered.

The floors and walls were widely bloodstained – which Haarmann at first explained away as a result of his illegal trade as a butcher. However, clothing and personal effects of missing youngsters were also found. Further, Haarmann's landlady's son was wearing a coat that parents of a missing boy confidently identified.

In custody, the bestial butcher confessed. Asked the number of his victims, he replied: 'Thirty or forty, I don't remember exactly.'

The Hannover police were able to establish the identities of 27 missing youths, whose murders had occurred only in the years 1923 4 although there must have been many more. Haarmann implicated Gans as his accomplice and as the perpetrator of three killings. On December 4, 1924, he stood trial, accused on 24 counts.

The trial lasted two weeks, although the outcome was a foregone conclusion. In court, Haarmann stood puffing on cigars and complained that too many women were present. Yet he freely admitted his guilt, and was sentenced to death. Gans was found guilty of complicity to murder and sentenced to life imprisonment, which was later commuted to twelve years. Haarmann was beheaded in Hannover prison on April 15, 1925. At last, the citizens of Hannover could sleep more easily.

CARL PANZRAM

TOTALLY UNREPENTANT

Carl Panzram was unusual, even among hardened serial killers, in that he never expressed the slightest regret for his actions:

> *'My conscience doesn't bother me. I have no conscience. I believe the whole human race should be exterminated. I'll do my best to do it every chance I get.'*

On death row, his greatest fear was that 'do-gooders' might manage to get his execution commuted to life imprisonment. He wrote:

> *'I wish you all had one neck, and I had my hands on it.'*

The son of Prussian immigrants, Panzram was born in Minnesota – at East Grand Forks, just inside the state line with North Dakota – on June 28, 1892. While in his final prison cell he wrote a 145-page autobiography, in which he stated: 'All of my family are as average as human beings are. They are honest and hard-working people. All except me. I have been a human animal ever since I was born. When I was young, 5- or 6-years of age, I was a thief, a liar, and a mean despicable one at that. The older I got, the meaner I got.'

This was not strictly true. His father left home when Carl was about seven years old, leaving his mother to work the poor farm and bring up Carl and his five siblings. After school, he and his sister were ordered to work in the fields, where the rest of the family had laboured throughout the day. As he said later, his pay consisted of plenty of work and a good sound beating every time he displeased someone older and stronger: 'It seemed to me then, and still does now, that everything was always right for the one who was strongest.'

Aged eight, Panzram was arrested for drunk and disorderly conduct. Three years later, he spent a period in the county jail for incorrigibility and burglary and was then transferred to a reformatory, where he was beaten regularly. After some two years, he was paroled into his mother's custody but ran away from home not long afterward and rode the rods westward. He said later how he had lived that part of his life: '. . . sleeping in box-cars, barns, sheds, haystacks or most anywhere at all.'

As an under-age vagrant, Panzram spent time in several juvenile institutions over the next few years, often threatening and assaulting his instructors. At age 14, full-grown and lying about his age, he volunteered for the U.S. Army – while drunk. Inevitably, he could not adjust to military discipline and in April 1907 he was court-martialled for theft of Army property and served three years in Leavenworth.

Released and discharged, he embarked on a career of robbery and indiscriminate killing, receiving further jail sentences for burglary and escaping several times before being recaptured.

Escaping from state prison in Salem, Oregon, in May 1918, Panzram took the name of 'John O'Leary', obtained seamen's papers and passenger passports and travelled through South America, Europe and Africa. In Scotland, in 1919, he was arrested for theft and spent ten days in Glasgow's Barlinnie prison.

Back in the US in 1920, according to his confession, he was sufficiently in funds after a burglary in New Haven, Connecticut, to buy a yacht. He lured sailors on board with promises of employment, drugged and raped them, and then dumped their bodies out at sea. In what was then Portuguese West Africa, he hired eight natives in a hunt for crocodiles, killed and sodomized them and fed their bodies to the ravenous creatures.

Panzram's detailed account of his activities filled many pages of his autobiography. He stole another yacht and murdered several teenage boys, as well as a woman in Kingston, NY. The only explanation he ever gave for this was: '. . . for the fun it gave me.'

Finally, on August 16, 1928, he was arrested for a series of burglaries in Washington, D.C. He was sentenced to 20 years in

Leavenworth, and on entering the facility announced: 'I'll kill the first man that crosses me.'

He was sent to the prison laundry, where he worked sullenly and silently, saying little to anyone. In his cell, he completely ignored his cellmate and spent his time brooding and reading the works of German philosophers such as Nietzsche and Schopenhauer.

On June 20, 1929, without apparent provocation, Panzram wrenched an iron bar from a packing case and beat to death Robert Warnke, the civilian laundry supervisor. Then he shuffled off – his ankles had been broken in an attempted escape from another prison – and demanded to be taken to an isolation cell.

Panzram's trial for Warnke's murder was held on April 15, 1930, and – though judged insane – he was sentenced to be hanged. In his death cell he wrote: 'In my lifetime I have murdered 21 human beings, I have committed thousands of burglaries, robberies, larcenies, arsons and last but not least I have committed sodomy on more than 1,000 human beings. For all these things I am not in the least bit sorry.'

During his few last months, Panzram received more humane treatment that he had ever had in his life. He wrote: 'If in the beginning I had been treated as well as I am now, then there wouldn't have been so many people in this world that have been robbed, raped and killed.'

He was content to face his own death and, as he mounted the scaffold on September 5, 1930, he turned to the hangman and snarled: 'Hurry it up, you Hoosier bastard. I could hang a dozen men while you're fooling around.'

PETER KURTEN

VAMPIRE OF DÜSSELDORF

In 1929, the German city of Düsseldorf was seized with fear, as a succession of frenzied attacks left the bloody and violated bodies of victims to be discovered in the streets or nearby green spaces. There were rumours that the murderer had drunk the blood that spurted from their wounds, and the press dubbed him the 'Vampire'. There were no witnesses, and few suspects, and it was a remarkable coincidence that finally led to his identification. His name was Peter Kurten.

In May, 1930, 20-year-old Maria Budlies took the train from Cologne to Düsseldorf in search of employment. As she left the train she was approached by a man who, under the pretence of helping her to find a lodging, attempted to lead her into Volksgarten Park. She naturally refused and a second man intervened. Grateful for the assistance of this other stranger, who seemed friendly enough, Maria accepted his offer of refreshment at his apartment. There he attempted to rape her and then dragged her to a nearby wood, where he began to strangle her. Unaccountably, he suddenly stopped and asked her if she remembered where he lived. When she assured him that she did not, he let her go.

Maria did not report the attack to the police, but described it in a letter to a friend. By great good fortune, the letter was wrongly addressed, and found its way to the 'dead letter' department at the post office, where a clerk opened it to discover the address of the sender. When he read its contents, he immediately handed it to the police, who were able to track down Maria. She did, in fact, remember sufficient details of the man's address and was able to lead detectives there. She was shocked to see her attacker leaving the premises, which he shared with his wife, and his name, said the landlady, was Peter Kurten. Next morning, Frau Kurten went to the police and told them that her husband was the terrible 'Vampire of Düsseldorf'.

It was blood that fascinated Peter Kurten. In his confessions, he told how, as long ago as 1913, he had spotted 13-year-old Kristine Klein asleep near the window of her father's inn at Köln-Mulheim, and had strangled her before cutting her throat with a pocketknife. By a strange irony, he dropped his handkerchief, embroidered with the initials 'PK', and the child's uncle, named Klein like his niece, was charged with the murder. The evidence, however, was considered insufficient, and he was cleared – while Kurten went unsuspected.

The so-called 'Vampire' was born in Köln-Mulheim in 1883. He was one of 13 children born to a sand-moulder, and they all lived together in a single room. His father was a brutal alcoholic, who beat and abused both his wife and his children, and was later imprisoned for an attempt to rape his own daughter. Even as a young child, Kurten revealed a violent disposition. Reports vary as to whether, at age nine, he attempted to drown two playmates by holding them under the waters of the River Rhine, or actually did so, their deaths being recorded as 'accidental'.

Kurten was a very early sexual developer. He said that he had first derived sexual pleasure from helping the local dogcatcher torture and kill strays, and by the age of 13 he was practising bestiality, stabbing the animals to death to heighten his excitement.

Later, he became an arsonist: 'The sight of the flames delighted me,' he said, 'but above all it was the excitement of the attempts to extinguish the fire, and the agitation of those who saw their property being destroyed.'

In 1894, the family moved to Düsseldorf, where Kurten later found brief employment as a molder's apprentice. But he soon ran away, and lodged with a masochistic prostitute. He became a thief, and served his first term of many imprisonments in 1899. He had recently visited the Chamber of Horrors in a local waxworks museum, and told a friend: 'I am going to be someone famous like those men, one of these days.'

Later, the story of Jack the Ripper excited him: 'When I came to think over what I had read, when I was in prison, I thought what pleasure it would give me to do things of that kind when I got out again.'

After his release, Kurten claimed, he committed his first murder in November 1899, strangling a girl during sex; but no body was found, and it may well be that she survived. He continued his thefts and sexual attacks, in and out of prison, for the next twenty years – time in which he indulged in fantasies of extreme violence. But, on his release in 1921, he relocated to Altenburg, where he married, and apparently settled down. Neighbours described him as a mild, conservative, soft-spoken man, a churchgoer, and a lover of young children. (Nevertheless, he was twice charged with sexually assaulting servant girls.)

The Kurtens moved back to Düsseldorf in 1925. In the following three years, he later claimed, he was responsible for four attempted strangulations of women and a string of fires that destroyed two homes and fifteen other premises. But he did not begin his horrific career as the Vampire until the early weeks of 1929.

On February 23, Kurten stabbed a young woman 24 times in the street, but her screams scared him off and she eventually recovered after several months. A week later, the body of eight-year-old Rosa Ohliger was found behind a hoarding on a construction site; she had been raped and stabbed 13 times with a pair of scissors. Kurten had returned later and had attempted to burn the body by dousing it with kerosene and setting light to it. And, on the night of February 12, a drunk named Rudolf Scheer had the misfortune to stumble against the killer, who turned and stabbed him repeatedly with the scissors.

Over the next few months, Kurten satisfied his lust with compliant servant girls, who nevertheless protested vigorously when he attempted to heighten his pleasure with 'playful' strangulation. On August 11, however, he met Maria Hahn, and took her for a walk by the river before leading her into a field where he choked her and stabbed her in the throat with his scissors. She begged him to spare her, but he stabbed her repeatedly, twenty times in all, rolled her corpse into a ditch, and covered it with undergrowth. The following day, he returned to the scene with a shovel to bury the body.

After his arrest in the following year, he said: 'I went to the grave many times afterwards, and kept improving on it; and every time I thought of what was lying there and was filled with satisfaction.'

In the following days, at least two women and a man survived stabbing attempts. Then, on August 24, Kurten came upon two young girls, 13-year-old Luise Lenzen and five-year-old Gertrud Hamacher. He lured them into a field, where he strangled and stabbed Luise and cut Gertrud's throat. The next day, Gertrude Schulte was accosted on her way to a fair by Kurten, who crudely suggested sex. When she said she would rather die, Kurten replied: 'Well, die then,' and he drew a knife and stabbed her several times before fleeing. She was able to give the police a description of her attacker, but they had nothing else to go on.

During September there were three more assaults on women, one of whom was pushed into the river, but all survived. On September 30, Kurten changed his choice of weapon. He left home in the evening with a heavy hammer in his hip pocket, accosted Ida Reuter at the train station and invited her for a drink. In the darkness, he struck her on the right temple with the hammer and dragged her into a field. She was still alive, so he struck her repeatedly and then raped her corpse.

Elisabeth Dorrier suffered a similar fate on October 11. Kurten picked her up outside the theatre in Düsseldorf and they took a train to nearby Grafenberg, where he killed her with the hammer and left her body in a field.

His last known killing took place in the early evening of November 7. He lured five-year-old Gertrud Albermann into a vegetable garden, where he strangled her and stabbed her 36 times. It may well be his admiration for Jack the Ripper that then led him to send a sketch map to the newspaper *Freshet*, with details of where to find Gertrud's body, as well as that of Maria Hahn. The police had also received anonymous correspondence after Maria's death, and a handwriting comparison showed that they had come from the same hand.

During the first months of 1930, a further series of violent attacks and strangulations was reported, until, in May, Kurten's assault on Maria Budlies led to his arrest. He was charged with nine murders, and calmly gave a detailed confession. In court on April 13, 1931, he wore a neat suit, shirt and tie, and, it is said, smelled of eau de Cologne – the very picture of a respectable citizen. He gave an account of his terrible childhood and entered a plea of insanity. This was rejected, and after eight days the jury took only 90 minutes to declare him guilty and he was sentenced to be beheaded.

THE PSYCHOLOGY OF A KILLER

Many academic studies of 'criminality' were carried out during the early years of the 20th century, but the specific investigation of what circumstances can lead to the development of a serial killer, and what goes on in his mind – now known as 'psychological profiling' – is more recent. The first reported face-to-face interview by a psychologist with a convicted killer was made in 1930, but it was to be some time before the practice was adopted by others.

The 1930 examination was conducted by German psychiatrist Professor Karl Berg, who questioned Peter Kurten in prison before his execution. He wrote a landmark book on the case, but it was not published in English – and so made available to other criminologists – until 1945. Its title was *The Sadist*. Professor Berg described Kurten as a 'narcissistic psychopath', and 'a king of sexual perverts'.

Awaiting his execution, Kurten talked freely with Professor Karl Berg. The psychiatrist was struck by the serial killer's frankness and intelligence, and his ability to recall his criminal activities over the past twenty years. He told Berg how he had stared with desire at the bare throat of the police stenographer who took down his confession, and longed to strangle her. During his trial, he had stated: 'I did not kill either people I hated, or people I loved. I killed whoever crossed my path at the moment my urge for murder took hold of me.'

Kurten ate a hearty breakfast before his beheading on July 2, 1931, and on the scaffold he turned to the executioner and asked: 'Will I still be able to hear for a moment the sound of my blood gushing? That would be the pleasure to end all pleasures.'

LEONARD EARLE NELSON

GORILLA MAN

By August, 1926, elderly lady rooming-house owners in California, particularly in the Bay area, were in a state of fear. Few were prepared to accept any new male lodgers, and some gave up letting rooms in any circumstances. A mysterious Bible-toting stranger, dubbed by the press as 'The Dark Strangler', was roaming the state. A near-silent, relatively young man, declaring himself a Bible student who needed a quiet place to read, was taking whatever room was on offer and, within hours of moving in, had departed again, leaving the raped and throttled body of the landlady behind him. It was nearly a year later that Earle Nelson was arrested and charged with 22 brutal murders.

The early days of Earle Nelson epitomize the unhappy background from which so many serial killers emerge. He was born in Philadelphia on May 12, 1897. Before he was 18 months old both his parents had died from syphilis. He was fostered by his aunt, Lilian Fabian, and taken to California, where he grew up. Mrs Fabian was a fanatically religious woman, and insisted on frequent Bible-readings with the young boy, planning that he would one day become a minister. Earle was later described as a 'quiet and morbid' child, and throughout his life he was a regular reader and quoter of the Bible.

At the age of 10, while he was playing in the street, he was struck by a passing trolley and dragged 50 yards. He remained unconscious for six days with a hole in his temple and suffered for ever after with crippling headaches and dizziness. As an adult, he felt such pain that at times he was unable to walk. The moody behaviour he had exhibited as a child grew worse, with wild mood swings in his teenage years.

Physically, however, Nelson grew into a stocky, powerful man, proud of his strength. He liked to demonstrate by walking on his hands or picking up heavy objects with his teeth. But his appearance was odd – his swarthy complexion, receding forehead, protruding lips and huge hands led to the eventual nickname of the 'Gorilla Murderer'.

Nelson attempted to enlist in the US Navy but was turned down as an 'unstable personality bordering on insanity' – an event that increased his moodiness. A short time later, on May 21, 1918, he attempted to rape his neighbour's daughter, but her father was alerted by her screams. Taken to court, he scandalized everybody by his outbursts of violent profanity interspersed with long, brooding silences, and was committed to a mental institution. Three times, however, he contrived to escape, and on the third occasion successfully evaded recapture and was pronounced discharged in his absence.

Early in 1919, in San Francisco, giving his name as 'Earle Fuller', Nelson married a woman 36 years his senior; but the marriage lasted no more than six months. While his wife was in hospital he attempted to rape her there, and was once more committed. Yet, in November 1923, he escaped again.

Nothing is known of Nelson's movements over the next two years, during which time he adopted the name 'Roger Wilson'. However, on February 20, 1926, Clara Newman, a spinster aged 60, opened the door of her San Francisco rooming house to a quietly-spoken young man with no luggage other than a Bible clutched to his chest. He was seen by Clara's nephew, Richard Newman, who was off to Sacramento for a few days to visit relatives. When he returned, he found his aunt's body in an upstairs lavatory. She had been strangled, either before or during rape. But the vague description Richard was able to give of the likely perpetrator was insufficient for the detectives who sought the suspect.

The hunt was now on in earnest. Landladies all over San Francisco and the surrounding districts were put on their guard. It was probably for this reason that the strangler travelled north to Portland, Oregon. There, in the three days from 19–21 October, he killed three times. Beatrice Withers was the first victim. Her body was found crammed into a locked trunk in the attic of the house she had advertised for sale. Money, clothing – including a coat – and jewellery were missing. The local police at first declared the death suicide, but they were unable to explain how the woman could have locked herself into the trunk.

The next victim was Virginia Grant, who had announced that her house was for rent; her body was discovered stuffed behind the furnace in the basement. The killer had again taken a coat and jewellery. The next day, he called on Mabel Fluke. Her corpse was later found in the attic of her home. She had been brutally beaten and strangled with her own scarf.

Because of the similarity of the cases in the two cities, the Portland police requested the assistance of detectives from San Francisco. But, while they headed north, the killer was back in the Bay city where he strangled the wife of William Edmonds on November 18.

Investigators were puzzled by the mobility of the strangler and wondered whether he might be a travelling salesman, or even a railroad employee. As if to support this theory, he turned up next in Seattle, where Florence Monks had also advertised her house for sale. This time, however, he was nearly caught in the act when a realtor arrived with a potential buyer to find Mrs Monk's body, still warm, rolled in a carpet in her kitchen. The house had been ransacked, and again jewellery had been taken. A few days later, in nearby Oregon City, rooming-house owner Blanche Myers met a similar fate, strangled with her apron and hidden under the bed of the room she had advertised for rent.

At last the police were able to get a line on the probable killer. Details of the stolen jewellery were circulated up and down the West Coast and three elderly ladies who ran a guesthouse in Portland reported that they had bought some from a lodger the day after Florence Monks was found dead. They described his unusual appearance: dark, untidy hair, staring blue eyes, a jutting jaw and long, powerful arms. An intense search for the strangler was mounted at once.

While police dragnets trawled the West Coast, the killer, however, was travelling east, no doubt hitchhiking or riding the rails. Stopping briefly in Council Bluffs, Iowa, on December 23, where he killed another landlady, Elizabeth Brerard, he reached Kansas City in time for Christmas. Young Bonnie Pace was newly married and she and her husband had decided to take in a lodger to improve their finances. They picked the wrong one: Mr Pace returned home from work the day after Christmas to find Bonnie strangled and rolled in a rug.

Two days later, the killer struck again. It was another young woman, Germania Harpin, in her rooming house, leaving the body under her bed. Even more horrifyingly, he also throttled her eight-month-old daughter in her cot. Rumours that the child had been raped brought the horror of the citizens to an even higher pitch.

The strangler was now travelling widely, and Philadelphia was the next city he visited. Perhaps the three killings in quick succession in Kansas City had temporarily sated his lust, for it was not until April 27, 1927, that Mary McConnell was discovered strangled in her guesthouse. A month passed before Jennie Randolph was murdered in Buffalo, NY, but two days later landlady Fannie May and her sister, Maureen Oswald, were both killed and raped in Detroit, 250 miles away. And only two days passed before Cecilia Setsima, another younger woman, was strangled in her rooming house in Chicago. By now, the manhunt involved police forces across the United States, but their quarry swiftly crossed the border into Canada.

On 8 June, a youngish, heavily-built man in workman's clothes and carrying nothing but a Bible, presented himself at the door of Mrs Catherine Hill's lodging house in Winnipeg, Manitoba. He said his name was Woodcots, and that he was 'a good Catholic with high ideals' who needed a room – any room would do – to study. The next morning he left early, on his way to work, Mrs Hill assumed.

Later that day, another of Mrs Hill's lodgers, Mrs Cowan, reported that her 13-year-old daughter Lola was missing. However, the police were diverted from their street enquiries when a distraught William Patterson came to tell them of the discovery of the body of his wife Emily. He had returned from work to an apparently empty home, and by late evening was frantically worried. Searching desperately through the rooms, he noticed what appeared to be a bundle of clothing stuffed under the bed. It was his wife. She wore only a blouse and a petticoat and had been beaten, strangled and raped.

The police began to wonder whether the Dark Strangler had come to Winnipeg. A shirt and suit were missing, and they issued a description of the clothing. A second-hand dealer recalled buying them from a man on June 10, and was able to provide a fairly detailed description. An artist's impression was quickly drawn and circulated throughout the province.

It was not until June 12 that the police were able to again take up the search for Lola Cowan. When they went to Mrs Hill's lodging-house she mentioned how 'Mr Woodcots' had not returned, and they asked her to open his room. Under the bed lay the putrefying body of Lola, typically strangled and raped.

The killer's trail was picked up in Regina, more than 200 miles to the west. On June 13 a man sold a gold wedding band, claiming that he had just got divorced. It was Mrs Patterson's. Then, on June 15, a storekeeper in a small rural town some 80 miles from Winnipeg recognized the strangler from a Wanted poster in the local post office. The police caught up with him as he walked along the road out of town. He said his name was Virgil Wilson, from British Columbia, working for a local farmer. When he was told that he was being held as a murderer of many women, he laughed and replied: 'I only do my lady-killing on Saturday nights.'

Held in jail in the nearby town of Killarney, he soon escaped by picking the lock of his cell with a nail, and a 500-strong posse was quickly deputized to search for him. Fortunately, he was recaptured the next morning and transferred to Winnipeg, where, giving his true name of Earle Leonard Nelson, he stood trial on November 1, 1927. He pleaded insanity, but only two witnesses – his aunt and his ex-wife – were called in his defence. He was declared sane, sentenced to death after only four days trial, and hanged on January 13, 1928.

MARCEL PETIOT

VANISHING REFUGEES

On March 11, 1944, the chimney of a house in the Rue Le Sueur, in the heart of Nazi-occupied Paris and only a few blocks from the Gestapo headquarters, caught on fire. Neighbours summoned the fire brigade, who broke into the house through the cellar and very soon called for the gendarmerie. A heap of dismembered human bodies lay beside the furnace, ready to be fed into the flames.

The owner of the house, who was absent at the time, was a Dr Marcel Petiot. He was very soon contacted for an explanation, and he whispered confidentially to the gendarme in charge that these were the bodies of pro-Nazi collaborators who had been executed by the French Resistance and entrusted to him – a true patriot – for disposal.

This story was, at least temporarily, accepted by the gendarmerie, who allowed Petiot to escape Paris. The newspaper *Paris Soir* reported that two vagrants had broken into the house and been burnt to death when their clothes caught fire as they warmed themselves beside the furnace. In his flight, Petiot made contact with the Resistance and was able to publish several letters in their clandestine magazine *Resistance,* under the name of 'Capitaine Henri Valery', in which he proclaimed the 'innocence' of the missing Dr Petiot. In November, however, some months after the liberation of Paris by the Free French Army, he was found, arrested and charged with the murder of 27 Jewish refugees.

Marcel Petiot was born on January 17, 1897, in the town of Auxerre, some hundred miles south of Paris. Stories from his childhood have survived: he was a late bed wetter and he delighted in taking young fledglings from their nest, poking out their eyes and watching them distractedly hurling themselves against the bars of a cage. He was expelled from school after school for unacceptable behaviour and at age 16 was charged with stealing mail from a letterbox. A court-appointed psychiatrist found Marcel to be: '. . . an abnormal youth suffering from personal and hereditary problems, which limit to a large degree his responsibility for his acts.'

Consequently, the charge was dropped, and – after further problems with his schooling – he eventually graduated in July 1915.

Drafted into the French Army in January 1916, Petiot was wounded and gassed in the trenches and by 1918 was diagnosed as suffering from 'neurasthenia'. At the time he was on a charge of stealing drugs from casualty clearing stations and selling them. However, a commission of enquiry decided that this was a result of his psychological state, and he was discharged with a disability pension.

After his release, Petiot enrolled in medical school on a fast-track course of study and received his degree from the Faculté de Medecine in Paris in December 1921. He set up a practice in the town of Villeneuve-sur-Yonne, where he distributed leaflets extolling his own abilities. He soon had numerous patients, and in 1927 he was elected mayor and married. The couple had a son and in 1933 they relocated to Paris. There the 36-year-old doctor advertised again, claiming that he could cure: '. . . fungi, red spots, goitre, tattoos, scars, tumours both benign and malignant, arteriosclerosis, anemia, obesity, diabetes, cardiac and renal deficiencies, arthritis, nervous depression, senility, colds, pneumonia, emphysema, asthma, tuberculosis, appendicitis, ulcers, syphilis, bone diseases, ailments of the heart, liver and stomach . . .'

Despite the success of his practice, Petiot attracted the attention of the law on a number of occasions. In 1935 one Anna Coquille lodged a complaint concerning the death of her daughter, who had been treated by him for a mouth abscess, had not recovered consciousness and died several hours later. The charge was dismissed, as was a charge in the same year of illegal handling of narcotics. But in 1936 Petiot was arrested for stealing a science textbook from a stall on the Boulevard Saint-Michel. He pleaded 'absentmindedness' due to his mental state at the time, and was committed to a private psychiatric hospital. Seven months later he was discharged and shortly afterward fined 25,000 francs for making false income tax returns – something, as he pointed out, that many other respectable French citizens did regularly.

For several years after Petiot lived a blame-free life. He was relatively wealthy, owned several properties in and around Paris, and bought and sold valuable pieces of jewellery at auction. His many patients spoke fulsomely of his courtesy and attentiveness – although there were complaints that his methods of treating drug addiction were far from ethical. Then came the war with Germany, the surrender of the French Army and the occupation of Paris in 1940.

Over the next four years, as the Gestapo – and their French collaborators – began rounding up Jewish citizens and dispatching them to the death camps, Petiot was in his element. He discreetly let it be known that he had access to an escape route to South America via Spain. He made appointments for refugees at his house on Rue Le Sueur – ironically, its name means 'sweat' – and, perhaps, persuaded them to have inoculations against diseases endemic in their destination. As a patriot, he asked no more than the costs of the journey, but inevitably they brought with them whatever valuables they could carry. None were ever heard of again.

Even as Petiot disappeared into the Paris night, the gendarmes were investigating the house on Rue Le Sueur. It was obvious that no-one had lived there for several years: dust lay everywhere, and the many rooms were crowded with pieces of furniture and piles of ornaments. At the rear was a courtyard enclosed by a high wall so that it was concealed from the view of the neighbours. The outbuildings, which had originally housed the stable and servants' quarters, included the only clean room: a converted passage that was neatly furnished as a doctor's office.

In the adjoining garage was a huge pile of quicklime in which fragments of bone and flesh were visible. In the former stable was a manure pit, half-filled with lime and more human remains. On the landing was a sack containing half a headless corpse and at the bottom of the staircase, beside a pile of coal and bodies, was a bloodstained hatchet.

Searching further, the investigators found a strange triangular chamber close to the doctor's office. It was empty except for eight iron rings fixed to the wall, opposite a double wooden door – which had no handle on its inside. A small spy hole through the wall gave a clear view of the iron rings.

Investigators also found a banal collection of personal belongings on the premises. They included 22 used toothbrushes, seven pairs of eyeglasses, five cigarette holders, five gas masks, seven pocket combs, a black satin evening gown, a woman's hat, a man's white shirt and a three-piece suit. The remains from the lime-pit and stove were examined by experts in forensic anthropology. Dr Albert Paul reported that they had been able to identify the bones of only ten subjects, but 'the number ten is vastly inferior to the real one'. There were no signs of knife or gunshot wounds, and someone with a knowledge of anatomy had dissected the corpses with professional care. But the identity of the victims remained unknown.

Petiot's trial opened on March 18, 1946, and lasted nearly three weeks. Searching one of the houses that Petiot owned near Auxerre, the police had recovered more than 80 suitcases containing some 2,000 items of clothing, including several German uniforms. These were to prove dramatic evidence – and, tellingly, only one former member of the Resistance appeared in support of Petiot.

His first victim was a patient, a Polish furrier named Joachim Guschinow. Petiot claimed that he had been paid with five matching sable furs, and that he had subsequently received three letters from the furrier in South America. The roll-call of the missing continued. All of them, said Petiot, had been working for the Germans in one way or another. However, his defence began to fall apart when the final victims were named. These were the Kneller family, German Jews who had fled from their homeland before the war. They had a seven-year-old son, whose pyjamas had been found in one of the suitcases. How could a young child be accused of collaboration? Petiot claimed: 'Kneller told me he wanted to escape . . . I paid for his false papers out of my own pocket, and asked him to leave me his furniture as collateral . . . Look, I'm not really very proud of this. They were Germans . . . They've probably already returned and are getting ready for the next war.'

On the fifth day of the trial, the court removed to Rue Le Sueur, and 300 policemen were stationed outside to hold back the crowds who turned up. They were unsuccessful, and soon chaos reigned as morbid spectators forced their way into the house. Lawyers and jurors had to enter the triangular cell, in which – presumably – the victims had died, in three shifts. In front of the manure pit, Petiot nearly fainted, but it was claimed that he was only weak from hunger.

Throughout the following week, and into the third, some 80 witnesses were heard. They included relatives and friends of those who had disappeared, as well as psychiatrists and handwriting experts. Petiot maintained his calm, contemptuous pose, insisting that his killings had been patriotic.

On April 3, the court heard the closing speeches for the prosecution and defence, and the jury duly retired. When Petiot was called to appear for the verdict, he was discovered sleeping peacefully. He was found guilty, with no mitigating circumstances, of the willful murder of 26 of those named in the charges.

Petiot lodged an appeal against the verdict, but it was turned down on May 15, and on May 25, 1946, he went to the guillotine. Dr Paul, the forensic expert, who was one of the official witnesses of the execution, later said: 'For the first time in my life I saw a man leaving death row, if not dancing, at least showing perfect calm. Most people about to be executed do their best to be courageous, but one senses that it is a stiff and forced courage. Petiot moved with ease, as though he were walking into his office for a routine appointment.'

JOHN GEORGE HAIGH

ACID BATH MURDERER

When Mrs Olive Durand-Deacon, a wealthy 69-year-old widow, failed to turn up for breakfast at the Onslow Court Hotel, London, on February 19, 1949, the staff were surprised. So was her friend Mrs Constance Lane, another resident at the hotel – and she became even more concerned when she learned from the chambermaid that Mrs Durand-Deacon's bed had not been slept in.

O nslow Court was a discreet private hotel a few minutes stroll from South Kensington London Underground station, its clientele almost entirely elderly, well-off widows and spinsters, who had nowhere else to spend their declining years. An unlikely resident was 40-year-old John Haigh, a dapper self-styled 'engineer', with a fashionably trimmed moustache. Handsome in the current style, debonair and well-mannered, he had been declared charming by the elderly residents – none more so that Mrs Durand-Deacon, who had spent many hours with him 'talking business'.

The 'business' had concerned a scheme for the manufacture of artificial fingernails, and Mrs Durand-Deacon had left the hotel the previous day, saying that she was on her way to visit Haigh's factory in Crawley, Sussex. He said that she had failed to turn up, and he hoped 'that she was all right'.

The following day, when there was still no sign of Mrs Durand-Deacon, Mrs Lane asked Haigh – whom she instinctively disliked – to drive her to nearby Chelsea police station. There, he reported that he had arranged to meet the lady on the afternoon of 18 February, had waited an hour, and had then driven down to Sussex alone. Four days later, on February 24, when Mrs Durand-Deacon was officially declared a missing person, a woman police sergeant was sent to make enquiries at the hotel and she became convinced that Haigh was lying. Her report persuaded her boss to request Scotland Yard's Criminal Record Division for a check on Haigh, and they revealed that he had been in prison three times: twice for fraud and once for theft.

So, on February 26, two sergeants from the Sussex Constabulary visited Haigh's premises in Leopold Road, Crawley, which were located in the backyard of a small engineering company. The keys to the small brick-built storehouse were not available, and – somewhat unofficially – they broke open the door. They found the expected clutter of workbenches, carboys of chemicals. But some things did seem out of place: a hatbox and an expensive leather briefcase. In the briefcase was a collection of documents, including food ration books and other papers. The hatbox contained several passports, driving licences, a cheque book and a marriage licence – none of them in the name of John George Haigh – and at the bottom was a revolver and eight bullets.

Hasty police enquiries traced Mrs Durand-Deacon's jewellery to a nearby Sussex dealer and her fur coat to a dry cleaner's. On February 27, Haigh was invited back to Chelsea police station in London where he calmly admitted that he was responsible, and said: 'Mrs Durand-Deacon no longer exists. She has disappeared completely and no trace can ever be found. I have destroyed her with acid. You will find the sludge that remains at Leopold Road. Every trace has gone . . . How can you prove a murder if there is no body?'

John George Haigh was born in 1909 to parents of the very strict Plymouth Brethren sect. As a boy, he won a choral scholarship to Wakefield Grammar School, in Yorkshire, and this meant that he was required to sing in Anglican services in the city cathedral. He later claimed that the contrast produced a state of mental confusion, in which he had strange visions of forests with the trees dripping blood.

He married in 1934, but soon after was jailed for fraud and deserted his wife on his release in November of that year. Over the next eight years he served at least two more terms of imprisonment

– but in 1943 declared that he was 'going straight'. He moved into the Onslow Court Hotel and rented a basement workshop a short distance away, in order to develop his 'inventions'.

World War II was in its darkest days, however, and Haigh had to survive. It seems likely that he made a living stealing and trading in food and clothing ration books and coupons. On September 9, 1944, he lured an old acquaintance – William McSwan, manager of a local pinball arcade – into his basement. There, he bludgeoned him, cut his throat and dissolved his body in concentrated sulphuric acid, disposing of the resulting sludge down an adjacent manhole.

Haigh wrote several times to McSwan's parents, explaining that their son had gone into hiding in order to avoid being drafted. In 1945, he invited them to London, and murdered them in the same way. By forging documents, he managed to take possession of their estate, including five houses and a number of valuable securities; and then sold off everything. By 1948, however, his lavish lifestyle left him once more in debt.

He had met Dr Archibald Henderson and his wife Rosalie in November 1947, when he expressed an interest in the sale of their London house. On February 12, 1948, Haigh took Dr Henderson to the workshop in Crawley. There he shot him with Henderson's own revolver – which he had stolen – and dropped the body into a tank of acid. He then went back to the hotel in Brighton where the couple had been staying, and – on the pretext that her husband had been taken ill – drove Mrs Henderson to Crawley and dealt with her in the same way. Once more forging deeds of transfer, he then sold their London home. In the following year, he set his sights on Mrs Durand-Deacon.

Later, Haigh claimed to the police that he had committed three other murders: a woman and a youth in west London and a girl from Eastbourne in Sussex.

After he was charged on February 28, 1949, Haigh continued to insist that, despite his confession, if there was no body he could not be found guilty of murder. Although prosecutions for murder had occasionally succeeded in the absence of a corpse, the police realized that it was essential to establish that Mrs Durand-Deacon was indeed dead.

The official pathologist on the case, Dr Keith Simpson, travelled down to Crawley. Later, he would write of the investigation in his memoirs, *Forty Years of Murder*: 'I did not have much hope of finding much beyond residual acid sludge, but on the way down I pondered on what parts of the body might conceivably have escaped destruction.'

Examining the ground outside the Leopold Road workshop, Simpson picked up a polished pebble about the size of a cherry pit. It was a human gallstone: 'I was looking for it. Women of Mrs Durand-Deacon's age and habits – 69 and fairly plump – are prone to gallstones, which are covered with a fatty substance that would resist the dissolving action of sulphuric acid.'

The sludge lay some four inches deep, but Simpson was able to extract some eroded bones that proved to be part of a left foot. The rest, nearly 500 pounds in all, was dug up and removed to the Metropolitan Police Laboratory for further examination.

Over the next three days, Simpson found more incriminating items in the sludge. There were two more gallstones and eighteen fragments of partially-dissolved bone. A piece of pelvis was identified as female, and this was confirmed by the discovery of the handle of a red plastic handbag and the metal cap of a lipstick case. A plaster cast was constructed from the foot bones and it fitted a left shoe that had belonged to Mrs Durand-Deacon. However, the most dramatic discovery was a set of dentures, which were positively identified by the dead woman's dentist. There might not be a body, but there were sufficient remains to confirm identification.

Haigh's trial opened at Lewes Assizes on July 18, 1949. His defence was based upon the claims he had made during his police interrogation, that after each murder he had drunk the victim's blood – grounds for a plea of insanity. However, the experts who examined him had all concluded that he was sane. At last, Dr Henry Yellowlees testified that Haigh suffered from 'pure paranoia', which led to a compulsive Jekyll and Hyde existence. But his evidence was dismissed by prosecuting counsel Sir Hartley Shawcross with just two questions: 'Were his conclusions based solely on things Haigh had said to him in three interviews? Was he aware that Haigh was a habitual liar?'

On only the second day of the trial, the jury took just 13 minutes to find Haigh guilty. He took the verdict calmly, remarking: 'It's no use crying over spilt milk.'

From prison, Haigh wrote to his parents: 'It isn't everybody who can create more sensation than a film star. Only Princess Margaret or Mr Churchill could command such interest.'

Also from prison, he bequeathed his favourite suit and tie to the Chamber of Horrors at Madame Tussaud's famous London waxworks, requesting that the model made of him should show at least an inch of shirt cuff.

Before his execution, Haigh asked the prison governor if it was possible to stage a rehearsal of his hanging: 'My weight is deceptive, and I would not like there to be a hitch.'

However, his request was denied, and, on the morning of August 10, arrogantly swaggering as ever, he went to the gallows.

WILLIAM HEIRENS

'FOR HEAVEN'S SAKE CATCH ME'

Young Billy's domineering mother, Margaret Heirens, told her son:

'All sex is dirty. If you touch anyone, you get a disease.'

This advice impressed him so deeply that, as an adolescent, he would be physically sick if he tried even to caress a girl. But he soon found other ways to arouse his instinctive sexual emotions.

Many serial killers come from poor, deprived backgrounds, but William Heirens was not like that. Born on November 15, 1928, he was the child of a well-heeled couple from the affluent Chicago suburb of Lincolnwood. Nevertheless, relations between his parents were unsettled, and his mother discouraged any show of emotion. Within a few years he was getting his excitement from firesetting, and then from breaking into neighbours' homes to steal female underwear.

In 1942, aged 13, Heirens was found carrying a loaded pistol at school. When police officers came to search his home, they discovered a rifle and three other pistols hidden behind the refrigerator and four more weapons on the roof. Taken into custody, William confessed to six acts of arson and eleven counts of burglary. Because of his young age, he was put on probation and sent to a correctional school in Terre Haute, Indiana.

Returning home eleven months later, the 14-year-old reverted to his old habits of night-prowling and burglary. Quite soon, he was detained in a hotel corridor; in his pocket was a bunch of keys, each taken from a local apartment that had recently been burgled. Psychiatric reports at this time revealed that Heirens often wore the stolen female underwear while deriving excitement from leafing through a scrapbook in which he had pasted photographs of high-ranking Nazis. In juvenile court, Mrs Heirens made an emotional appeal to the judge and William was once more put on probation – this time for 18 months – and sent away to St Bede's, a Catholic boarding school.

This was at the height of World War II, when many young men were being drafted, direct from school, to fight in the Pacific and Europe. Consequently, the University of Chicago found itself short of students and therefore offered places to younger candidates, if they could pass an entrance examination. Heirens had secured good grades at St Bede's, and in September 1945, not yet 17 years old, he was enrolled.

But already a critical change had occurred in his behaviour. On June 5, 1945, before entering university, he broke into the fifth-floor Chicago apartment of Josephine Ross, a 43-year-old widow who lived with her two daughters. When Mrs Ross woke and caught him in the act, he cut her throat and stabbed her, then tried fruitlessly to bandage her neck – after which, in an excited state, he spent two hours idly trailing from room to room of the apartment.

Four months later, on October 5, having entered the apartment of 27-year-old army nurse Lieutenant Evelyn Peterson, he was again surprised. He knocked Lieutenant Peterson unconscious and fled, leaving behind fingerprints. Surprisingly, the police failed to match them with his records.

On December 10, 1945, 33-year-old Frances Brown came out of her bathroom to find Heirens in her apartment. He shot her twice, then finished her off with a knife from the kitchen. He dragged her body into the bathroom, tried clumsily to wash away her blood, then left her, half in and half out of the bathtub with her bathrobe draped over her. With Frances's lipstick he scrawled desperately across the wall:

For heaVenS SaKe (*sic*) catch Me Before I Kill More. I cannot control myself.

The Chicago police were still trying to find the 'Lipstick Killer' when, on January 7, 1946, Heirens found his way into the bedroom of six-year-old Suzanne Degnan. He carried her off, leaving a note demanding $20,000 ransom, and strangled her in a nearby basement. He then dismembered her body with a hunting knife, wrapping the remains in paper and disposing of them down storm drains.

It was not until June 26, 1946, that police, answering a call concerning a prowler in an apartment on Chicago's North Side, found Heirens. He brought out a pistol, but the weapon misfired twice and he was finally overpowered. On July 12, the police announced that they had matched his fingerprints to the ones found in Frances Brown's apartment.

In jail, the 17-year-old killer attributed his actions to an alter-ego, 'George Murman', (short for 'Murder Man'?), under whose influence he had carried out his crimes: 'When I went out on a burglary, it seemed that George was doing it.'

In August, 1946, his lawyers offered a plea bargain, saving Heirens's life against a detailed confession. Eventually, he was indicted for three murders, four assaults, and 22 burglaries.

On September 5, the day he was formally sentenced, Heirens attempted to hang himself in his cell with a bed sheet – but without success. He was sentenced to three consecutive life terms and in 1965 he was placed on institutional parole for the murder of Suzanne Degnan, but continued to serve time for the Ross and Brown murders. In April 1983, a federal judge ordered his release on the grounds of his alleged rehabilitation, but the order was overturned on appeal by the State of Illinois.

Soon after his imprisonment, Heirens retracted his confession of murder, admitting the burglaries but insisting that he had never been violent. Despite the activities of a number of friends on the outside, who continue to believe him innocent, his 30 petitions for parole have been rejected.

In jail, William Heirens proved a model and intelligent prisoner. On February 6, 1972, he became the first inmate in an Illinois prison to gain a college degree. Taking courses offered by visiting professors and through television, he accumulated the necessary credit hours to be granted a Bachelor of Arts. Following this, he took part in the development of educational programmes and assisted other inmates to pass examinations. He was transferred to a minimum security unit in 1975.

JOHN REGINALD CHRISTIE

DEATH IN 10 RILLINGTON PLACE

Anyone who searches for Rillington Place in modern-day west London will find no trace of this once notorious address. The decrepit homes that once made up this area were pulled down many years ago and replaced by housing developments, while 'gentrification' is steadily creeping northwards up the Portobello Road from Notting Hill. In 1953, however, the three-storey houses that had once been occupied by respectable Victorian families were uncared for, divided into low-rent apartments, many occupied by immigrants.

One of these immigrants was Beresford Brown, newly arrived in London from Jamaica. On March 24, 1953, his landlord told him that he could make use of the first-floor kitchen, as the previous tenant had left owing several weeks rent. Brown happened to tap on a section of wall, and when it rang hollow he discovered that the door of a kitchen closet had been papered over. Stripping off some of the paper, he pulled open the door and found hidden inside the bodies of three women.

The missing tenant was John Reginald Halliday Christie, 55, who had lived in the apartment with his 54-year-old wife Ethel since 1938. A balding, neatly dressed office worker, he was a familiar figure in the neighbourhood, and claimed to have some medical knowledge. Ethel, he said, had left for surgical treatment in Sheffield, Yorkshire, shortly before Christmas.

A nationwide hunt for the killer was mounted, but he had not gone far, having booked into a local refuge under his own name. On March 31, he was spotted by a police constable, dirty and dishevelled, and readily admitted his identity.

Very soon after Brown's grisly discovery in the kitchen closet, the police arrived, accompanied by Home Office pathologist Dr Francis Camps. The first body, half naked and propped up in a sitting position by a string attached to her bra, showed little sign of decomposition; the woman had been dead only a couple of weeks. The two bodies behind her were wrapped in blankets and were also well-preserved. They were all identified as prostitutes well known to the police.

Tearing up the floorboards in the bedroom, the investigators discovered a fourth body, which proved to be that of Ethel Christie. The following day, they turned their attention to the backyard, and soon found a mass of bones, mostly human. One femur was propping up the garden fence. Dr Camps was eventually able to reassemble the bones into the skeletons of two females, although one skull was missing.

Even before Christie was in custody, the police had turned up his extensive criminal record. In 1921, aged 23, he was working as a postman and had been imprisoned for the theft of postal orders. Two years later he was put on probation for obtaining money by false pretences. In 1924, he was given two short prison sentences for petty theft, and in 1929 – separated from his wife – he served six months hard labour for assaulting a prostitute with whom he was then living with a cricket bat. His last criminal record dated from 1933 when he served a three-month sentence for stealing a car. From prison, he had written to his wife and persuaded her to rejoin him. It was also discovered, to the embarrassment of the police, that he had volunteered – and been taken on – as a special constable in the War Reserve Police at the outbreak of World War II in September 1939.

Confronted on March 31 with the discovery of his wife Ethel's body, Christie readily provided an explanation: 'On December 14 I was awakened by my wife moving about in bed. I sat up and saw that she appeared to be convulsive, her face was blue and she was choking . . . It appeared too late to call for assistance. That's when I couldn't bear to see her, so I got a stocking and tied it round her neck to put her to sleep.'

He alleged that Ethel appeared to have taken more than 20 phenobarbitone tablets – but no traces were found in her body. He remembered some loose boards in the room and put the corpse below them: 'I think that in my mind I didn't want to lose her.'

Confessing to the deaths of the three women found in the kitchen closet, Christie attributed each to the fact that they had become violent and attacked him. He claimed that his memory was failing: 'I don't remember what happened but I must have gone haywire . . . I know there was something in the back of my mind . . . She started struggling like anything . . . She then sort of fell limp as I had hold of her . . .'

But the autopsies showed that all three had been rendered unconscious with the domestic gas supply and strangled. And they had all been sexually assaulted, either before or shortly after death.

As for the skeletal remains found in the backyard, Christie eventually provided full details. In August 1943, he had strangled 21-year-old Austrian girl called Ruth Fuerst during sex. Knowing that his wife was about to return, he concealed the girl's body under the floorboards until he had the chance to bury her the next day. On his requested release from the War Reserve Police in December 1943, he found work with a radio company. There he met Margaret Eady, who was in her early thirties. She suffered from catarrh and he had told her that he had something to alleviate it. 'She became sort of unconscious and I have a vague recollection of getting a stocking and tying it round her neck. I believe I had intercourse with her at the time I strangled her.'

In the chaos of the regular bombing of London, it had been assumed that both women had been killed in air raids, and not subsequently identified.

Finally, Christie confessed to gassing 20-year-old Beryl Evans in November 1949. He claimed that she had asked him to help her commit suicide. He then strangled her with a stocking – after a failed attempt at sex. But the examination of Beryl's body showed no signs of gas poisoning and she had been strangled with a rope. There was also evidence that she had been brutally beaten.

Beryl's husband, Timothy, had confessed at one stage to her death and had been found guilty. But neither Timothy Evans nor John Christie admitted killing the Evans's baby daughter, who had also been strangled along with her mother.

THE CASE OF TIMOTHY EVANS

On 30 November 1949, 24-year-old Timothy Evans, an illiterate truck-driver, walked into a police station in Merthyr Tydfil, south Wales, and stated that his wife was dead. He lived with her in the top floor apartment at 10 Rillington Place, and on November 8 he had returned home to find her body, which he had then hidden, he said, down a drain. On December 2, police officers visited the house and found the corpses of Beryl, and her 14-month-old daughter Geraldine, in the wash-house at the back of the Christies' apartment. Both had been strangled.

Evans now changed his statement, saying that Christie had killed Beryl in the course of performing an illegal abortion – but there was no evidence of this on her body. Finally, transferred to London, Evans confessed to both murders.

On January 11, 1950, Evans stood trial at London's Old Bailey. He had now retracted all his confessions, and blamed both deaths on his neighbour. Christie, however, appeared as a principal prosecution witness and Evans was found guilty. His appeal was turned down on February 20, and he was hanged on March 5.

After Christie had been convicted, and had confessed to the killing of Beryl, the Home Office ordered a re-examination of the evidence. The conclusion was that Evans had been justly executed, but several writers carried out their own investigations and the case for Evans's guilt was effectively demolished. On October 18, 1966, he was granted a posthumous free pardon.

THE NECROPHILE

One of the veterans of the FBI's psychological profiling pro-gramme, Roy Hazelwood, commented on the Christie case:

> The only classic sign of a necrophile is when you have a dead body and the person is known to have had sex with the dead body. We know, of course, of people who are necrophiliacs who hire prostitutes to pretend to be dead. We know of necrophiliacs who put chloroform over the victim's mouth and cause them to become unconscious so they could pretend that they were dead. It suggests necrophilia, but it's not a classic case of necrophilia . . . Knowing what I know about the case, I'd think it likely that Christie was a necrophile.

Claiming that he had only vague memories of killing his victims, Christie was obviously working towards a plea of insanity. He had served in the British Army during World War I and had been injured and gassed in France. He asserted that he had been blind for five months as a result, but there was no record of this in his discharge papers. The gas had certainly affected his voice, which seldom rose above a whisper during his trial, which opened in June 1953, when he pleaded not guilty to the murder of his wife.

The jury, however, took less than two hours to find him guilty. An inquiry into his mental state concurred with the decision and he did not appeal. He went to the gallows on July 15, 1953.

EDWARD THEODORE GEIN

GRAVEYARD GHOUL

In the 1950s, the town of Plainfield, Wisconsin – population some 800 souls – had just one bar, Hogan's Tavern, run by 51-year-old Mary Hogan. One afternoon in December 1954 she went missing from the premises, and a farmer entering the empty tavern found a pool of fresh blood on the floor. He at once telephoned the sheriff, who arrived a few minutes later with three deputies. They found a single shell from a .32 rifle on the floor and a trail of blood leading through the back door, across the snow-covered car park, to where a pickup truck had stood. No trace of Mary Hogan could be found at the time, and the case remained unsolved for three years, until sheriff's deputies found horrifying evidence at the home of local man Edward Gein.

Edward Theodore Gein was born on August 8, 1906, at La Crosse, Wisconsin, but in 1913 the family moved halfway across the state to a farm in Plainfield. Mrs Gein was the dominant personality in the household, with strongly-held religious views, while Ed's father, a drunk and a bully, worked the family farm, taking occasional work as a carpenter. He died of cirrhosis of the liver in 1940, his elder son Henry followed four years later fighting a barn fire, and Ed's mother passed away in 1945. At last, Gein was able to live as he wanted. Henry's body was found among the ashes with extensive bruising to the face. Despite the fact that it was known that Ed did get along with his brother, the coroner's verdict was death by asphyxiation.

In the early morning of November 16, 1957, 58-year-old Bernice Worden vanished from her hardware store in very similar circumstances to Hogan, a trail of blood leading out back to where her delivery truck had been. Bernice's son recalled that local handyman Ed Gein had mentioned the previous day that he needed antifreeze, and a sales receipt for antifreeze in his name was found in the store. Deputies set out for Gein's home to inquire after the missing woman. What they found there would be relived in their worst nightmares for the rest of their lives.

It was the first day of the deer-hunting season, and hanging by the heels from the rafters of a lean-to behind the house was the headless body of a woman, flayed and disembowelled as if it were a newly killed deer.

The house itself was in a state of indescribable squalor. In the kitchen, piles of clothing, unwashed pots and pans and crusted plates were covered with mould. Standing around was a collection of human skulls, some split into two to make feeding bowls, and a row of dentures was ranged along a shelf. Bernice Worden's head sat there, with twine attached to her ears, as if ready to be hung up like a gruesome ornament; and her heart was in a pan on the stove. In a cup on the table were four human noses, and a pair of lips hung from twine at the windowsill.

When scientific investigators arrived at the scene, they pointed out that the seat of one of the kitchen chairs appeared to be made of human skin, and they soon found that a lampshade, a knife sheath, a drum and a wastepaper basket were fashioned from the same material. After this, they discovered a skin apron, with its breasts still attached, and several pairs of skin leggings. And hanging along the wall in Gein's bedroom were nine shrunken heads – one of them that of Mary Hogan.

The basement was a slaughterhouse, with decaying parts of bodies hanging from hooks, and dried blood and human entrails covering the floor.

Taken to the jailhouse, Gein at first refused to say anything but, on November 18, confronted by the local DA, he gradually confessed to the two murders, together with a slew of grave robberies.

On January 6, 1958, a judge found Gein incompetent to stand trial, and he was committed to the Central State Hospital at Waupun.

It was a decade later, in mid-November 1968, that his case was eventually heard and he was judged insane and guilty of just one of the two murders to which he confessed.

Grave Robber

All his life, Gein had wished he were a woman – and had even thought, he said, of amputating his penis on several occasions. Between 1947 – shortly after his mother died – and 1954, he haunted the local cemeteries, digging up some 40 graves. He carried body parts, or whole corpses, away, flayed them, and sometimes made crude implements from the bones. Wearing the skin 'apron', complete with breasts, and a woman's scalp and face, he would go out into the moonlight and dance, female genitalia fastened over his own. He mounted skulls on his bedposts, and, around the house, he often wore a belt adorned with excised nipples. But, in the end, these ghoulish practices failed to excite, and he turned his attentions to living women, and so to murder.

Throughout his many interrogations, and at the subsequent hearing on 6 January, Gein remained calm and composed, chewing gum. Asked whether he had ever eaten any of the human remains, he appeared horrified. As for sexual relations with the corpses, he replied:

No! No! In any case, they smelled too bad.

But the doubt remains – had he killed more? The death of his brother Henry remains in question, but there were others, such as two men who inexplicably disappeared at a time they had hired Gein as their hunting guide. The jacket of one was found in the woods near Plainfield and, although Gein claimed to know the whereabouts of one body, a killing that he said was committed by 'one of his neighbours', the matter was never followed up by the police.

More telling was the discovery, at Gein's home, of the organs of two young women, which could not be matched to any of the bodies he had taken from the local cemeteries. The names of two possible victims have been proposed. One was Evelyn Hartley, abducted from La Crosse, Wisconsin, at a time when Gein was known to have visited relatives close by. A trail of blood was found leading from her home. Some time later, Mary Weckler disappeared in the town of Jefferson, and an unfamiliar white Ford car was reported in the vicinity. Following Gein's arrest, investigators found a white Ford sedan parked on his property – a car that no-one could recollect having seen him drive. These two cases remain unsolved.

He returned to Waupun, where he died on July 26, 1984. Gein was buried in an unmarked grave beside that of his mother in a Plainfield cemetery.

The name and deeds of Ed Gein soon became a part of Mid-West mythology. Mothers told their children: 'Don't go down to the river or play on the railroad tracks. Ed Gein will get you.'

His car was sold and displayed at county fairs and carnivals. Dolls were manufactured in his likeness. Robert Bloch wrote a novel about a young man who took on his domineering mother's persona, and killed a woman who came between them. He called it *Psycho*, and it became the basis of Alfred Hitchcock's famous film of the same name.

HARVEY GLATMAN

CHEESECAKE PHOTOGRAPHER

With his jug-handle ears, bulbous nose and weak chin, Harvey Murray Glatman was not a glamorous figure – nor were the final photographs that he took of his 'models'. Even as a youngster, he had equated sex with bondage: he enjoyed auto-erotic 'games', suspending himself from a beam in the attic of his home to reach orgasm. His parents were reassured by the family physician that he would 'grow out of' his fantasies, if they could find some means to 'keep him busy'. But the young boy was sufficiently busy by himself.

Harvey had been born in the Bronx, New York City, in 1927, but the family moved to Denver, Colorado, around 1938. At school, he was rated highly intelligent – his IQ was later assessed at 130 – but, with his odd looks, he was unable to attract girlfriends. It seems that, as an adolescent, he would creep into women's apartments after school, force them partially to undress, and then fondle them. At age 17, his idea of fun was to grab the purse from a good-looking girl and run off laughing before throwing it back to her. But, one day in 1945, he accosted a girl with a toy pistol in his hand and ordered her to strip. She yelled, he fled, and was arrested later the same day.

After spending time in the state prison in Boulder, he was released on bail and took off back to his native city. In New York Glatman committed a series of street robberies of women at gunpoint – this time with a real pistol – and earned the name of the 'Phantom Bandit', before being caught breaking and entering an apartment. Identified as a wanted man in Boulder, he was sentenced to five years in Sing Sing.

In 1951, Glatman was released from prison on parole and

travelled all the way across the country to Los Angeles, where he set up a TV repair shop. He took up photography as a spare-time interest and, for five or six years, led an outwardly innocent bachelor life while his lust was fuelled by studying glossy 'glamour' magazines and gloating over naked models in the studio of the photographic club that he joined.

On July 30, 1957, Glatman answered a TV service call to the apartment of Judy Ann Dull, a 19-year-old model who had recently arrived in Los Angeles from Florida. Calling himself 'Johnny Glynn', he told her that he was a photographer and had been commissioned to shoot a series of photos for a New York 'true detective' magazine: 'You know, the typical bound-and-gagged stuff.'

Two days later, Glatman called on Judy and drove her to his apartment. There she submitted to having her hands tied behind her, her legs roped together, and a gag put in her mouth. He pulled down her sweater, raised her skirt and took several photographs, after which he stripped her and, holding a gun to her head, raped her twice. It was his first experience of real – if not consensual – sex.

Both naked, Glatman and Judy sat on the sofa, watching television. Then, when she promised him that she would not report the rape if he let her go, he drove her 125 miles east of Los Angeles, into the desert near Indios. Once he had reached an isolated spot, he photographed her again, this time in her underwear. He then strangled her with a piece of rope and buried her body in a shallow grave. The grave was, in fact, so shallow that the desert winds blew away the sand to reveal her skeletal remains on December 29, 1957.

For more than six months, Glatman was apparently satisfied with the enlarged photographs that he hung on his apartment walls. Then, in search of another victim, he joined a 'lonely hearts' club, giving his name as George Williams. He met 24-year-old divorcee Shirley Ann Bridgeford and, on March 9, 1958, telling her that he was taking her dancing, he drove again far out into the desert – this time 55 miles away to Anza State Park, east of

San Diego. There he raped her repeatedly, tied her up, took photographs, and then strangled her with his piece of rope. He left her corpse behind a cactus clump, and took away her red panties as a trophy.

Glatman's third victim was a part-time stripper, Ruth Rita Mercado, 24, who advertised in the personal columns of the *Los Angeles Times* that she was looking for modelling work. On 23 July 1958, having made an appointment to interview her, Glatman went to her apartment, carrying his gun, and raped her; then he drove her out to the desert where he spent all day alternately photographing and raping her. He nearly let her go: 'She was the only one I really liked', he said in his later confession. 'I didn't want to kill her. I used the same rope, the same way.'

As with all serial killers, Glatman's need to satisfy his perverted lust was now accelerating. Realizing that the newspaper classified columns were a promising source of potential victims, he began to advertise, promising auditions for modelling opportunities for young women 'with no previous experience necessary'. A number answered the advertisements, but found him 'creepy', and refused to accept the assignments he offered them.

After several failed attempts, Glatman found 28-year-old Lorraine Vigil, who was desperately short of money and agreed to his offer of work. On 27 October 1958, he called for her in his car and set off at speed along the Santa Ana Freeway, on his way to the desert. But on the outskirts of Los Angeles, near the town of Tustin, she became alarmed, and begged him to stop. Glatman pulled onto the hard shoulder, brought out his gun and demanded that she strip.

Desperately, she grabbed at the gun: it went off and she was hit in the thigh, but bravely she held on and succeeded in levelling the gun at her abductor. He hurled himself at her and together they fell from the car, furiously wrestling for possession. At that moment a highway patrol drew up on the other side of the freeway and the driver, pulling out his gun and firing a warning shot, ran across the road. Glatman surrendered quietly – although he later claimed, vainly, that he could have shot the officer if he wished.

INVESTIGATING THE VIOLENT CRIMINAL

The arrest and interrogation of Harvey Glatman was eventually a factor in the setting-up of the FBI Violent Criminal Apprehension Program (VICAP), and the establishment of the National Center for the Analysis of Violent Crime (NCAVC) (see Introduction).

In 1958, Los Angeles homicide detective Lieutenant Pierce Brooks was the investigating officer into the apparently unrelated murders of two women in the Los Angeles area. However, he felt that both might well have been committed by the same man, who could also have committed more. On his own initiative, he spent a long time searching through local newspapers and police files, looking for similar killings. He had already put together a file of related evidence when Glatman was arrested on October 27.

With his file at hand, Brooks interrogated the killer and obtained a full confession. It was among the first full studies of a serial killer's mentality since Professor Karl Berg's pioneering work on Peter Kurten in 1930 (see pages 37–42).

In 1983 Brooks, now retired with the rank of Commander after 35 years in police service, at last succeeded in persuading the Justice Department – after much lobbying – that a VICAP Task Force should be set up, under his administration, at Sam Houston University in Texas. He and Roger Depue, then head of the FBI Behavioral Science Unit, appeared before a Senate sub-committee, in Washington, D.C., in July. Funding was agreed and VICAP was adopted. Nine months later the NCAVC was set up.

In Glatman's apartment, the police found the many photographs that he had taken of his three victims, stripped, bound and gagged, and he readily confessed to their murder. His trial in

November 1958 lasted only three days and he refused to accept the advice of his appointed lawyers that he should appeal. He asked for the death sentence and went to the gas chamber in San Quentin on August 18, 1959.

ALBERT DESALVO

BOSTON STRANGLER – OR NOT?

For eighteen months, a growing wave of terror swept the city of Boston, Massachusetts. Between June 1962 and January 1964, thirty women, mostly elderly and nearly all living alone, were murdered in their homes. In every case they were sexually assaulted – sometimes beaten, bitten or stabbed – and strangled, and their near-naked bodies laid out, as if for a pornographic photograph. Even when he had strangled them with his bare hands, the killer left his 'signature' of an item of their clothing, such as their stockings or pantyhose, tied as a neat bow beneath the victim's chin.

The first murder took place on June 14, 1962. That evening, Juris Slesers called for his mother, 55-year-old divorcee Anna Slesers, originally from Latvia, to take her to church. He found her lying naked just outside her bathroom door, her housecoat spread out under her, and the belt knotted tightly round her neck – and tied in a bow. There was no sign of a break-in, although the apartment was in a state of disarray, and the police concluded that a robber had been challenged by Mrs Slesers. Finding her in a state of undress, he had raped her, then strangled her so that he would not be identified.

Some two weeks later, on June 30, 68-year-old Nina Nichols called her sister, Mrs Marguerite Steadman, at 5 p.m. to say that she would be over for dinner in an hour. She cut short the telephone conversation, saying: 'Excuse me, there's my buzzer. I'll call you right back.'

By 7 p.m. the Steadmans were worried that Mrs Nichols had not arrived and called the janitor of her apartment building. He used his pass key to open her door, but had no need to enter. The apartment had been ransacked and in front of him on the bedroom floor lay the naked body of Nina Nichols, with a pair of her stockings finished with a characteristic bow knotted fiercely around her neck.

This time, the police decided that it was not a case of attempted robbery. Nothing, it appeared, had been taken, and the killer had intended only to make it seem so. It began to appear that a sexual psychopath was on the loose in the city.

Only two days passed before police received a call that 65-year-old Helen Blake had not been seen since June 30 and it was feared that her apartment had been burgled. When they arrived they found Helen lying face down on her bed, naked except for a pyjama top. She had been strangled with her stockings and her brassiere was also knotted around her neck in a bow.

After the discovery of Helen Blake's body, the police questioned all known sex offenders and investigated any men, aged 18 to 40, who had been released from a mental institution in the preceding two years. They issued an appeal to all women, especially those living alone, to keep their apartments locked, to admit no strangers on any pretext, and to report any suspicious occurrences. They were overwhelmed with the response but none of their identity parades, or lie-detector tests of suspects, produced a positive result.

After three weeks, when the Strangler had not struck again, it was hoped that the killings were at an end. Then, on August 21, the corpse of 75-year-old widow Ida Irga was found in her apartment. She had been dead for two days and had been strangled by hand, but a pillowcase, in the characteristic bow, was round her neck.

The body of the next victim was discovered at the end of the month, but 67-year-old Jane Sullivan had then been dead for over a week. Strangled with her own stockings, she had been dragged into the bathroom and dumped half-kneeling in the bath tub, with her face and arms under the water.

For a time there were no more killings, but the city remained in panic. The *Boston Advertiser* published an appeal to the Strangler: 'Don't kill again. Come to us for help. You are a sick man. You know it.'

EXPERTS DISAGREE

Around the time that the third murder of an elderly woman occurred, the state authorities requested a panel of psychiatrists to assess the cases. Their majority opinion was that two separate persons, both unmarried, were responsible: one a schoolteacher and the other a man living alone. Both were filled with hatred of their mothers, who were probably deceased. The panel suggested that, during the childhood of the killers, their mothers had 'walked about half-exposed in their apartment, but punished them severely for any curiosity'. As a result, the stranglers acted out their repressed emotions in adulthood, killing elderly women in a way that was 'both loving and sadistic'. And both, the panel concluded, had a weak and probably absent father.

One member of the panel disagreed. He was psychiatrist Dr James A. Brussel, who had scored a famous success in his psychological analysis of the 'Mad Bomber of New York', George Metesky, in 1957. Following the final murder, but before the perpetrator had been apprehended, he published his 'psychofit' of the Boston Strangler. The crimes were committed by only one man, he said, a well-built 30-year-old, of average height, clean-shaven and dark-haired, probably of Spanish or Italian heritage. This decription closely fits DeSalvo.

In some desperation, the police had also consulted the Dutch 'psychic detective' Peter Hurkos. He described a lightly built man, weighing 130 to 140 pounds, with a pointed nose and a scar on his left arm – 'and he loves shoes'. Remarkably, such a man was on the suspects' list, a mentally unstable salesman of women's shoes. But he was not the killer.

But there was no response – and the killer's choice of victim changed dramatically.

On December 5, 1962, he murdered 20-year-old Sophie Clark, an attractive black student whose body, sexually assaulted and strangled, was discovered by one of the two friends with whom she shared an apartment. And on New Year's Eve Patricia Bissette, 23-years-old and white, was left on her bed, strangled and assaulted, but covered with a blanket.

On May 8, 1963, 23-year-old Beverley Samans, became the eighth victim. She was found by her fiancé, spread-eagled and naked on a sofa-bed in the living room – her wrists bound behind her back with silk scarves and a bloody stocking and two hand-kerchiefs tied at her neck. She had not been strangled, however, but stabbed 22 times in her throat and left breast.

'The Strangler' then reverted to type when he next struck. A neighbour discovered 58-year-old divorcee Evelyn Corbin, her body exposed in the typical 'Strangler' pose. She had again been strangled and grossly sexually violated. The police remained as frustrated as ever: in none of the cases had anyone been seen entering a victim's premises, and there were no physical clues.

Then more young women became his victims. On November 23, 1963, he killed 23-year-old Joann Graff, leaving her naked on a day-bed with her own black leotard knotted around her neck and his bite marks on her breasts. And on January 4, 1964, two girls who shared an apartment with 19-year-old Mary Sullivan returned from work to find her brutally murdered. She was dis-covered propped up against the headboard of her bed, with her knees up, violated with a broom handle. A stocking and a silk scarf were tied together in a large floppy bow, and a greeting card reading 'Happy New Year!' was laid against her left foot.

The continuing failure of the police to apprehend the Strangler, and the intense public outrage, prompted the Attorney General of the Commonwealth to take charge of the investi-gation and set up a task force, who worked throughout 1964, tirelessly sifting through reports. They examined dozens of sus-pects, 'weirdos' of all kinds, and the usual number of oddballs who arrived to confess to the crimes. But all were released, and for ten months the cessation of Strangler killings suggested that he might have left the area, perhaps committed suicide or, sated, had just given up.

Then, on the morning of October 27 everything changed. A young wife called the police to report a sexual attack in her apartment. She had seen her schoolteacher husband off to work and was dozing in bed when a man appeared at the bedroom door. He was around 30-years-old, medium build, wearing green pants and large sunglasses. He told her that he was a detective then lunged forward and held a knife at her throat, saying: 'Not a sound, or I'll kill you.'

He gagged her with her underwear and tied her wrists and ankles to the four bedposts, after which he began to kiss and fondle her. Suddenly he stopped, saying that he was sorry, and fled. After giving details to detectives, the young woman worked with a police artist to put together a likeness of her attacker. A detective took one glance at it and concluded: 'That looks like the Measuring Man.'

Albert DeSalvo, a handyman age 33 with a police record, was picked up at once. He denied his involvement; but his victim identified him immediately.

Between 1958 and 1960, police had handled many reports of the activities of one who had been nicknamed 'Measuring Man'. He had gained the name because, armed with a clipboard and tape measure, he would call on attractive young women, representing himself as an agent of a modelling agency. Telling them that they had been selected as possible models for TV commercials, he would then proceed to take their 'vital measurements'. He did not attempt rape, but succeeded in seducing many of them – and sometimes, he later claimed, it was he who had been seduced.

In March 1960, Albert DeSalvo was arrested following a break-in and admitted he was the Measuring Man. He was convicted of breaking and entering and indecent assault and sentenced to two years. He was released on parole after 10 months.

But he now became more aggressive, breaking into apartments, tying up and raping his victims. After his arrest for the last sexual assault, the police teletyped his picture to neighbouring states. They were amazed at the response.

Reports came in from New Hampshire, Rhode Island and Connecticut that DeSalvo had been identified as the 'Green Man' responsible for assaults on hundreds of women. His nickname came from his habit of wearing a green work shirt and pants. It was estimated that, over the past two years, he had committed more than 300 sexual assaults. He himself later bragged that he had raped six women in a single morning, and put his 'score' at over 1000.

DeSalvo was committed to Boston State Hospital for psychiatric observation and was found to be 'overtly schizophrenic and potentially suicidal'. He was therefore sent to the mental institution at Bridgewater, Massachusetts, on 4 February 1965 and ordered to be detained indeterminately. The police had not yet identified DeSalvo as the Strangler. Indeed, by rights, he should have been picked up in the dragnet instituted nearly three years earlier, but he had been listed on the computer for his breaking-and-entering crimes and not as a sexual offender. Then came a breakthrough.

In Bridgewater, DeSalvo talked constantly to another inmate, George Nassar, about sex and violence and hinted that he was the Boston Strangler. There was a $100,000 reward for anyone who provided information leading to the apprehension and conviction of the Strangler, so Nassar told his attorney, young F. Lee Bailey – later to become famous in many prominent cases – about the conversations.

Bailey interviewed DeSalvo several times in the institution, tape-recording what he had to say. DeSalvo claimed that he was indeed the Strangler and divulged details of the murders that had not been made public, and that only the killer could have known. He also claimed two further killings which, because they had not shown any of the Strangler's characteristic touches, had not been considered related.

Bailey turned over copies of his tapes to the Attorney General's Office and the police. When questioned, DeSalvo sketched plans of the different apartments in which the murders had taken place, and under hypnosis described the stranglings in horrific detail.

Assistant Attorney General John Bottomley spent a long time in many interviews with DeSalvo, and was convinced that he was the Strangler; but the suspect was known as an inveterate bragger, and there was no corroborating evidence. However, there were many fat files on his other crimes, and on June 30, 1966, a hearing began to consider DeSalvo's fitness to stand trial.

The judge accepted the prosecution's argument that he was competent and the following year he was found guilty of armed robbery, breaking and entering, theft, assault and sexual crimes on four women – who were fortunate enough to have survived and were willing to identify their attacker. He was convicted and committed to life imprisonment.

Nevertheless, he was never convicted as the Boston Strangler and he did not live out his prison sentence. On November 26, 1973, he was found stabbed to death in his cell in Walpole State Prison.

There are aspects to the Boston Strangler case that make DeSalvo's guilt not as clear-cut as has been made out. At the time, there was at least one murder every day in the city, and the remarkable difference of four young victims killed between December 1962 and November 1963 at least suggests the possibility that a copycat murderer was at work. It has also been claimed that DeSalvo's confession was, at least in part, fabricated by investigators.

The nephew of 19-year-old Mary Sullivan, convinced that DeSalvo was not the killer of his aunt, reported that he had personally confronted the man responsible. The man had been on the list of suspects, but further investigation was dropped following DeSalvo's full confession.

In December 2001, Miss Sullivan's body was exhumed for forensic tests by a team of scientists at George Washington University, D.C. DNA analysis of stains from her underwear matched neither her DNA, nor that of DeSalvo. Said Professor James Starrs, who headed the team: 'The evidence that has been found is quite clearly indicative of the fact that Albert DeSalvo was not the rape-murderer of Mary Sullivan.'

However, Frederick Bieber, associate professor of pathology at Harvard Medical School retorted: 'Finding someone's DNA at a crime scene doesn't tell you how it got there, and when. Similarly, not finding someone's DNA at a crime scene doesn't mean they weren't there.'

Who can say?

IAN BRADY & MYRA HINDLEY

MOORS MURDERERS

Few cases of serial killing in the UK have horrified the British public as deeply as that of the sadistic couple who became known as the 'Moors Murderers'. For two years they hunted down innocent youngsters, tortured and killed them for pleasure and buried the bodies on a vast stretch of Pennine moorland that lies between the counties of Lancashire and Yorkshire.

The dominant member of this lethal partnership was Ian Brady, born 1938; his willing accomplice was Myra Hindley, four years his junior. They met in 1961, when both were working for a Manchester chemical company, and soon became lovers. Brady, with a minor record for assault and theft, had ambitions to become a bank robber, but on July 12, 1963, he told Hindley that he had decided to commit the 'perfect murder'. In his mind, the plan was simple and infallible: Hindley would cruise the streets of suburban Manchester in a borrowed van, while Brady followed on his motorcycle. When he saw a possible victim he would flash his headlight and Myra would stop and lure their prey into the van.

Soon, Brady spotted a girl whom he recognized – 16-year-old Pauline Reade. Hindley knew the girl's mother, and Pauline was picked up on the pretext that Hindley had lost an expensive glove and would give her some pop music records if she would help to find it. Pauline was bound for a Saturday night dance, but good-naturedly she agreed. Hindley drove to a secluded spot on the edge of Saddleworth Moor, northeast of Manchester, and Brady arrived behind the van on his motorcycle. Myra introduced him as her boy-friend and he led Pauline off on to the moor to start the 'search'.

For what follows, we have to rely upon Hindley's confession some 24 years later. Brady returned to the van and told her to come with him. She saw Pauline lying on the ground, her skirt pulled up and her underwear in disarray, bleeding to death from her slashed throat. Producing a spade that he had left earlier at the site, Brady buried the girl in a makeshift grave. Back home the couple shared the tasks of destroying the evidence; Brady burned the blood-stained clothes he had been wearing, cleaned the spade and disposed of the knife he had used.

It was not until November that Brady had the urge to kill again. On November 23, the pair again hired a van and drove around for several hours before selecting 12-year-old John Kilbride, who was buying biscuits from a stall. Brady invited the boy into the van and – tragically – he accepted. Once again, they drove out to the moors to look for a lost glove. According to Hindley's account, Brady sent her away while he tried first to stab the youngster, and then strangled him with a piece of string. After sexually assaulting the dead child, Brady buried the body.

A major police investigation was mounted after John Kilbride's disappearance but, despite extensive enquiries, no clues were found. It later transpired that the search for his body had been called off only a mile from where he lay in a shallow grave.

On June 16, 1964, in a Mini pick-up that they now owned, the couple once again set out on the hunt and soon spotted 12-year-old Keith Bennett. He readily agreed to go with them to help shift some heavy boxes from a shop. As before, they drove out to the moors where Brady strangled Keith with string, sexually assaulted the body and buried it in a deep hole. He also took photographs which he developed at home and showed to his lover. Many years later she told detectives: 'The boy was lying on his back . . . there was blood on him so I wouldn't look closely. I couldn't say whether he was alive or dead when the picture was taken.'

By December 24, Brady's blood-lust had returned. Hindley, wearing an ill-fitting black wig to disguise her bleached blonde hair, accompanied him to a Christmas fair where they found 10-year-old Lesley Ann Downey, who had become separated from her two brothers. The couple were carrying boxes that looked like Christmas presents; Hindley dropped the parcels on the ground asking Lesley to help her pick them up and carry them to their car. Years later, Hindley said: 'She went with us like a lamb to the slaughter.'

What followed was, eventually, to bring hardened police officers to tears. In the couple's bedroom, Brady had set up his camera and lights, and a tape recorder. There he forced Lesley to strip and pose naked for pornographic photographs, while he tape recorded her terrified cries, before raping and strangling her. It had snowed heavily during the course of the evening and, after trying to reach the moors with Lesley's tiny corpse, Brady and Hindley were forced to turn back and return the next day, when she was buried like the others.

THE BEASTS

Ian Brady was the illegitimate son of a Glasgow waitress. He never knew his father, having been brought up by foster parents in a Gorbals tenement. While still a teenager, he was charged several times with theft and assault and spent some time in a Borstal correctional institution. By the time he met Myra Hindley in Manchester, Brady was a self-professed Nazi admirer and would quote long passages from Hitler's *Mein Kampf.* He already had a collection of books about torture and sadism, one of his favourites being *Compulsion*, the story of the senseless abduction and murder of a 12-year-old boy in 1924 by Nathan Leopold and Richard Loeb.

In contrast, Myra Hindley, born 1942, came from a respectable family in a Manchester suburb and regularly attended Mass, having adopted the Catholic faith in her teens. On meeting Brady she became convinced that he was an unrecognized genius, renounced her Catholic beliefs, and was easily persuaded to join in his perverted practices. She bleached her brown hair bright blonde and posed for him in jackboots as a Nazi concentration-camp guard. The relationship between the couple typifies the psychopathic phenomenon known as *folie à deux,* in which a man and woman derive mutual sexual excitement from their crimes.

Myra Hindley had a younger sister, 19-year-old Maureen, who had married 17-year-old David Smith. The two couples spent much time together, and David, a juvenile delinquent, greatly admired Brady. The older man possessed guns and took him out on the moors to practise with them, bragging about the robberies he was going to commit. Brady decided that he would gain complete power over David by making him an accomplice to murder.

On October 5, 1965, Hindley brought David Smith back to her home while Brady picked up a young apprentice, Edward Evans. Sitting in the kitchen with a glass of wine, Smith suddenly heard terrified screams coming from the living room and Hindley shouting: 'Dave, help him.'

Rushing into the room, he found Brady raining frenzied blows with a hand axe on Evans's head: 'It was a horrible scene. The lad was screaming and trying to get away. Ian just kept hitting him terrible blows on the head, neck and shoulders . . . I was frightened to death, my stomach was churning. There was blood everywhere, on the walls, the fireplace, all over.'

Finally, Brady strangled Evans with a length of electric flex, remarking: 'Well, it's done. It's the messiest yet.'

He told Smith to return next day to help dispose of the body, but the horrified teenager rushed home and roused his wife Maureen. In the early dawn light they left their home, in terror that Brady might have followed them, and telephoned the police, who arrived a few minutes later to pick them up.

After Smith had gasped out his night's experience, officers immediately went to the Brady house. Locked in an upstairs bedroom was the slaughtered body of Edward Evans. Close by was the axe in a brown paper bag and a box containing two fully loaded handguns. Brady was arrested at once and charged with murder; Hindley was taken in for questioning, but it was five days before she, too, was charged.

The house was searched from top to bottom. Detectives found a large collection of photographs: some of Hindley with her pet dogs, some amateurish pornography featuring the couple, and many moorland scenes. They also discovered a notebook with a list of names – one of which was John Kilbride – and a strange tape recording of Myra reading aloud newspaper reports about the disappearance of Lesley Ann Downey to a young girl.

Within a day or two the girl had been identified. She was the daughter of a neighbour and she told the police that Brady and Hindley had taken her for a car ride to Saddleworth Moor on Christmas Eve 1964 – two days before the disappearance of Lesley Ann. She took them to the spot, which was in the area where Smith said he had practised shooting with Brady. A wide search of that part of the moor was organized, with 150 police officers and dogs. On October 16, Lesley Ann's grave was found; she was naked, her clothes buried at her feet. But would it be possible to prove that Brady and Hindley were responsible?

Two days later, an officer flicking through a book belonging to Myra found two left-luggage receipts hidden in the spine. They were for suitcases lodged at Manchester Central Station, and when the cases were recovered they yielded a mass of incriminating evidence. There were bludgeons, wigs, masks, spare handgun ammunition and books about torture. There were also more photographs of Myra in obscene poses, and others of her on the moors. However, most horrific of all, there were photographs of Lesley Ann, naked and gagged with a handkerchief, suffering unspeakable sexual abuse – and a spool of tape. It ran for 13 minutes, recording the pitiful cries of the 10-year-old child as she pleaded for her life. Brady's recording of the last minutes of Lesley Ann Downey's life was meticulously analysed by horrified police technicians. A radio could be heard playing in the background, the voice of Alma Cogan, among others, singing 'Little Drummer Boy'. The broadcast was traced to Radio Luxembourg and a search of the play-lists quickly revealed this to be a Christmas broadcast which went out on the evening of December 26, 1964. The guilt of Brady and Hindley, whose voices, as well of that of the desperate child, could both be heard, was incontrovertible.

On October 21, police searchers found the grave of John Kilbride, some 400 yards from that of Lesley Ann – and they then realized that one of the photographs in Brady's collection showed Myra sitting on it with her dogs. Brady and Hindley were both charged with three murders: those of Edward Evans, John Kilbride and Lesley Ann Downey. The only emotion shown by Hindley was when she was told that one of her dogs was dead.

The trial of Brady and Hindley opened on April 19, 1966, at Chester Assizes. The much-publicised case had aroused violent hatred among the general public. In prison, the couple had been held under permanent guard to protect them from other prisoners, their food had been tested for poison, and in the courtroom the dock was enclosed in bullet-proof glass.

Both refused to swear on the Bible, protesting that they were atheists and both pleaded not guilty.

They continued to deny all the charges, and tried to put the blame on David Smith, who appeared as chief prosecution witness. In his summing up, the judge said: 'If what the prosecution has said is right then you are dealing with two sadistic killers of the utmost depravity.'

The jury took only four hours to agree. Brady was found guilty of all three murders, Hindley for the killing of Lesley Ann and Evans, and harbouring Brady after his murder of John Kilbride. Both were committed to imprisonment for life and Brady was later transferred to Broadmoor maximum security mental hospital.

The case continued to evoke wide interest, particularly as two bodies had not been found. It was not until 1985 that an investigative journalist obtained a series of interviews with Brady in Broadmoor, in which the killer admitted his crimes for the first time and confessed to the murders of Pauline Reade and Keith Bennett. On learning this, the head of Manchester CID, Detective Chief Superintendent Peter Topping, wondered if it was possible to re-open the case.

He visited Myra Hindley in prison and showed her many of the photographs of moorland taken by Brady. She said that, after 20 years, she could not recognize any of the scenes but offered to go with police to Saddleworth Moor. A new search of the moor began on November 20, 1986.

Then, on December 16, Topping received permission to take Hindley to the site. Heavily disguised and accompanied by an armed escort, she trudged about the moor in driving snow, but failed to identify any landmarks and was duly returned to prison.

Topping continued to talk with Hindley and at last, in February 1987, after two decades of maintaining her innocence, she announced that she would tell her story, and recorded 17 hours of terrible truth. Again she was taken to the moor; and again the search was fruitless. However, the police now called upon the advice of experts, who explained how disturbed soil could be spotted from changes in the pattern of vegetation. The RAF photographed the whole area from the air so that it could be compared with Brady's photographs – and Topping went to talk with Brady.

On July 1, 1987, a search team spotted a telltale difference in a patch of vegetation and, after carefully excavating the site, exposed the body of Pauline Reade.

When the find was announced, Brady contacted the Chief Superintendent and said he could show where Keith Bennett lay buried. For the whole of July 3, Brady tramped the moor with his police escort, but failed to find the spot. He was taken back to the moor on December 8, but without success, and the search for Keith's body was finally called off. It has never been discovered. Ian Brady died at Ashworth Hospital on 15 May 2017.

Hindley's case for parole was championed by Lord Longford, often to much press and public derision. From prison, she had gained an Open University degree – but in 1994 she still described herself as being 'wicked and evil' and as having behaved 'monstrously'.

In 1998, the Appeal Court judges upheld the decision by the former UK Home Secretary Jack Straw that Hindley should stay in prison until she died, unless there were exceptional reasons to review the sentence.

Hindley lost her battle for parole. In 2000 she took her case to the House of Lords, but again failed when five law lords unanimously ruled that the former Home Secretary's decision had been lawful and justified.

Myra Hindley died in hospital in November 2002 following a chest infection. She was 60 years of age.

LUCIAN STANIAK

RED SPIDER

When his parents and sister were all killed in a Warsaw hit-and-run auto accident, young Staniak was consumed with rage against the driver. She was the young, blonde, wife of a Polish Air Force captain and, when she was cleared of criminal negligence, Staniak felt bitterly that justice had not been done. His rage grew into obsession and eventually he determined to take revenge on young blonde women wherever, and whenever, he could. In 1964 he wrote an anonymous letter to the Polish publication *Prezeglad Polityczny*. It was written in red ink, in a wavering hand that was to earn him the name of 'Red Spider'. He wrote:

> *There is no happiness without tears, no life without death. Beware! I am going to make you cry.*

Working as a translator for the state publishing house, Staniak travelled throughout Poland in the course of his profession. His first victim was a 17-year-old student, Danka Maciejowitz, whom he raped and viciously disembowelled at Olsztyn, some 150 miles north of Warsaw, on July 22, 1964, during the twentieth anniversary celebration of Polish liberation from the German occupation. The following day, the state newspaper *Kulisy* received another anonymous letter, written in a spidery hand with red ink as before, and in a style reminiscent of Jack the Ripper: 'I picked a juicy flower in Olsztyn and I shall do it again somewhere else, for there is no holiday without a funeral.'

Staniak liked to select national holidays for his murders – perhaps because these were days when there were many more young women about, taking to the streets without thought of danger; or perhaps because this was the only time when his professional duties left him free to kill.

His second victim was 16-year-old Aniuta Kaliniak, another blonde, who marched proudly at the head of a student parade in Warsaw on January 17, 1965. On the following day, there was another anonymous letter, this time to the police, telling them that they could find her body, garroted with wire and with an iron spike thrust through her genitals, in the basement of a factory close to her home.

On All Saints' Day, November 1, 1965, a blonde hotel receptionist, Janka Popielski, fell to Staniak's murdering lust in Poznan, 135 miles west of Warsaw. Janka had gone to the local freight terminal, looking for a free lift to visit her boyfriend in a nearby village, but instead she encountered the Red Spider. She was suffocated with chloroform, raped and her body brutally mutilated with a screwdriver before being stuffed into a packing crate. The injuries she sustained were so horrifying that the police suppressed all details. They searched all the trains and buses leaving Poznan, looking for a man with bloody clothing, but found no suspects and were once again frustrated. The following morning the local newspaper *Courier Zachodni* received another typical letter with a quotation from a novel by a well-known Polish writer: 'Only tears of sorrow can wash out the stain of shame, only pangs of suffering can blot out the fires of lust.'

May Day 1966 was marked by the rape and disembowellment of 17-year-old Marysia Galazka, whose mutilated body was dumped in a tool shed behind her home, with her entrails draped across her thighs. On December 24, 1966, the sadistically mutilated body of Janina Kozielska, 17, was found in a train compartment in Krakow; she was the sister of 14-year-old Aniela, who had been murdered in Warsaw two years earlier. This time, the brief note from the 'Red Spider' was found pushed through the slot of the mail car: 'I have done it again.'

Investigators discovered that the compartment had been reserved by a man and his wife, and theorized that Janina had arrived as the killer's companion.

Major Ciznek of the Warsaw Homicide Squad took charge of the Red Spider case. A nationwide search for similar crimes turned up 14 more murders that seemed to fit the Red Spider's *modus operandi*, although none of them had been followed by the characteristic letters to newspapers. Dating from April 1964, five of the murders had occurred around Poznan; there had been two at Bydgoszcz; and single killings had taken place in districts such as Bialystok, Kielce, Lomza, Lublin and Radom. Plotting the murders on a map, Ciznek noted that most of the crime scenes lay south and west of Warsaw, in towns connected by direct rail lines to Katowice and Krakow.

The coincidence of two sisters being murdered gave them their first positive clue. Both had posed as artists' models for the Art Lovers Club in Krakow, and an analysis of red ink used by the Spider revealed that it was artists' oil paint, thinned with solvent. Every one of the more than 100 members of the club was questioned, and very soon the police picked upon 26-year-old Lucian Staniak, a keen painter.

Staniak's canvases were extraordinary; they made much use of blood-red paint, applied with a knife.

One painting in particular was dramatically revealing. Entitled 'The Circle of Life,' it depicted a cow eating a flower, the cow attacked and devoured by a wolf, a hunter shooting the wolf, the hunter run down by a female car driver, and finally a disembowelled woman with a bunch of flowers springing from her open belly.

The sadistic killer was apprehended in Lodz on February 1, 1967, hours after he had murdered student Bozena Raczkiewicz, 18, at the railway station. He had knocked her unconscious with a vodka bottle and – the clinching evidence – had left his fingerprint on the glass. In interrogation, he very soon admitted his identity as the Red Spider and claimed that he had committed this last killing because publicity for his recent actions had been lacking. A check on his movements over the previous two years fitted closely with the scenes of the succession of unsolved murders.

Confessing to 20 murders in all, Staniak was tried for six and found guilty. However, he was subsequently judged insane and committed to an asylum in Katowice for life.

JEROME BRUDOS

SHOE FETISHIST

The motive driving serial killers almost always includes a powerful sexual element. However, few cases have proved so bizarre as that of Jerome Brudos, obsessed collector of young women's shoes and underwear.

B orn in South Dakota in January 1939, Brudos moved with his family to California as a child. He grew up with a deep hatred of his domineering mother, yet from the age of five he developed a strange fetish for women's shoes. As a young boy he picked up a pair of high heels from a local dump and brought them home, where his mother promptly burned them. Then he stole shoes from his sister. By the age of 16, now living in Salem, Oregon, he began to steal from neighbours, sometimes also taking underwear from their washing lines.

Aged 17, Brudos forced a girl at knifepoint to strip while he took photographs. Taken to juvenile court, he was diagnosed as suffering from 'early personality disorder' and ordered to attend the state hospital in Salem for therapy. In March 1959 he joined the army, but was discharged in October the same year, after telling an army psychiatrist his dreams of a beautiful Korean girl creeping into his bed.

Back home with his parents in Salem, where he took to living in the family tool shed, Brudos began to stalk local women, knocking them down and half-suffocating them before making off with their shoes. These attacks ceased for some years after 1961, when he met a young woman called Ralphene, made her pregnant and married her. They relocated to the Portland suburb of Aloha and, for a time, Brudos seemed to have settled down.

Then, in 1967, while his wife was in hospital for the birth of their second child, he began to complain of migraines and 'blackouts', and started his night prowling again, stealing shoes and underwear. One woman awoke to find Brudos ransacking her closet; he choked her until she was unconscious, raped her, and made off with his plunder. Around this time, he used to make Ralphene walk about the house naked while he took photographs, and he also posed himself, wearing some of his stolen underwear.

Events began to accelerate the following year. On January 26, 1968, 19-year-old student Linda Slawson came to the Brudos front door selling encyclopedias. Jerry took her into the basement garage, beat her, raped her and strangled her. He then sent Ralphene out for hamburgers while he dressed Linda's corpse in some of his collection of clothing. After photographing her, he cut off her left foot as a trophy, locked it in the freezer and dumped the remains in the nearby Willamette River.

In July, 16-year-old Stephanie Vikko disappeared; her remains would not be discovered until the following March. On 26 November, another student, Jan Whitney, aged 23, vanished while on a drive from McMinnville, south of Portland. Her car was found abandoned on the road north of Albany. It was later established that Brudos had taken her to his garage where he had killed her and left her body hanging from a hook, dressed as he liked, for several days. He then cut off one of her breasts in order to preserve it and disposed of the rest of her corpse in the river.

Up to this time, the police had been investigating a succession of disappearances but, with the discovery of Stephanie Vikko's body on March 18, 1969, one case at least was now clearly homicide. Nine days later, Karen Sprinker, aged 19, vanished from a department store parking lot, leaving her car abandoned.

At about the same time, two witnesses reported seeing a large man – dressed in women's clothes – loitering in the lot. Brudos had taken Karen to his home, raped her and forced her to pose for photographs before hanging her. He then cut off both her breasts, dumping her body in the Long Tom River.

Meanwhile, Brudos's wife Ralphene had dark suspicions of her own. Tidying around their home, she had turned up a host of her husband's photographs of himself in his victims' underwear, together with Jan Whitney's preserved breast – which she assumed was plastic, and which he assured her was an innocent paperweight.

Fortunately for her peace of mind, she did not discover Brudos's store of photographs featuring himself posing with his victims' bodies, but disturbing doubts lingered.

Brudos claimed his final victim on April 23 when, posing as a plainclothes police officer, he 'arrested' 22-year-old Linda Salee in a shopping mall on suspicion of shoplifting. He took her to his garage, and eventually killed her; but he had a problem: 'Her breasts were all pink – the nipples weren't dark like they should be . . . I didn't cut them off because they didn't appeal to me.'

Instead, he tried, unsuccessfully, to make plaster casts of them.

On May 10, fishermen hauled up Linda Salee's body from the Long Tom River. It was weighed down with part of an auto transmission. Two days later, and only 50 yards downriver, Karen Sprinker's corpse was recovered by a team of divers.

Interviews with local co-eds yielded tales of an ageing 'Vietnam Vet', who hung around campus asking for dates. Answering their descriptions, Brudos was picked up by police on May 25, and questioned closely before being let go. Five days later, he was again arrested on a concealed weapons charge. This time he broke down and confessed in detail to the murders.

A search of the Brudos home revealed his huge collection of women's shoes and underwear, and hundreds of incriminating photographs. One in particular proved irrefutable evidence. While photographing one of his sexily dressed victims hanging from a hook, Brudos had placed a mirror below her – and had unsuspectingly caught a reflection of himself.

He pleaded guilty on three counts of first-degree murder on June 17, 1969, and was sentenced to life imprisonment.

ZODIAC KILLER

AS YET UNSOLVED

On October 14, 1969, the editor of the *San Francisco Chronicle* received a long letter. It was not the first of its kind, nor the last; but it sent a particular shiver of fear through families in the Bay Area. It began:

This is the Zodiac speaking . . .

and concluded:

. . . Schoolchildren make nice targets, I think I shall wipe out a school bus some morning. Just shoot out the front tire & then pick off the kiddies as they come bouncing out.

This was a clear and chilling threat that the man already known as the 'Zodiac Killer' was about to widen the range of his targets.

Over nearly three years, the targets had been young women, often together with their male companions. Originally, the first had seemed a single random victim – and it was many months before the police suspected that her death marked the beginning of an accelerating series of murders.

On the evening of October 30, 1966, Cheri Jo Bates, an 18-year-old freshman at Riverside City College near Los Angeles, left the campus library to discover that her parked car would not start. She did not know, but the distributor had been disconnected. Someone – presumably a man – approached her, and probably offered her a ride. He dragged her into some nearby bushes, kicked her in the head, stabbed her twice in the chest and slashed her throat so viciously that she was almost decapitated.

A few days later, the police received a letter. It was a blurred carbon copy of a document typed all in capitals, and therefore impossible to trace back to its source. It gave details of Cheri Jo's murder that only the police and the killer knew. It began: 'She was young and beautiful but now she is battered and dead. She is not the first and she will not be the last.'

After a detailed description of the killing, the writer admitted: 'I am not sick. I am insane. But that will not stop the game . . .'

Six months after Cheri Jo's death, the local *Riverside Press-Enterprise* published an article on the unsolved murder. The following day, the newspaper, the police and the girl's father received identical crudely pencilled notes on lined loose-leaf paper:

BATES HAD TO DIE THERE WILL BE MORE

Each was signed with what could have been a figure 2 – or a small letter 'z'.

More than eighteen months passed. On the evening of December 20, 1968, David Faraday, 17, and Bettilou Jensen, 16, attended a end-of-term concert in their high school at Vallejo, on the north side of the San Francisco Bay area. After the concert, David suggested that they should drive up to Lake Herman reservoir, to 'look at the view' over Vallejo. As the teenagers sat kissing, they were suddenly illuminated by the narrow beam of a flashlight. The driver's door was wrenched open and David was shot point-blank in the head. Bettilou was able to run just 10 yards before she was gunned down with five shots in the back from a .22 automatic pistol.

A few minutes later, a passing motorist spotted Bettilou's body and raced off in search of a patrol car. When the police reached the scene of the attack, Bettilou was dead. David was still alive and able to give brief details of the shooting, but not of his attacker, and he died shortly after reaching hospital. The police were stymied; there were no witnesses and no apparent motive. Neither victim had been robbed and Bettilou had not been sexually assaulted.

Just over six months later, on July 4, 1969, Mrs Darlene Ferrin, 22, had a date with 19-year-old Michael Mageau – one of a number of boyfriends she hoped her husband wouldn't find out about. They drove out of Vallejo together and parked at Blue Rock Springs, a local beauty spot only two miles from where David and Bettilou had been killed. On the way they had been followed by another car, which now parked only a few feet away. Darlene seemed to know the other driver and reassured Michael, saying 'Don't worry about it'.

However, ten minutes later a blinding white spotlight shone in on them from the other car. Without a word, a man appeared in the dark and started shooting. Darlene was hit nine times and died soon afterwards. Michael took a bullet in the neck, which shattered his jaw and ripped away part of his tongue. Other shots hit him in the leg, elbow and shoulder. The gunman left him for dead, but he survived and was able to give police details of the attack and even a partial description of the killer.

Within an hour of the shooting, Vallejo PD received a call from a pay phone. A man speaking softly, and without an accent, told them: 'I want to report a double murder. If you will go one mile east on Columbus Parkway to the public park, you will find kids in a brown car. They were shot with a 9-mm Luger. I also killed those kids last year. Goodbye.'

The police traced the call to a booth in front of the Vallejo Sheriff's Office and within sight of the house where Darlene lived with her husband Dean. A passerby had noticed a 'stocky' man using the phone at the critical time, but this was the only clue the police had.

Suspicion naturally fell upon Dean Ferrin, but he had a cast-iron alibi for the time of the shooting. Discussing the murder later, several of Darlene's friends recalled that she had received anonymous telephone calls in the preceding weeks and threatening visits from a heavyset man she referred to as 'Paul'. On one occasion she told her babysitter; 'He doesn't want anyone to know what I saw him do. I saw him murder someone'.

The police could only add the killing to a list of unsolved murders. Apart from the telephone call, they had no evidence to connect the shooting of Bettilou Jensen with that of Darlene

Ferrin. But everything changed on 1 August, when the editors of the *Vallejo Times-Herald*, the *San Francisco Examiner* and the *San Francisco Chronicle* each received a letter.

The letters were signed with a cross over a circle – presumably intended to be a sign of the zodiac, although also significantly similar to a gun sight – and were crudely written and carelessly spelt. The letter received by the *Chronicle* began: 'Dear Editor This is the murderer of the 2 teenagers last Christmass at Lake Herman & the girl on the 4th of July near the golf course in Vallejo To prove I killed them I shall state some facts which only I & the police know'. The details – the ammunition used, and the position of the bodies – made it clear that the writer must indeed be the killer.

Each newspaper also received one third of a message in cipher, a sheet of random symbols with no overt meaning. The murderer's letters concluded: 'I want you to print this cipher on the front page of your paper. In this cipher is my identity. If you do not print this cipher by the afternoon of Fry. 1st of Aug 69, I will go on a kill ram-Page Fry. night. I will cruse around all weekend killing lone people in the night then move on to kill again, untill I end up with a dozen people over the weekend.'

The three newspapers published their separate parts, while the police sought the help of Naval Intelligence, the CIA and the National Security Agency. Not one of these highly experienced organizations was able to break the code – probably because it was so unsophisticated. Donald Harden, a high school teacher in Salinas, and his wife cracked it in a day and a half. Each third of the message consisted of eight lines of 17 symbols each, and it was written in a simple substitution cipher.

On 7 August, the killer wrote again, for the first time identifying himself by his nickname. He gave many details about the Vallejo killings, explaining that he had been able to aim his gun accurately by taping a pencil flashlight to the barrel. But although he wrote that when the police cracked the code they would 'have' him, the deciphered message contained no clue – unless it was hidden in the final cluster of 19 apparently meaningless letters.

ZODIAC'S CIPHER MESSAGE DECODED

> I like killing people because it is so much fun it is more fun than killing wild game in the forrest because man is the most dangeroue anamal of all to kill something gives me the most thrilling experence it is even better than getting your rocks off with a girl the best part of it is thae when I die I will be reborn in paradice and the I have killed will become my slaves I will not give you my name because you will try to sloi down or atop my collectiog of slaves for afterlife ebeorietemethhpitti [*sic*].

The Harden decoding was confirmed by Naval Intelligence. It's apparent that, even with the substitution table at his side, the killer made several errors.

Cipher experts concluded that this was common practice, to fill out a message to the desired length; but when the deciphered message was published on August 12 amateurs from all over the Bay Area were sure that it was an anagram of the Zodiac's real name – the only plausible rearrangement, however, being 'Robert Emmet the hippie' – and no-one answering that description could be found.

The intervals between the murders was decreasing, and Zodiac struck again on September 27. In the early evening two students, 20-year-old Bryan Hartnell and 22-year-old Cecelia Shephard, were picnicking by Lake Berryessa, 20 miles north of Vallejo. Out of the trees came a heavily built man, around six feet tall, wearing a black hooded cape, like a medieval executioner; on its front was a white cross and circle. A long knife in a sheath hung at his left hip and in his right hand he held a semi-automatic pistol, which was pointed directly at the couple.

The man said he was an escaped convict from Deer Lodge, Montana, where he had killed a prison guard, and needed Bryan's car to get to Mexico. 'I'm going to have to tie you up,' he said, producing several lengths of clothesline. When they were both bound, and lying face down on the ground, he said 'I'm going to have to stab you people,' and began stabbing Bryan repeatedly in the back. The young man, unable to move, decided that the wisest action was to pretend to be dying. But the assailant then turned to Cecelia and began to stab her over and over again. Finally, he walked to the car and wrote a message on the door with a black felt-tip pen.

A little over an hour after the attack, the Napa Sheriff's Office received a phone call, later traced to a pay booth in Napa. 'I want to report a murder – no, a double murder,' said a quiet voice. '. . . I'm the one that did it.' At the crime scene, the investigating detective found the message on the car door. There was a crude drawing of male genitals with the customary Zodiac symbol and the words:

Vallejo
12-20-68
7-4-69
Sept 27-69-6.30
by knife

They were the dates of three Zodiac killings – and they were coming closer together. Cecelia died the following afternoon but Bryan survived.

The pay phone in Napa yielded a good palm print from the receiver. In the sand around the murder scene the police found a trail of footprints. They were size $10\frac{1}{2}$, and very deep.

Tests by the heaviest officer present established that the killer weighed around 220 pounds. The tracks were identified as made by a boot called 'Wing Walker', but over a million pairs of these boots had been manufactured to government contract, and 103,700 pairs had been delivered to Navy and Air Force establishments on the west coast. Was the killer a military man?

Two weeks later, on October 11, a San Francisco cab driver, Paul Stine, was killed with a 9mm pistol, and ballistics tests showed that it was the same gun used to kill David Faraday and Bettilou Jensen. The killer had wiped the interior of the car with a piece of fabric torn from the victim's shirt. It was three days after the killing that the *Chronicle* received a chilling letter beginning: 'This is the Zodiac speaking I am the murderer of the taxi driver . . .'

It concluded with the threat to shoot children on a school bus and contained a piece of the cloth torn from Stine's shirt.

In the Napa Valley area, thousands of children rode daily in school buses, many along deserted country roads. Urgent instructions were issued to all school bus drivers: in the event of an attack, they were to continue driving, even on flat tyres, with all lights on and sounding the horn, and they were not to stop until they reached a well-populated area, where police officers could be notified. Fortunately, the Zodiac did not carry out his threat.

The police issued a composite-based image during this stage of the investigation. At the time the case was being headed up by State Attorney General Thomas Lynch, in an effort to pick up the Zodiac's trail before he killed again. Then, a startling development came in the early hours of October 22. A man telephoned the police in Oakland: 'This is the Zodiac speaking. I want to get in touch with F. Lee Bailey . . . if you can't come up with Bailey, I'll settle for Mel Belli. I want one or the other to appear on the Channel 7 talk show. I'll make contact by telephone.'

Belli, one of America's most famous lawyers, agreed to appear on the show the next day. At 7.40 am, a man called in to the radio station. He had a long conversation with Belli about the murders and said he suffered from blinding headaches. He ended by agreeing to meet the lawyer in front of a store in Daly City – but, predictably, he failed to turn up. The police, already convinced that the call was a hoax, eventually traced the caller to Napa State Hospital, where he was a mental patient – and certainly not the Zodiac.

In the second week of November, the *Chronicle* received two communications from the Zodiac, one of which was a commercially printed greeting card. One side had the printed words:

Sorry I haven't written, but I just washed my pen . . .

Inside was a Zodiac cipher text together with the scrawled message:

and I can't do a thing with it . . .

This the Zodiac speaking I thought you would need a good laugh before you hear the bad news you won't get news for a while yet PS could you print this new cipher on your front page? I get awfully lonely when I am ignored, so lonely I could do my **Thing**!!!!!!

Dec July Aug Sept Oct = 7

There were two killings unaccounted for in August, when a couple of girls, aged 14 and 15, had been found frenziedly stabbed, but the police were far from sure that these could be attributed to the Zodiac. In fact, the true killer was traced two years later.

The second letter mailed to the *Chronicle* was seven pages long. In a diatribe against the police, the Zodiac wrote how he would never be caught, leaving no fingerprints: 'The police shall never catch me because I have been too clever for them . . . I wear transparent finger tip guards. All it takes is 2 coats of airplane cement . . .'

He then threatened to bomb a bus, and included a sketch of the construction of the bomb and a plan of how it would be laid.

Nothing more was heard of the Zodiac for some weeks, then Melvin Belli received a Christmas card with another scrap of Paul Stine's bloodstained shirt. The full-page message inside wished him 'a happy Christmas' and continued: 'The one thing I ask of you is this, please help me. I cannot reach out for help because of this thing in me wont let me. I am finding it extreamly difficult to hold it in check I am afraid I will loose control again and take my nineth + posible tenth victom.'

On March 15 and 17, 1970, a man in a white Chevrolet was reported following women motorists and trying to make them stop. On March 22, Mrs Kathleen Johns and her 10-month-old daughter were offered a lift to a service station near Modesto by a man who told her that the rear wheel on her car was loose. Instead, he drove her away through a maze of winding lanes, calmly remarking every now and then: 'You know I'm going to kill you.'

By mistake, the man drove on to the exit ramp of a freeway and, as he stopped, Mrs Johns gathered up her daughter, jumped from the car and took terrified refuge in an irrigation ditch. When she later reached a police station and gave a description of her abductor, she spotted an artist's portrait of the Zodiac on a 'wanted' poster and cried out: 'That's him right there!'

When her car was recovered the interior had been completely burned out.

Nine more letters were received from the Zodiac between April 1970 and March 1971, and there were several unsolved killings during this time, but the police were confident that at least one was a 'copy-cat' crime. In the first of these letters, the Zodiac claimed the following about his tenth victim: 'It would have been a lot more except that my bus bomb was a dud.'

Journalists and the police continued to receive Zodiac letters, but most were judged to be hoaxes. However, unsolved murders continued in the Bay area, and in January 1974 the *Chronicle* received a letter that was considered genuine: it ended with the score 'Me-37 SFPD-0'. Then, nothing for four years until on April 25, 1978, a letter arrived at the *Chronicle* with the chilling words: 'I am back with you.'

The police speculated that the killer might have been in prison, or even being treated in a mental institution. Significantly, the letter ended: 'I am now in control of all things.'

After that there were no more Zodiac murders.

ZODIAC IDENTIFIED?

Robert Graysmith, a cartoonist on the *Chronicle*, published a detailed investigation of the Zodiac murders in 1986. He named the killer as 'Robert Hall Starr', whose erratic behaviour had caused his family to inform the police of their suspicions that he could be the Zodiac.

'Starr' was a loner who hunted game and resembled the descriptions of the killer. The police had two partial fingerprints from Paul Stine's cab, but they did not match the suspect's and their investigation went no further. But the most significant piece of circumstantial evidence was that, in the period 1974–78, 'Starr' had been committed to an institution for child molestation.

HENRY LEE LUCAS

'I HATED EVERYBODY'

Henry Lee Lucas was born on August 23, 1936, in a remote two-room dirt-floored shack near Blacksburg, Virginia. There were eight other children, some deposited with relatives or foster homes over the years, but Henry Lee remained at home with his parents: Nellie Viola, who ran the household and the family's moonshine still with an iron hand, and Anderson Lucas – known as 'No Legs'– the result of a drunken encounter with a freight train.

Nellie, who also scored tricks as an occasional neighborhood prostitute, treated her youngest son – according to his account, which is not always to be believed – with violence, both physical and emotional. He later said: 'I hated all my life. I hated everybody. When I first grew up and I can remember, I was dressed as a girl by Mother. And I stayed that way for three years.'

He alleged that Nellie sent him for his first day at school wearing a girl's dress, and with his hair curled. 'After that I was treated like what I call the dog of the family; I was beaten; I was made to do things that no human being would want to do . . .'

Medical scans of Lucas's brain, much later, revealed extensive damage to the areas that control emotion and behaviour, attributable to his mother's beatings. As a child, he lost an eye when one of his brothers accidentally stabbed him. While still a youngster, he began to indulge in all kinds of sadistic and sexually deviant activities. He claimed that, at the age of 13, he killed his schoolteacher when she spurned his advances; she was found, alive and well, in 1985. And in 1951 (if he is to be believed) he picked up 17-year-old Laura Burnside near Lynchburg and, when she refused his clumsy attempts at sex, strangled her and buried her corpse in the woods near Harrisonburg.

In June 1954, Lucas was sentenced to six years for a series of burglaries around Richmond. He escaped twice and was finally released from prison on September 2, 1959. Four months later, on January 11, 1960, he finally stabbed his 74-year-old mother to death in a drunken quarrel. He was found guilty of second-degree murder, and committed to Ionia State Psychiatric Hospital in Michigan, but was paroled on June 3, 1970, despite his pleas to the hospital authorities: 'I'm not ready to go. I know I'll kill again.'

That day, he claimed, he killed a young girl within sight of the hospital gate.

Lodging with relatives in Tecumseh, Michigan, Lucas was booked for molesting two teenage girls in December 1971, but the charge was later reduced to kidnapping and he spent a further three and a half years in prison in Jackson. On his release, he travelled to other relatives in Maryland and Pennsylvania, before returning to Michigan with his newly-wed wife, a 39-year-old widow, and settling in Port Deposit.

The marriage lasted only 18 months. Meanwhile, according to his own account, Lucas continued a career of random murder, taking time off from work with his brother-in-law to roam and kill as he desired. After his divorce, he spent the next six years on the road, joining forces with Ottis Toole, a man he met at a soup kitchen in Jacksonville, Florida.

The pair survived by armed robbery of convenience stores and gas stations, swiftly travelling from one jurisdiction to another to avoid pursuit. According to both their confessions, they then began to kill for sheer pleasure. On November 5, 1978, for example, they were driving on Interstate 35, north of Austin, Texas, when they picked up a teenage couple whose car had run out of gas. Toole at once produced his .22 semi-automatic and Lucas, who was driving, pulled off the highway into a side-road. Toole dragged the boy from the car and shot him. Some distance further north, nearing Waco, Toole ordered the terrified girl from the car and pumped six shots into her.

In 1979, Lucas moved in with Toole's family in Jacksonville, working on and off as a roofer. Next door lived Toole's mother

OTTIS TOOLE

Born on March 5, 1947, in Jacksonville, Florida, Toole was a true psychopath with whom the wily Henry Lee Lucas cannot compare. His father, like Anderson Lucas, was an alcoholic and soon left home, leaving young Ottis in the care of his religious fanatic mother and a sister who liked to dress him in her clothes. He alleged that his grandmother was a Satanist who took him to graveyards to obtain parts of human bodies for use in magic charms. As a youngster, he got satisfaction from setting fire to empty houses near his home: 'I just hated to see them standing there,' he later said. He claimed to have committed his first murder at the age of 14. It is arguable that much of Henry Lee Lucas's description of his early years was derived from Toole's reminiscences – or vice versa.

An overt homosexual – he was married for just three days – Toole drifted around the western states for ten years, and was suspected of committing at least four murders during that time. For six years he and Lucas were bosom companions until, on June 6, 1983, he was arrested for arson in Jacksonville, Florida. He freely confessed to setting some 40 fires over the preceding twenty years, was convicted on August 5, and sentenced to a term of 20 years. In prison, he confessed to 25 murders in 11 different states, and admitted involvement with Lucas in a further 108 homicides. He died in prison, of cirrhosis of the liver, in September 1996.

with her second husband, her drug-addict daughter Drusilla, and her two children, 12-year-old Frieda – who called herself 'Becky' – and 10-year-old Frank. Toole and Lucas would often take the children off on their criminal trips, and the events that Frank witnessed would later drive him into a mental institution.

In October 1979, the strange foursome were once again on Interstate 35, near Austin, when they spotted 34-year-old Sandra Mae Dubbs peering into the engine compartment of her car. A few days later, her naked body was found in a field some 50 miles away. She had been stabbed 37 times. Several months later, in Georgia, a 16-year-old girl was abducted and killed, her body dumped in an artificial lake. Refused beer at a store in Brunswick, Toole shot the cashier in a rage. And south of Savannah 'a young blondish girl' was killed and her body mutilated by Toole.

And so the killing spree continued until, in the late months of 1981, Toole's mother died. Drusilla committed suicide and Frank and Frieda Powell were taken into a children's home in Bartow, Florida. By now, Lucas was in love with Frieda, and he and Toole broke into the home in January 1982 and carried her off. They headed west through Texas and on January 26 they raped and decapitated a woman near Abilene, before driving on and dumping her head a long way further on in the desert outside Phoenix, Arizona. Here Toole left his companions, heading back to Jacksonville, while Lucas and his 'wife' continued into California.

One rainy night at the end of January, an antique dealer named Jack Smart found the pair stranded on a lonely road near Palm Springs. He took them back to his home in nearby Hemet and lodged them in a small apartment in return for their doing maintenance work in his shop and house. He was so impressed with their industry that, three months later, he sent them off to look after his wife's mother, 80-year-old Kate Rich, in Ringgold, northern Texas.

The new job did not last long. Within a month, two of Mrs Rich's other daughters found her home neglected and filthy and turned Lucas and Frieda out. They were taken in by a local preacher who ran a small religious community known as the House of Prayer outside nearby Stoneburg, and Lucas was hired as a handyman. But the atmosphere of the community so affected Frieda that she announced that she wanted to return to Florida and confess her sins – which, Lucas realized, included confessing his sins, too. He agreed to go with her and, in a field some miles away, he stabbed and dismembered her.

Three weeks later, Mrs Rich disappeared and in the following month her house was burnt out. Back in Stoneburg, Lucas said that Frieda had run off with a truck driver and denied all knowledge of Kate Rich's whereabouts.

Finally, on June 11, 1983, Lucas was arrested on a charge of illegal gun possession, and from jail he wrote to the sheriff: 'I have tried to get help for so long and no-one will believe me. I have killed for the past 10 years and no-one will believe me. I cannot go on doing this. I also killed the only girl I ever loved.'

Lucas took sheriff's officers to where he had disposed of Frieda, and also to the drain where he had dumped Mrs Rich's body – but it was missing, and it later transpired that he had removed it and burnt it in a stove at the House of Prayer. In the evening, he began a videotaped confession which lasted for many hours as he admitted to killings in nearly every state. Over the next 18 months, following his conviction and sentencing to death, Lucas raised his body count from an original 75 to 'way over 500' – many of them, undoubtedly, murders committed by others. He was convicted of eight deaths and formally charged with 30 more.

Lucas claimed that some of the murders were committed under orders from a nationwide Satanic cult, the 'Hand of Death', to which Toole belonged. He said that Toole sometimes ate the flesh of the victims, but 'I don't like barbecue sauce'.

The Texas Rangers received inquiries from police in many states, in the hope of clearing numerous unsolved cases. Lucas was frequently allowed to leave his Houston jail cell on nationwide tours, escorted by armed guards. Robert Ressler, of the FBI Behavioral Science Unit, later wrote: 'He was conveyed to distant locations by airplane or car, stayed in motels, ate well in restaurants, and was generally treated as a celebrity.'

There were odd discrepancies in Lucas's 'confessions'. For example, he provided a wealth of details concerning the murder of 19-year-old Lisa Martinez in Kennewick, Washington State, on November 4, 1978, and the shooting of two teenagers outside Austin, Texas – some 2,000 miles away by road – on the following day.

It has been suggested that he possessed a condition called hypermnesia – the ability to recall in remarkable detail. Possibly, he managed to pick up enough from his Texas Ranger escort during his first interrogation by local police, and from the tales of other vagrants he met on the road, to consruct a plausible tale.

With Lucas providing details 'from memory', police in 35 states eventually decided that they could close their files on some 210 cases.

The FBI, however, were doubtful of many of Lucas's claims. Interviewing him in Houston, an agent asked him if he had committed murders in Guyana. (He meant Jonestown, Guyana.) Lucas agreed – though he wasn't sure – was Guyana in Louisiana or Texas? It was, in fact, in South America, where cult leader Jim Jones had persuaded hundreds of his followers to commit suicide at their Jonestown settlement in November 1978.

On April 15, 1985, two journalists from the Dallas *Times-Herald* published a damning analysis of Lucas's many confessions. Piecing together existing records of his employment, payment receipts and other evidence, they concluded that much of his story was untrue. Lucas himself confused the matter further by recanting his guilt in any murder – including that of his mother, for which he had already served time, and of Frieda and Kate Rich, both of whose remains had been recovered on his information.

Robert Ressler was finally able to obtain an interview with Lucas, who admitted that he had killed 'a few' since 1975. He said he had told lies 'to have fun', and highlight the 'stupidity' of the police. Ressler wrote: 'If we had had VICAP [see Introduction] up and running at the time Lucas made his first startling admission, it would have been easy to see what was truth and what was falsehood in his confession.'

Lucas spent 15 years on death row, but on June 26, 1998, George W. Bush – then governor of Texas – commuted his sentence to life imprisonment. Lucas died in prison in 2001.

EDMUND KEMPER

CO-ED KILLER

Ed Kemper was 14 years old when he was sent to stay with his paternal grandparents at their remote farmhouse in the Sierra Mountains of California. He found the life there dull – even though his grandfather gave him a .22 rifle to go out shooting – and his grandmother seemed to spend all day working on the children's storybooks that she wrote. On August 27, 1963, young Ed wondered 'how it would feel to shoot Grandma', and he did just that. When his grandfather returned from shopping at the local town store, he shot him too. In due course Ed was diagnosed as a paranoid schizophrenic and committed to the state hospital for the criminally insane at Atascadero.

K emper lived with his grandparents because his home life was in disarray. His father and mother were divorced after years of a tempestuous relationship; both had remarried and he did not get on with either of his step-parents. Born in Burbank, California, in December 1948, he had spent his early years dominated by his mother, whose standards of behaviour he found impossible to meet. This made him timid in nature, with feelings of inadequacy coupled with a deep-down resentment of his treatment.

With his two sisters, young Ed would often play out a game of execution, in which he was the victim. On one occasion he cut the head and hands off one of his sisters' dolls. By the age of 10, he had buried the family cat alive, only to later cut off its head and display it in his bedroom. Another cat was dismembered with a machete and the pieces hidden in a closet until they were discovered by his mother. At the same time, he enjoyed fantasies of sex and violence. When one sister teased him about his crush on his grade-school teacher, and asked why he didn't give her a kiss, he calmly replied: 'If I kiss her, I would have to kill her first.'

Even his mother described Ed as 'a real weirdo', and eventually sent him to live with his father, from where he was soon moved to his grandparents' – and the subsequent murders.

After spending five years in Atascadero the 21-year-old was released in 1969 – against his doctors' advice – into the custody of his mother, who had relocated to Santa Cruz and was working at local Merrill College as an administrator. He had grown into a giant, 6 ft 9 ins in height and weighing some 300 pounds. After incessant arguments with his mother, he moved to Alameda, near San Francisco. He then bought a car and cruised the highways, at first just giving rides to young female hitch-hikers while learning conversational ways to put them at ease.

Then, on May 7, 1972, Kemper picked up two 18-year-old co-eds, Mary Anne Pesce and Anita Luchesi, not far from Stanford University. He drove them to an isolated spot and drew a 9mm Browning automatic that he had borrowed from a friend. He then took out a pair of handcuffs and secured Mary Anne's wrists behind her, and locked Anita in the trunk at gunpoint. Producing a plastic bag, Kemper thrust it over Mary Anne's head and wound a cord around her neck. As she fought for her life he stabbed her many times, and finally cut her throat. Opening the trunk, he stabbed Anita to death as she tried to climb out, threw the knife inside with her body, and drove home.

The friend with whom Kemper shared an apartment in Alameda was away, so he carried the bodies, wrapped in blankets, to his room, where he dismembered them, taking Polaroid photographs as he worked. He stuffed the remains in garbage bags and drove off to bury them in the mountains – but he kept the heads for some time before finally tossing them into a lonely ravine. Mary Anne's head was discovered some months later and identified from dental records, but the police were without further clues.

For some months Kemper did not go out looking for likely hitch-hikers and turned his attention, with his mother's backing, to getting the murder of his grandparents expunged from his record.

appropriate as much as she'd bitched and screamed and yelled at me over so many years.'

There was no going back now. Kemper called a friend of his mother, Sally Hallett, and invited her over for a 'surprise dinner'. When Mrs Hallett arrived she said: 'Let's sit down, I'm dead' – and he took her at her word and strangled her. He then left for a drink at the 'Jury Room'. On his return he cut off the woman's head and left her body in bed.

At dawn next morning, Easter Sunday, without an idea of what to do, Kemper set off driving aimlessly eastward for many hours, having left a note for the police beside his mother's corpse: 'No need for her to suffer any more at the hands of this "murderous Butcher". It was quick – asleep – the way I wanted it. Not sloppy and incomplete, gents. Just a "lack of time". I got things to do!!!!'

Keeping himself awake with caffeine tablets, Kemper at last arrived in Pueblo, Colorado, where he pulled over to a roadside telephone booth and called the Santa Cruz police to confess that he was the 'Co-ed Killer'. At first they did not believe him, and it took several more calls before the local police arrived to arrest him.

At his trial, Kemper outlined his motive in killing young women: 'Alive, they were distant, not sharing with me. I was trying to establish a relationship. When they were being killed, there wasn't anything going on in my mind except that they were going to be mine . . . That was the only way they could be mine. I had their spirits. I still have them.'

Judged sane by state psychiatrists, Kemper was convicted on eight counts of murder. Asked what he considered suitable punishment, he replied starkly: 'Death by torture'.

However, there was no death penalty at that time in California, and he was sentenced to life imprisonment.

ARTHUR SHAWCROSS

ROCHESTER RAMPAGER

It was on April 28, 1987, that Arthur Shawcross walked out of Attica prison in upper New York State, released on parole. He was a few weeks short of his forty-second birthday, prematurely aged, pot-bellied and grey-haired, looking some twenty years older than his true age after serving nearly 15 years of a 25-year sentence. He didn't appear a threat to anyone, yet he was a convicted killer, and there was one desire that dominated his thinking – to kill again.

Like many other serial murderers, Shawcross claimed that it was his domineering mother, whom he could never please, who ruined his childhood. He was born in Portsmouth, New Hampshire, on June 6, 1945, and was the eldest of the family. He grew up near Brownville, outside Watertown, NY. At school, he was known as 'Oddie' and had no friends, and even in his teens he was still wetting his bed.

In 1964, Shawcross married for the first time, but the marriage lasted only two years and he had already been on probation twice – for burglary and assault. He was then drafted and served a spell in Vietnam, before returning in September 1968.

His second marriage was no more successful than the first, and when his wife left him he lost control. Later claiming to have been badly affected by his war experiences, he began to drink heavily, started fires and stole from a local gas station. He was sentenced to two years in prison. Released at the end of his sentence, Shawcross settled in Watertown and married for the third time on April 22, 1972.

Just two weeks later, on May 7, 10-year-old Jack Blake went missing from his home late in the evening. His mother worried whether he had gone fishing – perhaps with the 'creepy' man he sometimes sold bait to, a man named Art. By midnight there was still no sign of Jack and his younger brother volunteered the information that Art lived in Cloverdale Apartments, a low-rent housing project. Mrs Blake contacted the police and went with an officer to knock at the door of the Shawcross apartment. When he opened the door, she asked Shawcross: 'Where's my son?'

Shawcross said that he had seen the boy playing earlier in the day, but had not seen him since. The police showed little interest and listed the boy as a runaway. Frantically, Mrs Blake organized search parties of family and friends, but months went by without any news.

On September 2, 1972, Stan Fisher drove his friend Helene Hill and her two daughters – Karen (8) and Chrissie (3) – to spend the Labor Day weekend with some of Helene's relatives in Watertown. Late in the afternoon, Karen went missing and her mother reported it to the police. They found a passer-by who claimed he had seen a little blonde-haired girl climbing over a fence by the iron bridge that crossed the Black River. Searching under the bridge, the police found Karen's body, face down in the mud and half-covered with paving slabs. Her bloodstained shorts and panties were found nearby. At the autopsy, it was established that Karen had been raped and strangled, probably with her own clothing.

When Mrs Blake heard of the crime, she immediately called the police and suggested that they should question Art Shawcross. He had previously been in trouble for child molestation, so they brought him in. At first he claimed to have an alibi, but some girls described a man they had seen climbing back over the fence by the bridge, wearing shorts, a T-shirt and sandals, and a nearby bicycle carrying fishing rods. Clothes answering the description were found in a laundry basket at Cloverdale. After an all-night inter-rogation by detectives, Shawcross finally whispered: 'I must've done it. But I don't actually recall doing it.'

Hearing a news report on the radio, a motel clerk remembered seeing a man stumbling out of woodland to the east of Watertown some months before – perhaps early May, around the time of Jack

Blake's disappearance. Luckily, he also remembered the man's name: Art Shawcross. Searchers were sent at once to the woods, and on September 6 they found a child's naked corpse buried in a shallow grave. Scattered in the undergrowth were the clothes that Mrs Blake had described Jack wearing.

The body was too far decomposed for the cause of death to be determined. And failure to establish the time of Karen Hill's death, or to blood-type the semen found in her body, made the case against Shawcross difficult to prove. The DA's office therefore cut a plea bargain: in exchange for his confession, the murder charges against Shawcross were reduced to manslaughter. And so he was sentenced to only 25 years, rather than the life imprisonment he would have faced for murder.

SHAWCROSS' SELF-ANALYSIS

A letter written by Shawcross in prison is revealing, indicating both emotional immaturity and literate sophistication, and a repressed and devious personality:

> Was it possible that some people were rotten from the start, hopelessly corrupt before environment had an opportunity to effect [sic] them? Was that a reactionary, medieval, thought? It's been said a great deal of a man with the XYY – is a genetically ordained criminal type that inspired so much scientific research over the past few years. Could it be some people can be born less human or civilized then [sic] others? Can it be caused by chemical or genetically reasons that no one had thought seriously about yet? This can be misinterpreted! If I am a chemical or genetic inferiority, then lets look into every aspect of others who may have what I do! Was I born to do evil or trained? . . . I am a special creature, born more or less than human . . .

By 1987, Shawcross succeeded in convincing the parole board that he was a reformed character. He had been corresponding for many years with Rose Marie Walley, a nursing aide, and on his release he met her for the first time and they made plans to get married. They set up home in Rochester, some 90 miles southwest of Watertown, and Shawcross was thought to be kind and considerate by his new neighbours, although he could sometimes appear cold and distant.

Rose found she was living with an unpredictable man. After his years in prison he was obsessively tidy and would lose his temper and smash things if everything was not to his liking. And sometimes he would stay out all night. Nevertheless, they were married in August 1989.

Beginning in October of that year, a succession of bodies began to turn up, many in or close to the gorge of the Genesee River on which Rochester stands. On October 21, fishermen found 'a bunch of bones in clothes'. It was the remains of a woman aged between 35 and 45, with her jeans unzipped and pulled down; but no ID was found, and her head was missing. Six days later, the body of known prostitute Patricia Ives was found on waste ground behind the local YMCA.

On November 5, another prostitute, Maria Welch, disappeared and on November 10 the asphyxiated corpse of 22-year-old Frances Brown, a 22-year-old high-school dropout and heroin addict, was discovered near the Genesee. Panic began to spread in the city's red-light district.

The police, realizing that a serial killer was at work, mounted heavy surveillance in the quarter, noting the licence plates of every car that stopped in the area, but they obtained far too much information to deal with – and many of the prostitutes went into hiding, complaining that the police presence was driving their customers away.

On Thanksgiving Day, June Stott's body was discovered, wrapped in a rug near the mouth of the Genesee, where it flows into Lake Ontario. She had been mutilated and part of her genitals had been cut away. Four days later, another prostitute, Elizabeth Gibson, joined the killer's score. In the weeks before Christmas, three more prostitutes disappeared: one, June Cicero, had been talking to police only minutes before she was picked up by the killer.

On New Year's Eve, a pair of jeans was found containing the ID of another of the missing women, Felicia Stephens. State troopers launched an aerial search by helicopter and on January 3, 1990, spotted a corpse lying in the snow beside a creek. Standing close by was a man who appeared to be urinating. The helicopter followed as the man drove away in his car, and ground patrols were alerted. The body was identified as that of June Cicero, naked except for a pair of socks and a sweater: her face was frozen to the snow and her genitals had been excised.

Arthur Shawcross was found in the kitchen of a nursing home where a woman friend worked, and was arrested by the State Police. His interrogation was complicated by disputes between Rochester PD and the State Police as to who should interview him, but eventually, asked about Elizabeth Gibson, he said baldly: 'I killed her.'

He then went on to confess to at least eight – probably eleven – murders, providing intimate details of each one. When Shawcross came to trial, the only question that remained to be resolved was whether or not he was insane. In due course the jury found him sane, and he was sentenced to 10 consecutive life sentences – 125 years in total, without chance of parole.

JOHN WAYNE GACY

KILLER CLOWN

To the community of Des Plaines, Cook County, Chicago, corpulent and jovial divorcee John Wayne Gacy was a successful man with his own construction business, a pillar of the local Jaycees (Junior Chamber of Commerce), and a staunch supporter of the Democrats. He was forever active in local events and charities, visiting the sick in hospitals, and organizing parties for underprivileged children, at which he would appear as 'Pogo the Clown', and perform conjuring tricks. But his smile hid a dark and terrible secret.

It began in 1967, when the County Attorney's office heard suggestions that teenagers working under 25-year-old Gacy's management at the KFC outlets in Waterloo, Iowa, were being invited by him to parties, plied with strong alcohol and encouraged to take part in illegal sexual activities. Gacy was questioned several times by the police, but they could never gather sufficient evidence. They got it finally in 1968.

Gacy seduced the 15-year-old son of a fellow member of the Jaycees. At first the boy complied with his demands but eventually became frightened and confessed to his father, who immediately went to the police. While Gacy was in jail awaiting trial, another youngster came forward with a similar charge. Tried in November 1968, Gacy pleaded guilty to charges of sodomy, expecting only a suspended sentence, but to his dismay he was given a 10-year sentence in prison, with a recommendation that he be released on parole after six years – the maximum penalty under Iowa law.

However, he proved a model prisoner and the parole board released him after only 18 months. Unwilling to go back to Waterloo, he returned to Chicago, determined (it seemed) to put his past behind him. But he could not control his sexual cravings, and on February 12, 1971 he was charged with 'disorderly conduct' in Chicago with a young boy. His accuser did not put in an appearance, however, and the charges were dismissed. Gacy was discharged from his parole in Iowa on October 18, 1971, because the police in that state had not been notified of this latest misdemeanour.

THE BACKGROUND OF A MONSTER

John Wayne Gacy, Jr. was born on March 17, 1942, in Chicago. He was the third child, physically weak and running to fat, and his father, a drunk and a bully, treated him with contempt. He was called a 'sissy, dumb and stupid', and was frequently brutally beaten for the slightest offence. At the age of 18 he could take no more and headed for Las Vegas, where he took a succession of low-paid jobs before returning to Chicago and enrolling in the North Western Business School.

Gacy graduated near the top of his class and, within a year of being employed at a shoe company, was made manager of their retail store in Springfield, Illinois. In 1964 he married Marlynn Myers, daughter of a wealthy local businessman who appointed him manager of a string of KFC franchises in Waterloo, Iowa. He had grown into a personable – if plump – executive, and it was even suggested that he should run for mayor. But then rumours began to circulate about his sexual tastes . . .

According to his own account, Gacy committed his first murder on January 3, 1972. He had begun cruising the streets of Chicago and had picked up his victim – never identified – at the bus terminal. He had married again – to lend colour to his apparent respectability – and for a while, until the marriage ended in 1976, his homosexual conquests had to be limited to times when his wife was not at home or out of town. His methods were simple: sometimes he flashed what looked like a police badge and a gun, and 'arrested' his prey; other times, the victims were invited home, given drinks and shown tricks with his 'magic handcuffs'. Later came sex toys and temporary asphyxiation, until he finished off with strangulation. The bodies were dumped in the crawl space beneath his home, and the pervading odour of decomposition – one of the reasons why his wife left him – was blamed on sewer problems. Others were buried close to the house or disposed of in the nearby river.

From 1976, with his wife gone, Gacy was able to accelerate his murderous activities. Between April 6 and June 13 of that year, at least five youths were killed, and on October 25 he murdered two on the same evening. Later, Gacy broadened his range, picking up not just teenage runaways but ex-jailbirds and male prostitutes. Not all were killed. In December 1977, he abducted Robert Donnelly at gunpoint, tortured and sodomized him at his home, then let him go. Three months later, 27-year-old Jeffrey Rignall was chloroformed and bound to a homemade rack. Gacy enjoyed several hours flogging his victim, re-applying chloroform so often that his liver was permanently damaged. When Rignall recovered consciousness, dumped by a lake in Lincoln Park, he immediately informed the police – but it was four months before they charged Gacy with misdemeanour and the case was still on the books many months later.

Gacy made his first major mistake – one that was to lead to his final arrest – on December 11, 1978. That evening, Mrs Elizabeth Piest went to collect her 15-year-old son, Robert, from his spare-time work at the Nisson Pharmacy in Des Plaines. He told her to wait a few minutes while he went to see 'a man about a construction job', but did not return. By midnight, his parents had informed the police and they spent the rest of the night driving through the streets in search of their son.

The following morning, a police captain visited the Nisson Pharmacy but the proprietor was unable to tell him anything more. However, just as he was leaving, the officer noticed that the store had been recently redecorated and was told that the contractor's name was John Gacy. And, yes, the pharmacist remembered him offering Robert Piest some part-time work. Gacy was called and asked to come to the police station.

At headquarters, a confident, outgoing, model citizen, he recognized a photograph of Robert and confirmed that he had offered him a job. Asked if he would meet police later at his home, he agreed. The visit was not an official search and everything appeared quite normal. However, just as he was leaving the hallway, the police captain spotted a yellow slip of paper lying on the floor: it was a receipt for a roll of film to be developed at the Nisson Pharmacy and was in the name of Kim Beyers. Gacy shrugged nonchalantly, saying he had no idea how it came to be there.

However, the police went immediately to the Piest home, where Robert's mother broke down in tears: Kim Beyers was a girlfriend of her son and he had offered to get the film processed for her. This was probable evidence that Robert had been at Gacy's house, but it was only circumstantial, insufficient for a search warrant to be obtained. Over the next four days, Gacy was kept under surveillance while enquiries gradually uncovered details of his past record of sex offences, in both Iowa and Illinois. Putting up a bold front, Gacy filed a civil lawsuit of $750,000 against the city of Des Plaines, alleging illegal search and seizure, harassment and slander, on December 19, but on that same day the police obtained their search warrant.

As they searched the house, the police quickly became aware of the foul odour. A detective discovered a trapdoor in the floor of a cupboard, opened it, and reeled back from the stench that rose from the crawl space below. A brief examination revealed a mass of human remains in a sea of stinking black mud, and Gacy was at once arrested and charged with murder.

Next morning the Cook County medical examiner, Dr Robert Stein, brought his team to the house. Wearing gas masks and protective clothing, they undertook the appalling task of sorting out the rotting remains, bagging and labelling them and dispatching them to Stein's laboratory. By December 24, parts of 16 bodies had been dug out, either from the crawl space or the ground around the house, and a week later the total had risen to 27.

Meanwhile, taken to police headquarters, Gacy had begun to provide details of his many murders. He confessed to killing 32 young men and boys over the past seven years, after having forced them to have sex with him. Five bodies had been thrown in the Des Plaines river, including that of Robert Piest. He provided the full names of only six of his victims; most of the others he knew only by their first names. He was also able to identify two photographs of missing youths from the files. Four bodies were finally dragged from the river, although the fifth was not recovered, and the police eventually set Gacy's total at 33.

Committed to Cermak Mental Hospital in Chicago to await trial, he attempted to represent himself as insane, attributing his crimes to a sinister alter-ego, 'Bad Jack'. The examining psychiatrists were not impressed, but when Gacy stood trial on February 6, 1980, both prosecution and defence teams agreed that a verdict of guilty would hinge upon the question of his sanity. The prosecutor presented the accused as follows: '. . . [he is] quite simply an evil man.'

In mitigation, Gacy's attorney argued that: '. . . any man who could sleep in a house with 29 dead bodies was not evil but insane.'

Among the witnesses, two teenagers who had stayed at Gacy's home for a time described how he had made them dig trenches in the dirt of the crawl space on the pretext that they were for a new drainage system. The prosecution pointed out that this proved that the murders were premeditated. For the defence, Jeffrey Rignall and Robert Donnelly both described their experiences at Gacy's hands, and agreed: '. . . no sane man would have done what he did.'

Despite his confessions taken into evidence, Gacy did not take the stand, and the defence case relied largely upon the four independent psychiatrists called, who described him as psychotic, a paranoid schizophrenic. Testifying for the prosecution, psychiatrist Dr Robert Reifman described Gacy as: '. . . a specifically narcissistic type, so-self-obsessed that other people did not matter. I don't believe that you can have 33 cases of temporary insanity.'

THE TASK OF IDENTIFICATION

Even while Gacy was awaiting trial, Dr Stein, the Cook County medical examiner, was still faced with the problem of identifing the victims' remains. The killer had named just six, and identified two more – but which of these body parts belonged to whom, and who were the others? The police had a long list of missing young men but, because the murders had been homosexually-related, many families were reluctant to provide any assistance.

By the end of January 1979, only ten victims, including Robert Piest, had been identified from their dental records, X-rays, fingerprints, clothing fragments, or personal jewellery. After several months of frustration, Dr Stein sought the advice of Dr Clyde Snow, a leading forensic anthropologist, who was currently working on the identification of bodies from the O'Hare aircraft disaster of May 25, 1979. Dr Snow requested the assistance of Cook County radiologist John Fitzpatrick.

Snow's first task was to secure a match between bones and tissues. He then drew up a 35-point reference chart, listing the particular characteristics of each skull. It was soon confirmed that each was male. Many hours of painstaking work produced only five more positive identifications, one of 19-year-old David Tasma, who had broken his left arm as a boy and later suffered a minor skull fracture. Hoping that parents were anxious to obtain closure on the fate of their missing sons, Snow called in Betty Ann Gatliff, a leading facial reconstruction expert from the headquarters of the Civil Aeromedical Institute in Oklahoma and one of his former colleagues. She sculpted likenesses of nine of the unidentified skulls and photographs were published in newspapers.

Unfortunately, nobody came forward to say they recognized any of the photographs. As Gatliff recalled:

Two girls ... gave the same boy's name and said he was their brother. But when it came to list the parents they said, 'Oh no, I'm not going to tell you, because my mother just refused to talk about this'. Well, we asked, who was his dentist? They said, 'We don't have any idea'. We said, could you ask your mother? 'Oh no, she won't even talk about it'.

Some years later, a local newspaper reporter managed to identify one of the faces. The rest were simply buried as 'John Does'.

The jury found the defendant guilty, and on March 13, 1980, the judge sentenced him to death on 33 counts of first-degree murder. There were loud cheers from the public benches.

Over the following 14 years, appeal after appeal by Gacy's lawyers was refused. He now claimed that the bodies exhumed at his home had been planted during his absence. He described himself as 'the 34th victim' of a plot by unknown conspirators. Finally, on May 11, 1994, he was executed by lethal injection.

TED BUNDY

BETRAYED BY HIS BITE

On the night of January 15, 1978, terror erupted on the campus of the University of Florida, Tallahassee. In the Chi Omega sorority house, home to 40 co-eds, a man in a black mask roamed frenziedly from room to room, striking out at the occupants with a heavy oak tree branch. In one room, Karen Chandler and Kathy Kleiner suffered severe head injuries that left them disfigured for life. In another, Margaret Bowman and Lisa Levy were similarly bludgeoned, and both were raped as they lay dying. The man then ran away.

When the man ran from the sorority house at 3.15 am, he passed Nita Neary, who was returning from a late party. She raised the alarm and within minutes the approaches to the house were clogged with police vehicles and ambulances – but only four blocks away, in Dunwoody Street, another horror was being enacted. Cheryl Thomas, a ballet dancer, was found beaten, lying close to death in a vast pool of her own blood. Fortunately, she recovered and was able to testify later at the trial of her attacker. But who was he?

On February 6, a man had stolen a van and driven to Jacksonville, where he had attempted, unsuccessfully, to abduct a schoolgirl. Three days later, 12-year-old Kimberley Leach was kidnapped outside her school in Lake City. The van was found abandoned on February 13, and there was no sign of Kimberley. Finally, on February 15, police spotted the licence plates of a stolen orange VW Beetle parked in a Pensacola side street. After a chase, they were able to arrest the driver.

He claimed that his name was Kenneth Misner – but the ID he produced was stolen and his wallet was full of stolen credit cards. He eventually admitted his true name was Theodore Robert

Bundy – a wanted man who had escaped from prison in Aspen, Colorado – but he denied any responsibility for the Tallahassee killings or the abduction of Kimberley Leach. Her remains were found two months later in a derelict pigsty. She had been raped and suffocated in the mud, her body mutilated with a knife.

'Ted' Bundy was well known to police in several different states. He eventually confessed to between 20 and 30 murders, in Washington State, Idaho, Oregon, Utah and Colorado; but the real tally has been estimated at many more.

He was born Theodore Robert Cowell in Vermont, in November 1946. He never knew his father, and his mother Louise took her baby to live with her family in Philadelphia.

Even at three years old, he was behaving oddly. One morning, his young aunt found him slipping butcher knives into her bed: 'He just stood there and grinned. I shooed him out of the room and took the implements back down to the kitchen and told my mother about it. I remember thinking at the time that I was the only one who thought it was strange . . .'

In 1950, Louise and her son relocated to Tacoma, Washington, where she married John Bundy the following year. Young Ted achieved good grades at school, although his teachers remarked on his unpredictable temper. He enrolled in the University of Washington, gaining a scholarship to Stanford University in Chinese studies and graduating in 1972 with a B.S. in psychology. Ironically, he found early employment as a psychology assistant to the county crime commission.

Well-educated, good-looking, charming and witty with women, Bundy was nevertheless a lethal obsessive who was building up inside to explosion point. A series of gruesome events chronicled the process:

- Late 1973, young Susan Clark is found badly beaten in her bed in Seattle;
- January 31, 1974, Lynda Healy disappears from her lodgings nearby, leaving a bloodstained nightgown and pillow;
- March 12, 1974, Donna Manson, 19, is last seen crossing the

campus of Evergreen State College, Olympia, on her way to a jazz concert;

- April 17, 1974, Susan Rancourt, 18, similarly vanishes in Ellensburg;
- May 6, 1974, 22-year-old Roberta Parks fails to return to her dormitory at Oregon State University from an evening walk;
- June 1, 1974, 22-year-old Brenda Ball leaves the Flame Tavern in Seattle with an unknown man, whose arm is in a sling, and is never seen again;
- Ten days later, 18-year-old Georgeann Hawkins disappears on the way to her Seattle sorority house;
- March 1, 1975, the remains of Brenda Ball, Lynda Healey, Susan Rancourt and Roberta Parks are finally discovered in a forest on the Cascade Mountains, south of Seattle.

Although, in 1974, investigators could find no trace of the missing girls, nor any idea of motivation, they had plenty of evidence of the abductor's choice of victim. All the girls – four of them co-eds – were young and attractive, with shoulder length hair. As one writer has said: 'In their photos, laid out side by side, they might have passed for sisters, some for twins.'

The first lead came on July 14, when crowds gathered at Lake Sammamish to share the sunshine and water sports. Wandering among them was a tall, good-looking young man, with one arm in a sling, asking young women to give him a hand in roping his sailboat to his car. Several lucky girls refused, but at the end of the day Janice Ott, 23, and Denise Naslund, 19, were reported missing. Some people remembered having seen the man in conversation with Janice; and one had heard him introduce himself as 'Ted'.

The police received many calls from the public naming possible suspects. In fact, they had so many calls that, although Ted Bundy was among those named, the well-dressed young law student seemed the least likely killer. Then, on September 7, a small group of hunters found a shallow grave in woods some miles from Lake Sammamish. In it there were three bodies, reduced almost to skeletons. Only dental records identified Janice Ott and Denise Naslund; the body of the third woman was never identified.

On October 12, another hunter discovered the bones of two more women near the Oregon border. One was identified as Carol Valenzuela, 20, missing since August from nearby Vancouver; but the other body remained unidentified.

Police began to hope that the discoveries might lead them to the killer; but Bundy was already far away, having driven more than 1,000 miles to Salt Lake City, Utah.

In Salt Lake City, Bundy enrolled in the University of Utah in order to study law. Consequently, there were no more disappearances of young women in Washington State – but the pattern now began to be repeated in Utah.

Nancy Wilcox, aged 16, vanished from Salt Lake City on October 2, 1974. Next, on October 18, Melissa Smith, the 17-year-old daughter of the local police chief, was abducted. Her body was found nine days later, raped, battered and strangled, in woodland. On Halloween night, Laura Aimee, 17, disappeared. Her corpse, brutally mutilated in the same way, was only discovered almost a month later.

Eight days after Laura's abduction, 18-year-old Carol DaRonch was approached by a man in a Salt Lake City shopping mall. He said he was a police officer and told her to get in his car. He tried to handcuff her, but she fought back and managed to escape. However, just a few hours later, Debbie Kent, 17, was seized from her school car park at Viewmont, 15 miles away. She was never found, and the police had just a single clue – the handcuff key.

Come the New Year of 1975, Bundy was in the ski resort of Aspen, Colorado. First to disappear was 23-year-old Caryn Campbell, from a ski lodge at Snowmass, on January 12, 1975. Her raped and bludgeoned body was found five weeks later. On March 15, Julie Cunningham, 26, vanished in Vail. One month after that, Melanie Cooley, 18, went missing while riding her bicycle in Nederland, near Denver. Her corpse was discovered eight days later; her skull was crushed and her jeans pulled down round her ankles. Then, on July 1, 24-year-old Shelley Robertson joined the list of missing in Golden, just outside Denver. Her remains were found eight weeks later in a deserted mineshaft.

Finally, on July 4, gas station attendant Nancy Baird, 19, vanished from the forecourt where she worked in Bountiful.

By August, Bundy was back in Salt Lake City, where he was soon arrested on suspicion of burglary. Searching his car, the police discovered handcuffs and a pair of black pantyhose with eyeholes cut to make a mask. In the glove compartment were gas station receipts that linked him to a number of Colorado ski resorts.

Carol DaRonch identified Bundy as the man who had attempted to carry her off in November. As a result, he was convicted of attempted kidnapping and in January 1977 he was extradited to the jurisdiction of Colorado to stand trial for the murder of Caryn Campbell.

Held in prison in Aspen, Bundy announced that he would be defending himself, and asked for permission to visit the Court House library to read up the law. On June 7, 1977, he escaped from a third-floor window, dropping some 20 feet to the ground. He was recaptured eight days later, but on December 31, while still awaiting trial, he dug a hole through the ceiling of his cell and vanished into the night. Two weeks later he was in Tallahassee, nearly 2,000 miles away, posing as graduate law student Chris Hagen. And it was there that his final bloody orgy took place.

Examination of the body of Lisa Levy, one of the girls murdered on January 15, 1978, revealed a clear bite mark on her left buttock. When Bundy had been arrested and charged he refused to provide a dental impression. Detectives had to obtain a warrant, allowing them to use force if necessary, and Bundy reluctantly agreed. Odontologist Dr Richard Souviron made colour photographs of the uneven formation of his teeth.

Bundy's trial opened in Miami on June 25, 1979. With his knowledge of law, he opted to conduct his own defence with the assistance of attorney Margaret Good. As the judge said at the end of the trial: 'You're a bright young man. You'd have made a good lawyer.'

In his crucial testimony, Dr Souviron placed an acetate film of Bundy's teeth over an enlarged photograph of the bite mark and showed that they fitted exactly. Dr Lowell Levine, chief odontological consultant to the New York Medical Examiner, agreed. The evidence was indisputable, so the jury was unanimous in finding Bundy guilty of the murder of Lisa Levy and Margaret Bowman. He was sentenced to the electric chair.

In 1980, Bundy received a third death sentence for the killing of Kimberley Leach. He employed every possible legal loophole to escape execution, with appeals that went as far as the Supreme Court in Washington, D.C. When every one had been exhausted, he began to confess to many more killings – even the 'Green River' murders (see pages 196–8), of which he was certainly not guilty. As his execution drew near, he claimed responsibility for more than 20 additional murders and he is believed to have committed at least 9 of these. Some have set the figure at anything from 40 to 400.

Nearly ten years passed before Bundy's final appeal was set aside, and he was executed on January 24, 1989.

DAVID BERKOWITZ

SON OF SAM

For over a year, an anonymous gunman stalked the streets of New York City at night, from North Bronx to the southern edge of Brooklyn – although never taking his hunt into Manhattan. His prime targets seemed to be young women, but male companions were just as likely to be hit as he wildly fired bullet after bullet from his .44 Bulldog revolver.

The reign of terror began shortly after midnight on July 29, 1976. Donna Lauria, 18, and her 19-year-old friend Jody Valenti were sitting together in the front seat of Jody's car, which was parked outside Donna's home in North Bronx. As Donna said goodnight to her friend and began to open the car door to leave, a young man standing a few yards away pulled a gun from a paper sack, crouched, and fired without a word. The first bullet shattered the passenger window, and hit Donna in the neck. She raised her hand, and a second bullet struck her in the arm. She fell from the car as the gunman fired again, hitting Jody in the thigh.

Hearing the shots, and Jody's screams, Donna's father rushed from the house to find his daughter lying near death in a spreading pool of blood. Jody was hanging half out of the car, crying: 'We've been shot!'

By the time the emergency services reached the scene, Donna was dead. Jody's wound was fortunately not life-threatening, but she was hysterical and unable to give the police a coherent account for some hours. Finally she was able to give a description of the assailant: a white male, around 30 years, clean-shaven with black curly hair. She had never seen him before, nor, she believed, had Donna.

All the police could learn was that neighbours had noticed a yellow sedan parked some way behind Jody's car, and that it had raced away immediately after the shooting. They had got no further in their investigation three months later, on October 23, when a similar attack occurred – although, at first, there was no reason to connect the two. The shooting was in a different jurisdiction, a respectable suburb of the borough of Queens.

Rosemary Keenan, the 18-year-old daughter of NYPD detective John Keenan, had spent the evening with her boyfriend, Carl Denaro, 20. They were parked in a quiet side street and did not notice a man approaching the car from behind. Carl had shoulder-length hair – and could have been mistaken for another girl from the back. The gunman fired five times through the rear window of the car, shattering the glass without hitting his target. The target was Rosemary, but as Carl ducked to avoid the flying glass, the fifth bullet tore into his skull.

Rosemary was unhurt, but in a state of terrified shock. Carl was rushed to hospital, where it was found that the bullet had smashed the back of his head, but had not penetrated his brain. Lucky to survive, he eventually made a complete recovery. Detectives found a .44 bullet on the floor of the car and ballistics experts matched it to those from Donna Lauria's murder. Yet again, there was no obvious motive.

Another month passed before the police suspected that a serial killer was on the loose. Around midnight of November 26–27, 16-year-old Donna DeMasi and her friend Joanne Lomino, 18, were approached on the stoop of Joanne's home in Queens by a man who asked for directions. The two girls turned away, but as they did so he drew out a gun and fired twice. The first bullet hit Joanne's spine, leaving her permanently paralyzed; but the second only hit Donna's collarbone, breaking it but leaving her otherwise unharmed. Once again, the bullets were matched.

The fact that the victims of the shootings were probably of Italian extraction caused the police to wonder whether they were looking at a case of Mafia revenge; but they could find no connection. In addition, there was a problem of identification. Both Joanne Lomino and Donna DeMasi were adamant that their attacker had shoulder length blonde hair and an eyewitness confirmed that a man answering this description had run from the scene carrying a handgun.

The third attack in Queens came two months later, on the night of January 29, 1977. Again, a young couple in a parked car were the targets. It was a cold night and the car's windows were misted over – so Christine Freund, 26, and her 30-year-old boyfriend John Diel could not see the gunman approaching. Suddenly, three bullets burst in quick succession through the passenger window, mortally wounding Christine, who died in hospital four hours later. Diel could give no description of the attacker, and all an eyewitness could tell the police was that he was young, about 5ft 8in tall and wearing a black ski mask.

On the evening of March 8, Russian language student Virginia Voskerichian was shot through the head and died, a mere 300 yards from the scene of the January killing. Confirmation that the same gun had been used as in the previous shootings led the police to immediately set up a task force. Named 'Operation Omega', it was under the leadership of Deputy Inspector Timothy Dowd and was dedicated to tracking down the '.44 killer'. But although the announcement of this development was intended to reassure the public, it actually resulted in a deluge of calls which overwhelmed the police.

Soon, the killer struck again. In the early hours of April 17, 18-year-old Valentina Suriani and her boyfriend, Alexander Esau, were sitting in his car in North Bronx, just a few blocks from where Donna Lauria had been murdered. Without warning, three shots shattered the passenger window. The first two shattered Valentina's skull, killing her instantly, and the third hit Alexander in the side of the head. He crawled from the car before losing consciousness but died later in hospital.

As dozens of police arrived on the scene, one officer noticed an envelope lying a few feet from the car. It was addressed to Queens detective Captain Joseph Borelli, second-in-command of the Omega team, and was the first letter to identify the killer as 'Son of Sam'. There were four pages, all written in block capitals. It was a rambling, but coherent, letter that indicated an unhinged personality.

EXTRACTS FROM THE FIRST 'SON OF SAM' LETTER

I am deeply hurt by your calling me a wemon [*sic*] hater. I am not. But I am a monster. I am the 'Son of Sam'. I am a little 'brat' . . . 'Go out and kill' commands Father Sam . . .

I feel like an outsider. I am on a different wave length then [*sic*] everybody else – programmed too [*sic*] kill.

However, to top me you must kill me. Attention all police: Shoot me first – shoot to kill or else. Keep out of my way or you will die! . . .

I love to hunt, prowling the streets looking for fair game – tasty meat. The wemon [*sic*] of Queens are Z prettyist [*sic*] of all. I must be the water they drink. I live for the hunt – my life. Blood for Papa . . .

I dont [*sic*] want to kill anymore, no sir, no more but I must, "Honour thy father."

I want to make love to the world. I love people. I don't belong on earth. Return me to Yahoos.

To the people of Queens, I love you. And I want to wish all of you a happy Easter. May God bless you in this life and in the next and for now I say goodbye and goodnight.

Police – let me haunt you with these words;

I'll be back!

I'll be back!

To be interpreted as Bang, Bang, Bang, Bang, Bang – ugh!!

Yours in murder

Mr Monster

The contents of the letter were kept secret for several weeks, but one of the few outside the Omega task force allowed to read it was *Daily News* columnist Jimmy Breslin, who referred to its existence several times in his column. On May 30, he himself received a letter signed 'Son of Sam'. Like the first, it was long and written in block capitals.

> HELLO FROM THE GUTTERS OF N.Y.C ... [it began and later continued] ... J.B., I'm just dropping you a line to let you know that I appreciate your interest in those recent and horrendous .44 killings. I also want to tell you that I read your column daily and find it quite informative ... Mr. Breslin, sir, don't think that because you haven't heard from [*sic*] for a while that I went to sleep. No, rather, I am still here. Like a spirit roaming the night. Thirsty, hungry, seldom stopping to rest; anxious to please Sam. I love my work. Now, the void has been filled ...

The killer continued:

> In their blood and from the gutter 'Sam's Creation' .44 ...

Then, referring to himself as 'Sam's Creation .44', went on to suggest:

> ... some names to help you along: 'The Duke of Death', 'The Wicked King Wicker', 'The Twenty Two Disciples of Hell', 'John "Wheaties" – Rapist and Suffocator of Young Girls.'

Finally he promised:

> Upon my capture ... to buy all the guys working on the case a new pair of shoes if I can get up the money.

On the back of the envelope enclosing the letter were the words: 'Blood and family Darkness and death, Absolute depravity, .44.'

The *Daily News* published this letter a week later, on June 6. As a result, over a million copies of the newspaper were sold and public outrage intensified – but the police were no nearer apprehending Son of Sam.

Three weeks later, on June 26, Judy Placido, 17, who had been celebrating her high school graduation, was sitting with a friend, Sal Lupo, in his car in a Queens side street. 'All of a sudden I heard echoing in the car. There wasn't any pain, just ringing in my ears . . .'

Only when she looked in the rear-view mirror and saw her face covered in blood, did Judy realize she had been shot: three times in the head, neck and shoulder. Lupo had taken a bullet in his forearm but managed to reach a bar and raise the alarm. Both eventually recovered, but could not give any description of their assailant.

On July 31, 'Son of Sam' gained his last victim in south Brooklyn. As on every previous occasion, two people, 20-year-old Stacy Moskowitz and her boyfriend Robert Violante, were in a parked car. Robert later said he did not hear any shots: 'I heard like a humming sound . . . First I heard glass break. Then a humming.'

He had been shot twice in the face, effectively blinding him for life, while Stacy, shot in the head, died later in hospital.

Another young couple had witnessed the attack from their car. They had seen a stocky young man, with 'stringy' fair hair, fire four shots and then run away. The police now had two conflicting descriptions of the gunman. Did 'Son of Sam' wear a wig for some of his murders – or were two killers using the same gun?

There was another witness, Mrs Cecilia Davis, who told a friend that she was sure she had seen the gunman but was reluctant to go to the police because he had also seen her, and she feared for her life. Eventually she reported to an Omega detective that she had spotted a yellow Ford Galaxie parked beside a fire hydrant. A young man had torn a parking ticket from the windscreen and driven off. He was, she said, a white male in his early twenties, with dark curly hair.

It was not until August 9 that the parking ticket was traced.

It had been issued to David Berkowitz, 35 Pine Street, Yonkers. Following up this information as purely routine, a detective spoke to a dispatcher at Yonkers headquarters. Her name was Wheat Carr and she exclaimed: 'Oh my God, he's a psycho!'

Berkowitz was a neighbour of her father, Sam Carr, and over the past months the family had suspected him of sending them anonymous letters, starting a fire at their home, as well as shooting and wounding their dog.

The following morning, two detectives went to Pine Street, where a yellow Ford Galaxie was parked. On the back seat they found a duffle bag containing a semi-automatic rifle with four full magazines, a shotgun, and two .22 rifles. In the glove compartment was an envelope addressed to Inspector Dowd.

A squad of detectives waited outside the apartment for some hours, until a pudgy, dark-haired white male left the building, carrying something in a paper sack. As he got into the car, he was surrounded and asked: 'Are you Mr Berkowitz?' He turned round, smiled and said: 'No, I'm the Son of Sam.'

The paper sack contained a .44 Bulldog.

Berkowitz, a 24-year-old postal worker, cheerfully confessed – providing precise details – to all the 'Son of Sam' shootings. He was, he said, acting on the orders of his neighbour, Sam Carr – but the orders were received through Carr's black Labrador dog.

Despite his bizarre claims, several leading psychiatrists were unanimous that Berkowitz was not insane. He was arraigned on August 23, 1977 with a plea of guilty to six counts of murder and eight of attempted murder. Because of the plea, he was not committed to trial but sentenced immediately to 365 years in prison, without any hope of parole.

PETER SUTCLIFFE

YORKSHIRE RIPPER

Nearly a century after Jack the Ripper caused panic in the streets of Victorian London, a second 'Ripper' terrorized the women of cities and towns in the northern county of Yorkshire and in neighbouring Lancashire. For five years, the British police were unable to apprehend the killer and were even deliberately misled by a malicious deceiver. When the true felon was at last arrested, he admitted bludgeoning, stabbing and mutilating 20 women, 13 of whom he had killed.

The killings began in the city of Leeds on October 30, 1975, when part-time prostitute Wilma McCann – 28, and the mother of four – was making her way unsteadily home after a night out. Without warning, a heavy hammer smashed down twice into the back of her head, shattering her skull. Her attacker dragged her dead body into nearby playing fields, ripped open her jacket and blouse, and stabbed her 14 times in the chest and stomach.

Prostitutes pursue a dangerous trade; so the police considered this an isolated incident. Indeed, they would have similarly regarded the killing of another prostitute, 42-year-old Emily Jackson – found dumped on January 20, 1976, in the heart of the Leeds red-light district – but for one disturbing fact. Both women had been killed with blows from a ball-headed hammer and stabbed frenziedly many times with the sharpened point of a Phillips (cross-head) screwdriver.

At this time, and for several years after, the police made no connection to two previous attacks, in both of which the assaulted women had survived. On July 5, 1975, 34-year-old Anna Rogulskyj had been attacked with a hammer in Keighley; and, on August 15, 46-year-old Olive Smelt had been bludgeoned and slashed across the buttocks in Halifax. Both towns were within a half-hour drive of Leeds.

On the night of May 9, 1976, 20-year-old Marcella Claxton was assaulted in Roundhay Park, Leeds. She screamed and her attacker – whom she described as a man with a dark beard – ran off. Detectives were convinced that this had been an abortive attempt by the same killer.

THE MIND OF THE RIPPER

Peter Sutcliffe was born on June 2, 1946, the eldest of five children, in Bingley on the northwestern outskirts of Bradford. He was a loner, unhappy at school and centred his affections on his mother. Light in build, at 16 he worked out regularly to build up his physique. It was not until 1967 that he had a girlfriend, 16-year-old Sonia Szuma. The couple frequently broke up – Sonia spent two years training as a schoolteacher in London – and did not marry until 1974, after which they continued their furious quarrels.

Sutcliffe attributed his hatred of prostitutes to an occasion when he had given one a £10 note and asked for £5 change. She said she would repay it, but never returned.

> I felt outraged and humiliated and embarrassed. I felt a hatred for the prostitute and her kind.

Some indication of Sutcliffe's mind-set can be gleaned from the note he posted in the cab of his truck:

> In this truck is a man whose latent genius, if unleashed, would rock the nation, whose dynamic energy would overpower those around him. Better let him sleep?

For ten months there were no more reported attacks and the police began to hope that the murderer had been imprisoned for a different crime – or even committed suicide. Their hopes were dashed, however, when the characteristically mutilated body of another prostitute was found in Roundhay Park on February 6, 1977. Irene Richardson, 28, had been struck down with three massive blows from a ball-headed hammer. Some of her clothing had been torn off and she had been stabbed more than 20 times with a knife and a Phillips screwdriver. It was now that the press named the serial killer the 'Yorkshire Ripper'.

Following the killing of Irene Richardson, panic spread through the Leeds red-light district. Many of the prostitutes moved away, to London, Birmingham and Manchester, while others travelled only a few miles, to the neighbouring city of Bradford. But Bradford was not far enough away. On April 23, 32-year-old Patricia Atkinson, a divorced mother of three daughters who had taken up prostitution to make ends meet, was killed there in her own home. Her skull was shattered with four hammer blows and she had been stabbed seven times in the stomach.

Then, on the night of June 25, 16-year-old shop assistant Jayne MacDonald was walking home from a night out with friends when she was hammered to death and stabbed in the characteristic way. Detectives had to assume that this was a 'mistake' on the Ripper's part: Jayne lived close to the red-light district and only six houses away from the home of Wilma McCann. Her death provoked a public outrage, but the police were still no nearer finding the killer.

On the night of July 27, Maureen Long, 30, was walking home through the centre of Bradford when she was offered a ride home by a man. He drove to some wasteland and struck her from behind with a hammer. He then drove off, leaving her lying on the ground, apparently dead. But she survived and described her attacker as a man with blonde hair – a detail that added further confusion to the investigation.

After this, the Ripper changed his killing ground to Lancashire. On October 1, he drove over the Pennines to Manchester and picked up 20-year-old Jean Jordan. Taking her into a cemetery, he killed her with 11 ferocious hammer blows. Then, he dragged her body into some thick bushes, but without completing his ritual, he left. Back home in Yorkshire, he realized that he had given her a new £5 banknote from his wage packet, which might be traced to him. So, a week later, he drove back to the cemetery and found Jean's body where he had left it. But he could not find the note, which was hidden in a secret pocket in her purse. Now, however, he was overcome with the irresistible urge to mutilate the body, using a shard of broken glass that he found close by. The grotesquely slashed corpse was found the next day.

On discovering the banknote, the police traced it to a bank in Shipley, just north (and more or less part) of Bradford, were it had been issued in payrolls for factories in the area. Officers interviewed more than 5,000 men who might have received it. One of these was a truck driver named Peter Sutcliffe, who, although interviewed twice, answered the police questions so politely and openly that they dismissed him as a suspect.

The next killing, that of 22-year-old prostitute Yvonne Pearson, came on January 21, 1978. However, her mutilated body – beaten with a hammer but not stabbed – was not discovered for two months. Ten days later, Helen Rytka, 18, vanished and her body was found two days later, battered and stabbed. Uncharacteristically, it appeared that her killer had also assaulted her sexually, and so left evidence of his blood group – type B.

More than 200 detectives had by now been assigned to the case, and the UK press and TV coverage devoted to the 'Yorkshire Ripper' was constant, but without any evidence being forthcoming.

On May 16, the Ripper struck again – and once more in Manchester – when Vera Millward, a 41-year-old prostitute, was battered with a club hammer, her torso stabbed and slashed.

Then, for an inexplicable eleven months, the killings again ceased. However, the nightmare returned with a new, and even more sinister, variation: the Ripper had stopped stalking prostitutes and turned to attacking lone women at random. On the night of April 4, 1979, 19-year-old Josephine Whitaker, a clerk with a company in Halifax, was walking the short distance home from a visit to her grandparents. The Ripper struck her once with his hammer, dragged her body into thick undergrowth and stabbed it repeatedly with his screwdriver.

The investigation was misled for some months by several letters and a tape recording that allegedly came from 'Jack the

Ripper', and for a time police theorized that the killer lived in the northeast town of Sunderland, with a job that brought him frequently to Leeds. But, while squads of detectives turned their attention to the north, the Ripper continued his lethal campaign in the Leeds area.

There was only a single killing in the 16 months that followed the murder of Josephine Whitaker: on September 1, 1979, Barbara Leach, a 20-year-old student at Bradford University, fell victim to the Ripper, her body repeatedly stabbed with an identical screwdriver. But the terror returned on August 18, 1980. Government employee Marguerite Walls, 45, had stayed late in her office because she was going on holiday the following day. Her body was found two days later; she had been hammered to death and then strangled, but strangely her body was not mutilated.

Over the next two months there were two unsuccessful attempts by the Ripper; then, on November 17, he made his final killing. Jacqueline Hill, a 20-year-old student at Leeds University, was only yards from her hall of residence when she was struck to the ground with a hammer. The Ripper dragged her body into some nearby bushes, stripped her and stabbed her repeatedly.

It was on January 2, 1981, that the Ripper set out again, carrying his hammer and screwdriver in his coat pocket. In Sheffield, nearly as far from Leeds as Manchester, he picked up Olive Reivers and offered her £10 for sex. As he drove off, a police car pulled up in front of him, suspicious of the registration plates on the Ripper's car. The dark-bearded driver gave his name as 'Peter Williams', and asked if he might relieve himself at the roadside. When he returned to his car, the police had already checked the registration. The plates were stolen.

Arrested and taken to the local police station, 'Williams' again asked permission to go to the lavatory. Two 'Ripper Squad' detectives, learning of the arrest, arrived next day to interview him. Alerted, the police officers who had arrested him returned immediately to the site where they had picked him up. There they found, almost at once, a discarded ball-headed hammer and a sharpened screwdriver. Also, back at the police station, there was a knife hidden in the lavatory cistern.

A CRUEL HOAX

Over a period of 15 months, the team investigating the Ripper murders had received three letters – reminiscent of the letters sent during the reign of Jack the Ripper and signed with his name – that taunted their efforts. The letters were made public in the hope that someone would recognize the handwriting, but without success.

Then, on June 18, 1979, Assistant Chief Constable George Oldfield, in charge of the case, received a tape recording in the mail. A soft voice with a Northumbrian accent began: 'I'm Jack. I see you are having no luck catching me. I have the greatest respect for you, George, but Lord, you are no nearer to catching me now than four years ago when I started . . .'

And the recording ended: 'No good looking for fingerprints, you should know by now it's clean as a whistle. See you soon. 'Bye. Hope you like the catchy tune at the end. Ha. Ha!'

The 'catchy tune' was the song *Thank You For Being A Friend*.

The blood group B was found in the saliva used to seal all four envelopes, and Oldfield was convinced the tape was from the Ripper. Dialect experts reported that the accent was that of the Wearside area around Sunderland on the northeast coast. However, Detective Chief Inspector Zackrisson of the Northumbrian police pointed out that ten phrases in the letters were almost identical to phrases used in the original Jack the Ripper letters, and opined that the whole affair was an elaborate hoax. Hundreds of hours of police time were wasted, and a big publicity campaign organized, before the Ripper team gave up.

Nearly 30 years later, in 2005, a Wearside man, John Humble, confessed to the hoax, and in March 2006 was sentenced to a term of imprisonment.

'Williams' now gave his true name as Peter Sutcliffe, aged 34, and his occupation as a truck driver. Most importantly, he confessed to being the 'Yorkshire Ripper'. His full statement took 17 hours to record. He was charged with 13 murders and 7 attempted murders. However, the detectives were embarrassed by some of Sutcliffe's admissions.

In 1969, he said, he had stalked a prostitute and coshed her with a loaded sock. Further, in the same year, he had been arrested carrying his hammer (with his admitted purpose of having it with an intent to kill), yet fined merely for 'going equipped for burglary'. Yet, in 1971, he had clubbed another prostitute unconscious in Bradford.

Sutcliffe stood trial at London's Central Criminal Court, the Old Bailey, on May 5, 1981. He pleaded guilty to manslaughter, but on May 22, the jury found him guilty on all 20 counts of murder. He was sentenced to life, with recommendation that he should serve at least 30 years. Soon after, prison psychiatrists pronounced him insane and he was transferred to Broadmoor Hospital for the Criminally Insane. There, on March 10, 1997, he was attacked by another inmate and stabbed in both eyes, leaving him permanently blinded in the right eye.

The mountain of paperwork assembled by the 'Ripper Team' was one of the reasons why the investigation was unsuccessful for so long. It was one of the major factors that led to the British police forces – following an inquiry into the failings in the 'Yorkshire Ripper case' in 1982 – to set up the first UK centralized crime computer in 1987. It was originally named the 'Home Office Major Enquiry System'; but someone realized that, by adding the word 'Large' its acronym would be HOLMES – with all of its literary detection connotations – and as such it is known.

Documents released in 2006 under the Freedom of Information Act confirm the inefficiency of the 'Ripper' investigation. In a December 1981 report, an inspector of constabulary wrote: 'it is my firm conclusion that between 1969 and 1980 Sutcliffe was probably responsible for many attacks on unaccompanied women, which he has not yet admitted'. His inquiry found that a list had been made of 850 suspect vehicles whose owners had been seen picking up prostitutes and that, in March 1979, Sutcliffe was one of only three car owners who had previously been recorded as a 'triple area sighting'. In June 1980, he was interviewed for the eleventh time after behaving suspiciously and driving erratically and was held for drink-driving. However, he was released after he had been 'eliminated from the inquiry on handwriting' – that is, on the evidence of the hoax letters.

DEAN CORLL & WAYNE HENLEY

THE CANDYMAN

Early in the morning of August 8, 1973, the police of Pasadena, a suburb of Houston, Texas, received a call:

'Y'all better come right now. I killed a man.'

Arriving at the given address, they found two spaced-out young men and a girl in ripped clothes, sitting on the porch. Elmer Wayne Henley, 17, admitted the killing, but maintained it had been in self-defence. The tale he had to tell was a shocking one.

The dead man was 33-year-old Dean Corll, former owner of a failed candy factory. In the early hours of the morning, Wayne had taken a 15-year-old girl called Cora and another friend, Tim Kerley, to Corll's home for a paint-sniffing session. Around dawn, as Wayne regained consciousness, he found that his ankles were tied and his wrists were handcuffed. The floor of Corll's bedroom was completely covered with plastic sheeting. On it lay Tim, naked, and Cora, both still unconscious and tied up. Before he forced Wayne into the kitchen with a .22 pistol, Corll said: 'I'm gonna kill you all, but first I'm gonna have my fun.'

Thinking quickly, Wayne said that he would help the man if he were spared, and Corll agreed and released him. In the bedroom, he strapped the naked Tim face downward on a plywood board and handed Wayne a hunting knife, ordering him to cut off Cora's clothes while he himself stripped, saying: 'You take the girl, and I'll mess with Tim.'

As Wayne began to cut at Cora's clothing, he noticed the .22 lying on the bedside table. Seizing it, he told Corll to stop, but the naked man advanced upon him, taunting: 'Kill me, Wayne. You won't do it.'

Wayne pulled the trigger, again and again. Corll fell with six bullets in his body.

Inside the house, the police found all the trappings of sadistic sex. The plywood board had holes in the corners to take two sets of handcuffs, and two lengths of rope attached to other handcuffs. In the van parked outside the house were rings and hooks attached to the sides.

At Pasadena police station, Wayne had more to tell. Corll, he

A DEVELOPING HOMOSEXUAL

Dean Arnold Corll was born in Waynedale, Indiana, on 24 December 1939, the first son of Arnold and Mary Corll. His childhood was an uneasy one: his parents divorced, then remarried, and divorced again, after which Mary married a travelling salesman and relocated to Texas. In Houston, she opened a candy factory in the garage of her home and 15-year-old Dean worked happily there when he was not at school. Then his mother began a rival establishment after a quarrel with her husband and Dean was was made vice-president of the Corll Candy Company, with his own apartment above the factory.

From his earliest days Corll had been a loner, but one of his employees recalled: 'I never saw a man who loved kids like Dean.'

Corll began to give away candy to children from the school opposite his apartment and was always surrounded by young boys. He was drafted into the army in 1964 but served only 10 months, and it has been suggested that it was then that he had his first homosexual encounters.

Eventually the factory failed and Corll took work as an electrician. He grew moody and unpredictable, and in 1970 he committed his first known murder.

said, was 'into little boys', some of whom he had murdered. The names of several were listed at Houston headquarters as missing runaways.

Wayne led the police to Corll's rented boat shed, a long corrugated iron structure nine miles south of Houston. There was no boat inside: only a stolen vehicle, a child's bicycle, a plastic bag full of small male clothing and two sacks of quicklime. Excavation of the floor over the next two days revealed 17 boys' bodies, one who had been dead less than a week, but others too decomposed and their bones too mixed up for identification.

The following day, after a night in the cells, Wayne Henley began to reveal a very different character. He no longer appeared to be an innocent teenager who had been lured to Corll's home and there forced to defend himself. He now admitted that he had sometimes acted as a procurer of victims for the sadist – getting as much as $200 a head – and had himself assisted in the killing of some eight boys. Wayne insisted that there were 19 bodies hidden in the boat shed – two more than the police had exhumed – four or five near Lake Sam Rayburn, 120 miles north of Houston, and more in the sand of High Island beach on the Gulf coast. He also named David Brooks as an accomplice.

Hearing the news on local TV, Brooks went to the police and volunteered a statement. He said he had been one of the local boys offered candy by Corll, beginning in 1967 when he was 12. Three years later, he had moved in with Corll, who paid him a few dollars a time for oral sex. Late in 1971, Wayne Henley had begun to replace him in Corll's affections. After denying for some time that he had any knowledge of the killings, Henley finally admitted that he had been present on many occasions, as well as at the burial of the bodies, although he continued to claim that he had not participated in the murders. Brooks told the police: 'Most of the killings that occurred after Wayne came in the picture involved all three of us. Wayne seemed to enjoy causing pain.'

A search around Lake Sam Rayburn revealed four more graves, and six were found at High Island, bringing the total to 27. Henley continued to insist that there were two more bodies undiscovered in the boat shed, and two more at High Island, but the police called off any further searches. In August 1974, Wayne was sentenced to life imprisonment for multiple murder. Brooks received the same sentence in March 1975.

DONALD HENRY GASKINS

LETHAL PEE WEE

Little Donald Gaskins – who curiously described himself as 'born special and fortunate' – was known to everyone as 'Pee Wee' throughout his childhood. The runt of a large family, he was born to an unwed mother in South Carolina on March 13, 1933. She subsequently married a man who was a harsh disciplinarian, beating all his wife's family 'just for practice'. Young Pee Wee dropped out of school at the age of 11, joining up with two other adolescents to call themselves 'The Trouble Trio'. They indulged in a succession of local burglaries until a gang rape of one of the boys' young sister led to the other pair leaving the district leaving Pee Wee to operate on his own.

In 1946, during one of his burglaries, Pee Wee was interrupted by a former female classmate. She was waving an axe which he seized from her, hitting her on the head and arm before escaping. The girl survived and named him, and he was sentenced to South Carolina Industrial School for Boys until his eighteenth birthday.

Despite the fact that he was regularly homosexually raped while in confinement – or perhaps as a perverted result of this – Gaskins maintained a blind hatred of women. He said they gave him pains 'like hot lead' in his stomach and groin. Released in 1951, he found work on a tobacco plantation, but soon thought it more profitable to steal part of the crop and set fire to the barns in which it was stored to conceal his theft. He was arrested for arson and attempted murder of his employer's daughter the following year but was acquitted on the first charge and bargained the second down to assault and battery, for which he was sentenced to prison for five years – and then another year, when he swore at the judge.

In jail, Gaskins was again subjected to rape but retaliated by cutting the throat of his rapist. A bargain to a plea of manslaughter earned him a further nine years. He escaped from prison in 1955 but was soon recaptured in Tennessee and charged with a federal offence – driving a stolen car across the state line. The sentence of three years for this last offence ran concurrently with his existing sentences, and in August 1961 he was paroled and returned to Florence, South Carolina.

Gaskins returned to his career of burglary but was able to escape detection by taking a job as driver to a roving preacher, which made his crimes harder to trace as he travelled from town to town. In 1962, however, he was arrested on a charge of statutory rape of a 12-year-old girl. He escaped from a courthouse window while awaiting trial and joined a travelling carnival, but was recaptured not long after and received another prison sentence, this time of eight years.

Gaskins was paroled in November 1968, on condition that he did not return to Florence for at least two years. By now he was a raging psychopath with an obsessive hatred of everybody, and particularly women. His first known murder came in September 1969 when he picked up a female hitch-hiker on the road near Georgetown on the South Carolina coast. He tortured and disembowelled her, then dumped her remains in the ocean.

This was a turning point: Gaskins later described it as 'a vision' into the 'bothersome feelings' that he had felt throughout his whole life. Although he preferred women victims, by 1975 he had raped, tortured and butchered more than 80 young girls and boys he found along the Carolina highways.

Gaskins described himself as 'one of the few that truly understands what death and pain are all about. I have a special kind of mind that allows me to give myself permission to kill.' And, for nearly six years, he permitted himself an orgy of murder. In November 1970 he raped and murdered his own niece, Janice Kirby, aged 15, and her friend 17-year-old Patricia Alsbrook, in Sumter, South Carolina, burying their bodies out in the country. His next victim was 20-year-old Martha Dicks, who found him attractive and hung around the car repair shop where he worked part-time. In December, he tortured and killed 13-year-old Peggy Cuttino – a crime for which William Pierce, sentenced to life for a similar killing in Georgia, was held responsible – even though Gaskins confessed to it in 1977.

One of the most horrific of the murders to which Gaskins later confessed occurred in 1973 when he raped and killed both Doreen Dempsey, 23, who was pregnant, and her 20-month old daughter. But the year 1975 was what he described as his 'killingest'. An accomplice in a number of his 'serious murders' was Walter Neely, who helped to dispose of the bodies of three people he had killed when their van broke down on the highway. Later, Gaskins took a $1,500 contract to murder Silas Yates, a wealthy farmer, and when Neely's ex-wife Diane and her boyfriend attempted to blackmail him for the crime, he killed them both.

He also killed 13-year-old Kim Ghelkins and the investigation into this death led the police to a search of Gaskins's apartment, where some of Kim's clothing was discovered. Neely, implicated, turned state's evidence and led police to eight buried bodies. Gaskins, already being held on a charge of stealing cars, was indicted with all eight, but stood trial in May 1976 on only one count. This was for the killing of Neely's former brother-in-law, Dennis Bellamy. He was found guilty on 24 May and sentenced to death. Neely received a life sentence for this murder, claiming that he had been 'controlled' by Gaskins.

With a further seven indictments on his head, Gaskins began to bargain for his life by leading detectives to yet more graves. In November 1976, however, the U.S. Supreme Court declared South Carolina's death penalty law invalid, and Gaskins's sentence was commuted to life imprisonment. In April 1977, he was given a second life sentence for the murder of Silas Yates in 1975.

The death penalty for murder was reinstated in South Carolina later that year, and in 1978 Gaskins again bargained for leniency, providing details of many more buried bodies. He confessed to another 14 murders, but was charged with only nine, receiving sentences of life imprisonment in each case – considered sufficient, as there was no possibility of parole.

COASTAL KILLS AND SERIOUS MURDERS

On death row, Gaskins wrote his autobiography – semi-illit-erate, but dramatic. He divided his homicides into 'coastal kills' – committed on strangers of both sexes for pleasure – and 'serious murders', of people with whom he had been acquainted. He estimated that, by October 1970, he had already committed ten 'coastal kills', and these continued, on average, once a month thereafter. He did not embark upon 'serious murder' until November of that year, and his victims included neighbourhood acquaintances, personal enemies and criminal associates.

Altogether, Gaskins listed 31 'serious murders' – of which the police found 14 bodies, the others still remaining undis-covered – and some 80 'coastal kills'. As he did not know the names of any of these latter, and claimed he did not remember many details of how he had disposed of them, they could not be identified.

But Pee Wee did not live out his life in prison. On 12 September 1982, he took on a 'contract' to kill a prisoner on death row, Randolph Tyner, by wiring an explosive charge to Tyner's radio. Sentenced to death for this last outrage, he had his final appeal denied in June 1991. He attempted to delay his execution by slash-ing his wrists, but he was found in time and went to the electric chair on 6 September.

DENNIS NILSEN

KILLING FOR COMPANY

Muswell Hill remains a relatively quiet and salubrious suburb of north London. Ironically, it was developed at the beginning of the twentieth century, when a murder took place in the vicinity and city sightseers, taking the long tram-ride to the scene, were struck by the charm of the surrounding woods and fields. Eighty years on, a later generation of sightseers could be found outside 23 Cranley Gardens, one of the many streets of houses that had sprung up in the area. The resonance with the earlier 'pilgrimages' was both uncanny and depressing.

I t was a bitterly cold day on February 3, 1983, when the tenants of a house which had been converted into apartments, first complained of a blockage in the drainage system. Five days later, when an engineer came to inspect the drains he found the inspection pit deep in stinking, rotting flesh. As it was late, he decided not to report to his employers until the next morning. When he returned he found that most of the flesh had disappeared. However, some bones and a small piece of flesh had lodged in a pipe; so he contacted the police.

One of the ground floor tenants told them that she had heard quiet footsteps repeatedly passing her door in the night, seemingly coming from the top apartment. It was there that Dennis Nilsen, a polite, bespectacled 37-year-old civil servant lived alone. Learning from the police laboratory within hours that the bones and fragment of flesh were human, detectives were waiting for Nilsen when he returned home from work.

Chief Inspector Peter Jay greeted him: 'Good evening, Mr Nilsen. I've come to talk to you about your drains.'

When told of the grisly discovery, Nilsen replied calmly: 'Good grief, how awful.'

The conversation then took a startlingly dramatic turn: 'Don't mess around. Where's the rest of the body? In two plastic bags in the wardrobe. I'll show you.'

Taken to the police station, Nilsen was asked: 'Are we talking about one body or two?'

Nilson responded: 'Fifteen or sixteen, since 1978. Three at Cranley Gardens, and about thirteen at my previous address . . .'

This was a total that made him, at that time, Britain's most prolific serial killer. Over the next two weeks he provided gruesome details of his crimes.

A self-confessed homosexual, Nilsen was desperately lonely after leaving the army and settling in Cricklewood, north-west London. Working at an official employment bureau – a Job Centre – in central London, he constantly came in contact with equally lonely dropouts, and would buy them rounds of drinks before taking them to his apartment for companionship. Then, on December 30, 1978, after a solitary Christmas, he picked up a youthful Irish manual labourer in a local pub called the Cricklewood Arms, and became a killer for the first time. Waking in bed with the young man, he seized a necktie impulsively and strangled his sleeping victim. To make doubly sure, he then held the man's head in a bucket of water for some minutes.

Then began the extraordinary ritual that was to be repeated frequently in the next few years – and for which Nilsen was eventually to be described as 'killing for company'. He placed the corpse in the bathtub and carefully washed it; after drying it, he put it in his bed. Next day, he hid it beneath the floorboards in his room, but a week later he brought it out again and gave it another bath. After this, the corpse remained under the floor for eight months, until August 1979, when Nilsen cremated it in a bonfire.

Some time later in 1979, he picked up a student cook from Hong Kong, Andrew Ho, and attempted to strangle him, but the intended victim escaped. Ho reported the assault to the police, but they dismissed the incident after the student refused to prosecute.

A MORBID FASCINATION

Born in Scotland on November 23, 1945, Dennis Andrew Nilsen was the son of a Norwegian, Olaf Nilsen, and a local woman. His parents were divorced when he was aged four and he went to live for a time with his grandparents. A possible source of his psychopathic nature was the time when his fisherman grandfather drowned and, aged only 7, young Dennis was made to view the corpse. Following this he is reported as having hanged a cat to see how long it took to die. As an adult, his fascination with death led him sometimes to powder his naked body and regard his 'corpse' reflected in a mirror.

Nilsen loved uniforms and joined the army at age 16, serving 11 years as a regimental cook before volunteering for the police force. He soon resigned, however, and took up a civil service post at a job placement centre for the unemployed in London.

The second killing came on December 3, 1979, after Nilsen got into a lunchtime conversation with 19-year-old Canadian Kenneth Ockendon. Kenneth was due to fly home for Christmas with his family the next day, but was persuaded to go home with Nilsen to Cricklewood. After a meal and many drinks, he was strangled. Nilsen bathed him, slept with the body beside him and then hid it under the floorboards. Over the next two weeks he took up the corpse several times, sitting with it to watch TV shows.

Five months passed until, in May 1980, Martyn Duffey, 16, became the third victim. A few days later, 27-year-old Billy Sutherland joined Duffey under the floorboards. As for his next seven victims, Nilsen was infuriatingly vague. One was 'from the Philippines or Thailand'; one was yet another young Irish worker in London; the next a starving 'hippy type'; the fourth he could hardly remember; two were young Scotsmen that he had picked up; and the eleventh victim was a tattooed skinhead. The police were unable to make any identification of these victims from such unhelpful descriptions.

On November 10, 1980, 26-year-old Douglas Stewart had a narrow escape. After drinking with Nilsen in the West End of London, he agreed to return to Cricklewood, where he fell asleep in a chair. Waking, he found that his ankles were tied and Nilsen was trying to strangle him with a necktie. There was a struggle and Stewart broke free, escaping from the house to call the police. They, however, decided that the incident was a 'domestic' disagreement between two homosexuals and took no further action.

There were no more incidents – at least as far as Nilsen confessed – until September 17, 1981. He found Malcolm Barlow, 24, slumped in a drug-induced state close by his home as he left for work and sent him to hospital. On his return, he found Barlow once more at this door, invited him in and strangled him.

The following month, Nilsen was given notice by his landlord, with the offer of an alternative apartment in Cranley Gardens. By the end of the previous year he had already disposed of some of his victims' decomposing bodies in a second bonfire and now he consigned the rest to the flames.

After his arrest, he described to the police how he first cut off the hands and feet, washed and dried them and stored them in plastic bags. Then he removed all the major internal organs and tipped them into a narrow space between the yard fence and a wall – where they were soon consumed by rats, cats and foxes. The arms and legs were cut into pieces and the torso bisected; these were also put into bags, and finally burned. He laid old motor tyres on the bonfire, so that the smell of burning rubber covered the smell of roasting flesh.

Once settled in Cranley Gardens, Nilsen continued his cruising for likely victims. His first two attempts, on 25-year-old student Paul Nobbs and on a 'drag' artist, failed. For reasons that Nilsen himself could not explain, he gave up while trying to suffocate them. Oddly, neither of them approached the police until after the news of Nilsen's arrest.

The first murder in Cranley Gardens was that of John Howlett, well known in the West End as 'John the Guardsman'. When Nilsen attempted to strangle him with an upholstery strap, Howlett put up a fierce fight and was overcome only when Nilsen held his head under water in the bathtub for five minutes. In the top-floor apartment, there was no convenient space under the floorboards to hide the remains. So, after keeping the body in a closet for several days, Nilsen cut it into tiny pieces with a kitchen knife and flushed them down the lavatory. The head, hands, feet and ribs were boiled in a large pan on the kitchen stove in order to remove the flesh; and the larger bones were packed into a crate, where they remained until the police discovered them nearly a year later.

Nilsen treated the corpse of his next victim, drunken drifter Graham Allen, in the same way. After some time, his final killing took place on January 26, 1983.

Steve Sinclair was a 20-year-old drug addict. Nilsen picked him up, strangled him with a necktie and dressed the body in his own clothes, keeping it for several days before dismembering it. 'I put the head in a pot, popped the lid on and lit the stove. Later I listened to music and had a good drink, also watching some TV as the head was simmering.'

It was Allen's remains that blocked the drains and led to the gruesome discovery, and Nilsen's confession.

Nilsen stood trial on October 24, 1983, charged with the murder of six men – Ockendon, Duffey, Sutherland, Barlow, Howlett and Sinclair – and the attempted murder of Douglas Stewart and Paul Nobbs.

Despite his detailed confession, which was given in evidence in court, he pleaded not guilty to all counts. Psychologists and counsel argued over his cold, remorseless nature and whether or not he was insane. A plea of diminished responsibility was rejected, however, and Nilsen was finallly found guilty on November 4 by a jury majority of 10 to 2.

He was sentenced to life imprisonment, with a minimum of 25 years. As one commentator on the case wrote: 'Most people like someone to come home to, and so did Dennis Nilsen. He just preferred them to be dead.'

FRED & ROSEMARY WEST

HOUSE OF HORROR

There had been whispers among the neighbours before, but this time it was a police officer who heard them. On August 2, 1992, a young girl told him that she was worried that one of her friends had been 'mucked about with' by her father, who had videoed the incident. Four days later, armed with a warrant to search for pornographic material, the police called at 25 Cromwell Street, on the outskirts of Gloucester, England. There, Fred and Rosemary West were arrested on a charge of raping a minor, and their five youngest children taken into care. It was only later that the children began to talk of how their parents had threatened that they would end up 'buried under the patio . . . like Heather'.

What the police found at Cromwell Street they described as 'so disgusting and so vile and so difficult' to handle. There was a huge collection of rubberwear, 99 videotapes – both commercial and home-made – whips and bondage equipment and a hoard of photographs, including some of Rosemary in a variety of sexual poses and two of the West's daughters naked. While possession of such material in a private home was not in itself criminal, it was supporting evidence for the charges against the Wests.

There was already a case on file, dating from December 1972, when Fred and Rosemary had been charged with a vicious sexual assault on a 16-year-old girl. But she had chosen not to appear in court and the Wests had been fined a mere £25 on each of four minor counts.

However, this time, in 1992, they were put on bail. Rosemary was allowed to return home to a house where only two of her children remained; but Fred was sent to a hostel for ten months.

On June 7, 1993, they stood trial: Fred on three counts of rape and one of buggery against his daughter, and Rosemary on two counts, one of 'encouraging the commission of unlawful sexual intercourse' and one of cruelty to a child. Yet, at the last moment, the two children who were to have given evidence refused to appear, and the judge was reluctantly compelled to dismiss the charges. But, soon after, the police heard of the 'family joke' concerning Heather.

THE LETHAL PAIR

Frederick Walter Stephen West was born on September 29, 1941, the eldest son of a farm worker, in Much Marcle, on the county border between Herefordshire and Gloucestershire. In November 1962, he married 18-year-old Catherine Costello and they had two daughters – one of them not his. They lived for some time in Catherine's native Glasgow where she worked as a prostitute while Fred took a job as an ice-cream vendor; but he fell out with the local mobsters and the couple returned to Gloucestershire.

In January 1969, Fred told friends that Catherine had left him and he shortly took up with Rosemary Letts, aged 15. In March 1970 he obtained custody of Catherine's two children. Rosemary gave birth to Heather on October 17, 1970, and the couple married on January 29, 1972, finally moving into 25 Cromwell Street in July. They subsequently had seven more children.

Meanwhile, Fred had a variety of jobs, mostly as a builder. He made 11 court appearances, mainly for receiving stolen goods, petty theft and motoring offences, and spent six months in prison in 1971. Rosemary intensely disliked Fred's elder daughter Charmaine and, shortly after his release from prison, Catherine turned up to claim her. Neither she nor her daughter were ever seen again.

Heather Ann was the Wests' eldest daughter, aged 16 when she had disappeared seven years earlier. Her parents had maintained that she had left home without warning and that they had not heard from her since. On February 24, 1994, the police returned to 25 Cromwell Street and started digging. As they were removing the slabs of the patio behind the house, they uncovered a bone. Called to the scene, Home Office pathologist Professor Bernard Knight declared it to be human and female.

Fred was arrested, and admitted that he had killed Heather and that there were other bodies in the back yard. One was that of Shirley Robinson, who was six months pregnant when she died, and the foetal skeleton was found beside her dismembered bones. The other was Alison Chambers, who had disappeared in August 1979. The police soon realized that throughout Fred's interrogation this jaunty, grinning man was telling them what he chose and what he was sure they would in any case discover. They decided to seek the advice of forensic psychologist Paul Britton.

The police told Britton what they knew of the set-up in the West home. There was a bedroom on the top floor of the house that was fitted up like a brothel. Fred would bring men to Rosemary there and take photographs, and she also advertised in sex contact magazines as 'Mandy Mouse'. Britton told the police: 'You are looking at evidence of predatory and sadistic sexual psychopathy. We have a combined depravity – a husband and wife whose energy bounces off each other . . . They didn't just kill for the sake of taking a life, their victims were playthings who were tortured and abused.'

He went on to tell them that the three bodies under the patio would not be the only ones found: he had used the garden because the house was full.

As Britton advised, the police commenced an inch-by-inch search of 25 Cromwell Street. The skeletal remains of five young women were found in small square pits in the floor of the cellar, which Fred had later converted into a bedroom for his younger children. At the same time, the police received a report from a member of the public that the disappearance in 1973 of Lynda Gough, 19, might be connected. Her body was found in a similar pit beneath a bathroom that Fred had built in place of the garage. Circumstantial evidence provided by Lynda's mother linked Rosemary with the death. She and Fred – who had now confessed to nine killings – were both charged with this murder.

Britton had also suggested that the police search should extend to every place where Fred had lived or worked, and they launched an appeal for anyone who had known him over the past 25 years. They were particularly concerned to contact Catherine Costello, who had married Fred in 1962, and her elder daughter Charmaine. The younger daughter, Anne Marie, was already in touch.

Fred at last confessed that he had killed both of them, burying Catherine's body in a field near the village of Much Marcle where he was born. As for the fate of Charmaine, he told a variety of conflicting stories, apparently in the hope of exonerating Rosemary. Her remains were later found buried in a concrete floor at a house the couple had previously occupied. It took a month of digging to recover Catherine's body from the field. Fred then announced that there was another body in an adjoining field. It turned out to be that of Anna McFall, a girl with whom he had fallen in love with in Glasgow, and whom he later described as 'an angel'.

Eventually, the total of known victims reached 13. Dr David Whittaker, a forensic odontologist at University of Wales Medical College, applied a battery of tests that established the sex, age and medical history of each skeleton. Finally, he superimposed images of the victims upon photographs of their skulls. They all fitted.

However, before he could be brought to trial, Fred West hanged himself in his prison cell on the night of January 1, 1995.

In October, Rosemary appeared in court, charged with ten murders, all of which she denied. But, on the afternoon of November 22, convinced by Dr Whittaker's evidence, the jury reached a unanimous verdict on all counts, and Rosemary was sentenced to ten terms of life imprisonment.

KEN BIANCHI & ANGELO BUONO

THE HILLSIDE STRANGLERS

When, between October 1977 and January 1979, the strangled and brutalized – and usually nude – bodies of young women were found in the hilly areas that surround the centre of Los Angeles, the press attributed them to a killer they named the 'Hillside Strangler'. But, from quite early in the investigation, the police knew that they were looking for two sadistic murderers who were working together.

The first body was discovered on the morning of October 18, 1977, on the roadside close to Forest Lawn cemetery. Fingerprints quickly established the victim's identity as Yolanda Washington, 19, well known to the vice squad as a prostitute who practised her trade along Hollywood Boulevard. The murder of prostitutes was a regular occurrence in Los Angeles, and the killing was not considered of primary importance by the police.

On October 31, a second nude body, that of 15-year-old Judy Miller, was found dumped in Glendale. There were ligature marks around her neck, wrists and ankles, and an autopsy revealed that she had been sexually assaulted by two men, one of them a 'non-secretor' – that is, one whose blood characteristics are not found in other body fluids. A week later, on November 6, the body of a similarly murdered girl, 20-year-old Lissa Kastin, was discovered on a golf course in Glendale. She was not a prostitute, but had worked in Hollywood as a dancer and waitress and it was assumed that she had probably been known to the same men as the killers of Yolanda Washington and Judy Miller.

The absence of the three victims' clothing amongst other evidence made it clear that they had been killed elsewhere and later dumped where their bodies were found. The likelihood that they were specifically known to the killers was, however, put in doubt with the discovery on 20 November of the bodies of two school-girls, Dolores Cepeda, 12, and Sonja Johnson, 14. Then, within hours, the corpse of 20-year-old art student Kristina Weckler was found in the hills above Glendale. Three days later, the naked body of student Jane King, 28, was dumped beside the Golden State Freeway and on November 29 student Lauren Wagner, 18, was found strangled in Glendale. These latest victims had not only been sexually assaulted, but also tortured and mutilated.

The serial killings were now front-page news, and the citizens of Los Angeles were in a state of panic. The LAPD formed a special task force under Lieutenant Edwin Henderson, more than 100 detectives were recruited and a reward of $140,000 was offered for information leading to the arrest of the 'Strangler'.

There was not much evidence to go on. A boy reported that he had seen Dolores Cepeda and Sonja Johnson speaking to someone in a car on the night of their disappearance. Another witness was able to give a few more details. She had seen Lauren Wagner's car stopped by two men, who ordered her into their car. She described the men: one was around the age of 40, Latin-looking with bushy hair; the other was younger, with an acne-scarred neck. In Los Angeles this description could fit many persons, but next morning she reported that a man with 'a rough east-coast accent' had telephoned and threatened her with death if she told what she had seen.

Fortunately, the threat was never carried out. However, on December 14, the naked body of 17-year-old prostitute Kimberly Martin was discovered on a hillside construction site in downtown Los Angeles. She had been strangled and brutalized. It was established that she had been lured to her death by a telephone call to a local call-girl agency, asking for 'a young blonde, preferably wearing black underwear', and offering $150 for her services.

It was not until 17 February 1978 that the next victim was discovered. Police examining a car that had been pushed off a cliff in Angeles National Forest found the naked body of 20-year-old Cindy Hudspeth in the trunk. Cindy was not a prostitute, but a telephone operator, and she had been sexually assaulted by two men, one a non-secretor, and then strangled.

Following this, there were no more murders by the Stranglers in the Los Angeles area. However, nearly a year later, on 12 January 1979, two university students – Karen Mandic and Diane Wilder, both 22 – were found strangled and sexually assaulted in the back of a car in Bellingham, a small industrial town in Washington State, 1000 miles to the north. Karen's boyfriend told the police that the two girls had been hired the previous evening by a man from a local security company to 'house-sit' for a couple of hours. And the man's name was Kenneth Bianchi.

Bianchi was called in for questioning. He was relaxed and polite, and denied that he knew either of the dead girls. A search of his house revealed no evidence of the crime, but it uncovered a hoard of electrical goods that had been stolen from companies where he had worked as a security guard – and that was sufficient for him to be charged and jailed.

Meanwhile, the police learnt that the security company had one unoccupied property on their books, and they searched it. Forensic scientists found several blonde hairs that matched Karen Mandic's and a single pubic hair that proved to be Bianchi's. The girls' clothes also carried fibres that matched a carpet in the house. Bianchi still held a California driving licence and a check revealed that the address was of an apartment building where Kristina Weckler had once lived, where Kimberly Martin was last seen, and across the street from where Cindy Hudspeth had been abducted.

The case against Bianchi looked watertight, but then doubts were raised about his sanity, and a series of psychologists and psychiatrists were called in by his attorney. Bianchi agreed to be examined under hypnosis, and revealed an aggressive alter ego claiming to be 'Steve Walker', which resulted in a diagnosis, for the defence, of 'multiple personality disorder'. He confessed to many murders, implicating Buono as his partner and describing in lurid detail how the pair had used fake police badges in order to abduct young women. They had taken them to Buono's house in Glendale and subjected them to torture and sexual assault before killing them. 'Steve Walker' boasted: 'Angelo is my kind of man. There should be more people in the world like Angelo.'

The prosecution, however, were not convinced. In Bianchi's house, the police found a number of books on psychology and hypnosis, together with two novels that dealt with multiple personality. And, looking into the academic record he claimed from Los Angeles City College, they found it full of inconsistencies: it was obviously a forgery. Requesting an original copy from the college, they discovered that it belonged to a psychology graduate – named Steve Walker. Bianchi was found fit to stand trial on October 19, 1979, and transferred to jail in Los Angeles.

Buono was arrested on October 22, but what he did not know was that Bianchi had struck a deal to avoid the death penalty, agreeing to plead guilty to seven counts of murder and to give evidence against his adoptive cousin. However, the forensic team could find little incriminating evidence in Buono's home, except minute fragments of fibre on nine of the victims' bodies that matched a chair and a piece of fluff on Judy Miller's eyelid that was identical to the upholstery fabric in his workshop. In July 1981, the District Attorney filed a motion for dismissal of the charges of murder against Buono, on the grounds that the evidence against him was too slight.

The police, the press and the public were dismayed. Fortunately, in a very rare case of disagreement, the judge denied the motion and transferred the prosecution file to the office of the state's Attorney General.

Angelo Buono's trial opened on November 16, 1981, and dragged on for a full two years. Bianchi took the stand in June 1982. At first his testimony was vague and contradictory, but the judge pointed out that he could be violating his plea bargain and be returned to Washington, at which point he fully implicated Buono. On January 9,1984, the pair finally appeared for sentencing. Buono was guilty of nine murders, and was sentenced to life

THE TWO STRANGLERS

Kenneth Bianchi was the son of a prostitute in Rochester, NY, born on 22 May 1951. At the age of three months, he was adopted by Nicholas Bianchi and his wife Frances. Frances's sister was Jenny Buono; her son Angelo was born in Rochester on October 5, 1934, but the two moved to Glendale, California, in 1944–45.

As a child, Bianchi was intelligent but given to violent tantrums and compulsive lying. Handsome and charming, he married briefly at the age of 18, but the relationship soon broke up and he turned to casual encounters. He was arrested several times for petty theft, but never charged. In 1976, believing that he was a suspect in a series of brutal killings in Rochester, he left for Los Angeles where he joined up with his adoptive cousin, Angelo Buono.

Buono was now 42 years old, and Bianchi looked up to him like an elder brother. The senior man had been in trouble many times for stealing cars and brawling. He had been married four times, fathering eight children, but each of his wives had left him, citing physical cruelty and excessive sexual demands. His taste for young girls and sadistic sex gained him the local name of the 'Italian Stallion'. He was an established pimp and when he tired of a conquest, he would force the girl into prostitution. However, by 1976, he also had a flourishing business as a car upholsterer.

Bianchi applied to the Glendale and Los Angeles police departments but was turned down by both. He readily agreed to Buono's proposal that they should impersonate police officers, stopping cars and 'arresting' prostitutes and subjecting them to sexual assault and brutality. It was not long before they embarked on their horrific murder spree.

imprisonment without possibility of parole. He died of a heart attack at Calipatria State Prison in California.

Bianchi's worst fears were realized when he was sent back to Washington to serve a sentence of some 27 years before being eligible for parole.

RICHARD TRENTON CHASE

VAMPIRE OF SACRAMENTO

Faced with the need to understand the motivation and personality disorders behind the rapidly increasing phenomenon of serial killing, the FBI set up their Behavioral Science Unit at the Bureau's headquarters in Quantico, Virginia, in 1972. At first they studied the details of solved cases, such as that of Harvey Glatman (see pages 72–6), but gradually they began to extend their expertise to the prediction of the likely characteristics of active, unapprehended murderers.

On the evening of January 23, 1978, truck driver David Wallin, 24, returned to his home in Sacramento, California, to find his 22-year-old pregnant wife Terry butchered in their bedroom, her abdomen slashed open. An empty yoghurt carton beside the bed revealed that it had been used to drink the blood of the victim and several pieces of her body were missing. There was no other apparent motive for the murder.

The police contacted the local FBI co-ordinator for the BSU, Russ Vorpagel, and he called Robert Ressler, one of the leading psychological profilers, in Quantico. Ressler was about to leave for the West Coast for a lecture tour, but before he left he drew up a preliminary profile of the probable offender.

Then, even as Ressler was packing his bags for the California trip, the killer struck again. Around midday on January 26 three bodies were discovered by a neighbour in a home less than a mile away from the Wallin murder. The dead were Evelyn Miroth, 36, her six-year-old son Jason, and Daniel Meredith, 52, a family friend. In addition, Mrs Miroth's 22-month-old nephew, Michael Ferriera, was missing. All three dead victims had been shot with a .22 and Evelyn Miroth had been mutilated, in an even more

RESSLER'S FIRST ASSESSMENT

White male, aged 25-27 years; thin, under-nourished appearance. Residence will be extremely slovenly and unkempt and evidence of the crime will be found at the residence. History of mental illness and will have been involved in the use of drugs. Will be a loner who does not associate with either males or females, and will probably spend a great deal of time in his own home, where he lives alone. Unemployed. Possibly receives some form of disability money. If residing with anyone, it would be his parents; however, this is unlikely. No prior military record; high school or college dropout. Probably suffering from one or more forms of paranoid psychosis.

obscene manner than Terry Wallin. The killer had apparently left in Meredith's red station wagon, which was found abandoned not far away.

In the baby's playpen, there was a pillow heavily soaked in blood. The bathtub contained bloody water, as well as brain and fecal matter, and there were signs that blood had been drunk here, too. The local sheriff described the scene as: 'The most, bizarre, grotesque and senseless killings I've seen in 28 years.'

As soon as he was informed of the crime, Ressler at once added more details to his profile, stating that the killer was: '. . . single, living alone in a location within one-half to one mile from the abandoned station wagon.'

He told Vorpagel: 'Before this man had murdered, he had probably committed fetish burglaries in the area and, once he was caught, we'd be able to trace his crimes and difficulties back to his childhood.'

Fetish burglaries were those in which the stolen items were articles of women's clothing – rather than valuable items that could be sold – which the burglar took for auto-erotic purposes.

THE RISE OF 'DRACULA'

Born in 1950, Chase had been a well-behaved child, although he was still wetting his bed at the age of 8. Three or four years later, his parents began to quarrel violently, and psychiatrists who later interviewed her described Mrs Chase as 'highly aggressive . . . hostile . . . provocative'. The couple eventually divorced.

Chase was of normal intelligence, but in his second year at high school he grew 'rebellious and defiant, had no ambition and his room was always in a state of disarray' – perhaps not so uncommon in a teenager. He was arrested in 1965 for possession of marijuana. Nevertheless, he graduated from high school and found employment for several months in 1969 – the only job he kept for more than a few days.

Living alone in an apartment paid for by his mother, Chase began to kill rabbits and drink their blood: he believed that, if he didn't, his heart would shrink and his blood turn to powder. He was committed to a psychiatric institution, where he earned the nickname of 'Dracula' after he killed birds and was found with a bloody mouth.

Following a course of medication, Chase was released into the legal care of his parents in 1976. He received disability payments and his mother bought his groceries. He acquired a gun and shot neighbours' pets and continued to drink their blood.

On December 20, 1977 he took to the streets and fired, first at a Mrs Polenske in her home, and then at Ambrose Griffin, killing him. Very soon, his murderous rampage escalated.

Armed with this information, some 65 police officers began to question hundreds of people in the area around the station wagon. A valuable lead came from a woman in her late twenties, who, on the day of Terry Wallin's murder, had spoken to man she had known in high school some ten years earlier. She was shocked at his appearance: '. . . dishevelled, cadaverously thin, bloody sweatshirt, yellowed crust around his mouth, sunken eyes.'

His name was Richard Trenton Chase.

Two police officers staked out Chase's home, which was close to where the station wagon had been abandoned. When he came out, they arrested him in possession of a .22 pistol and the wallet of Daniel Meredith. His truck, parked close by, was 12 years old and littered with rubbish. There was also a 12-inch butcher's knife and rubber boots splashed with blood.

Chase's apartment was a filthy mess. Detectives found three food blenders with blood in them, bloodstained clothing, and a collection of newspaper articles about his murders. In the refrigerator were dishes containing body parts and a container with brain tissue. A calendar was marked 'Today' on the dates of the two previous killings – and, ominously, the same word was marked on 44 forthcoming dates throughout 1978. Some months later, the body of missing baby Michael Ferriera was at last found close to Chase's home.

Feelings against the 'Vampire of Sacramento' ran so high in the city that the trial was held in San Jose. It opened in January 1979, and Chase was charged on six counts of first-degree murder. On May 8 he was found guilty and sentenced to death.

DONALD HARVEY

'ALWAYS A GOOD BOY'

Donald Harvey did not have the dysfunctional family background typical of so many serial killers. He was the kind of boy who is a mother's darling and a teacher's pet. The principal of the elementary school he attended for eight years commented: 'He was always clean and well-dressed ... He was a happy child, very sociable and well-liked by the other children.' Said his mother, after he had been found guilty of some 70 murders: 'My son has always been a good boy.'

Harvey's killing career began in 1970, when his mother asked him to visit his grandfather in Marymount Hospital, London, Kentucky. While there, he was asked if he would be interested in working as an orderly and he accepted the offer. All went well for some months, and then, one evening, a patient in a private room smeared him with faeces. 'The next thing I knew, I'd smothered him. It was like it was the last straw. I went in to help the man and he wants to rub that in my face.'

When Harvey reported the death of the patient: 'No-one ever questioned it.'

Unsuspected, he killed again three weeks later, disconnecting the oxygen supply of an elderly woman. His confidence growing, he began to experiment. In the course of a year he murdered at least a dozen more patients, usually with drugs.

On March 31, 1971, Harvey was arrested for burglary. He was drunk at the time, and the police paid little attention to his incoherent confessions to the murders he had committed. At his trial, he pleaded guilty to a reduced charge of petty theft, and was fined $50. The judge recommended psychiatric treatment 'for his troubled condition'. Instead, Harvey decided to enlist in the U.S. Air Force.

He served ten months before being discharged in March 1972. His service records do not state the reason; although it may be that he was recognized as homosexual. At this time, Harvey fell into a deep depression and twice committed himself to a mental ward in Lexington for a few weeks in July and August 1972.

With his previous experience at Marymount, Harvey was able to find part-time work as a nurses' aide at Cardinal Hill hospital in Lexington, and in June 1973 took another part-time job at a second hospital. Between August 1974 and September 1975 he worked as a telephone operator and then took work as a clerk in St Luke's Hospital, Fort Thomas. For nearly three years he had little or no access to unattended hospital patients and his compulsion to kill was frustrated.

THE 'GOOD BOY'

Donald Harvey was born in Butler County, Ohio, in 1952, but very soon his parents relocated to Booneville, Kentucky. An intelligent boy, he was very much a loner at school, seldom taking part in extracurricular activities and preferring to read books. He entered high school in 1968 but, earning high grades with little effort, he dropped out and eventually moved to Cincinnati, taking a job in a local factory.

So, relocating to Cincinnati, Ohio, in September 1975, Harvey secured employment at the city's Veteran's Administration Medical Center. His duties were varied: as a nursing assistant, housekeeping aide, cardiac-catheterization technician and autopsy assistant. Now he was in his element, as he had access to nearly every part of the hospital and worked at night with little supervision.

Over the next ten years, Harvey murdered at least 15 patients. He kept a detailed diary of his methods: asphyxiation; adding rat poison to a patient's food; adding arsenic and cyanide to orange juice; adding cyanide to an intravenous feed; injecting cyanide into a patient's buttocks. He was never suspected and on one occasion he even told the nurses, jokingly: 'I got rid of that one for you.'

However, he earned the name of 'angel of death', because he was always around at the time someone died.

In the early 1980s, Harvey took a lover, Carl Hoeweler, and regularly poisoned him with doses of arsenic before nursing him back to health. He also poisoned Carl's parents and a female neighbour. After an argument with another neighbour, he laced her drink with hepatitis serum and she nearly died before the infection was diagnosed.

On July 18, 1985, Harvey was stopped by security guards as he left hospital with a suspicious-looking gym bag. It contained hypodermic needles, surgical scissors and gloves, several medical texts and other books – and a .32 calibre pistol. Fined $50 for carrying a firearm on Federal property, he was given the option of quietly resigning from his hospital job.

However, no mention of this incident appeared on his work record and in February 1986 he was taken on part-time at another Cincinnati hospital, soon earning a full-time position. Now his compulsion to kill took over completely, and in just over a year he murdered a further 23 patients.

The end came near on March 7, 1987, however, when John Powell – a patient who had been comatose for several months but was showing signs of recovery – died suddenly. At the autopsy, an assistant noted a faint smell of bitter almonds, a sure sign of cyanide poisoning. In April, investigators secured a warrant to search Harvey's apartment and found a wealth of incriminating evidence, including jars of cyanide and arsenic and a detailed journal of his killings.

Arrested on a charge of aggravated murder, Harvey at first pleaded not guilty by reason of insanity but, as the evidence mounted, he made a plea bargain to avoid the death penalty. On August 11, he confessed to 33 murders over the previous 17 years, and by the time his trial opened a week later he had raised the total to 70. When questions were asked as to his sanity, the prosecutor's office stated: 'This man is sane, competent, but is a compulsive killer. He builds up tension in his body, so he kills people.'

In the Cincinnati court, Harvey pleaded guilty to 25 counts of aggravated murder. He was given four consecutive 20-years-to-life sentences and fined $270,000, in addition. In Kentucky the following month, he confessed to 12 murders at Marymount Hospital, and was sentenced to eight life terms, plus 20 years. Back in Cincinnati in February 1988, he was sentenced for a further three homicides and three attempted, earning an additional three life sentences and three terms of 5–25 years.

Asked the question 'Why Did You Kill?' in 1991, Harvey replied: 'People controlled me for 18 years, and then I controlled my own destiny. I controlled other people's lives, whether they lived or died. I had that power to control . . . After I didn't get caught for the first 15, I thought it was my right. I appointed myself judge, prosecutor and jury. So I played God.'

His first parole hearing is scheduled for 2047. He died on March 30, 2017, having been found severely beaten in his cell.

WAYNE WILLIAMS

MUSIC-BIZ TALENT SCOUT

Between July 1979 and May 1981, more than 20 bodies, killed in a wide variety of ways, were discovered in Atlanta, Georgia – and the police were very soon confirmed in their fears that a serial killer of children was at work in the area. All the victims were African-American and the case was named the 'Atlanta child murders'. Yet, the killer was finally convicted on only two counts of the murder of young adults.

O n July 21, 1979, 14-year-old Edward Smith was reported missing. Alfred Evans, aged 13, was last seen alive on July 25. Three days later, a woman discovered their bodies half-concealed in roadside undergrowth: Edward had been shot with a .22 weapon, while Alfred had been strangled. On September 4, Milton Harvey, 14, vanished, his corpse being discovered three weeks later. The cause of death was given as 'unknown'. Nine-year-old Yusef Bell was last seen alive on October 21, and his strangled body was found in an abandoned school building on November 8.

The list of victims rapidly began to swell. Reported missing on March 5, 1980, 12-year-old Angel Lenair was found dead five days later, tied to a tree with her hands behind her back. She had been strangled. The following day, March 11, Jeffrey Mathis disappeared; his remains, reduced to a skeleton, were not recovered until 11 months later, and it was impossible to determine the cause of death. Eric Middlebrook, 14, who left home on May 18 after receiving a telephone call, was found the following day, bludgeoned to death.

By the end of July, the total of dead and missing children had reached 12. On June 9, Christopher Richardson, 12, disappeared, and on the night of June 22, LaTonya Wilson, 7, was abducted from her home. The following day, 10-year-old Aaron Wyche disappeared; his body was discovered, with a broken neck, on June 24. On July 7 the body of Anthony Carter, 9, was found; he had died from multiple stab wounds. And on July 31 Earl Terrell disappeared from a public swimming pool, his skeletal remains not being uncovered until January 9, 1981.

The mayor of Atlanta appealed directly to the White House for the FBI to be brought in. Although the Bureau seldom intervenes directly in murder investigations, there was justification in this case. At this stage, four children were still listed as 'missing', and might well have been kidnapped, a Federal offence. Many Atlanta citizens were convinced that the murders were racist, so that there was also the possibility of 'violation of Federal civil rights'.

By the time two leading psychological profilers from Quantico, John Douglas and Roy Hazelwood, arrived in Atlanta, the number of cases had risen to 15. Clifford Jones, 12, was abducted and strangled on August 20, and Darren Glass, 11, disappeared on September 14. Young Charles Stevens was found, strangled, on October 10, and the remains of LaTonya Wilson, abducted on June 22, were uncovered on October 18.

The two FBI agents soon discounted the possibility that the murders were racist: the crimes had all occurred in African-American neighbourhoods, and a white man prowling the area for prey would have been noticed. They also decided that the killings of the two young girls were likely unrelated, and drew up a profile of the murderer. He was African-American – relatively rare for a serial killer, but almost certainly true in this case – single and aged 25–29. He drove a police-type vehicle, and owned either a German shepherd or a Doberman dog. Lacking a girlfriend, he would be attracted to young boys, although there was no evidence that any of his victims had been sexually abused. Said Douglas: 'He would have some kind of ruse or con with these kids, I was betting on something to do with music or performing.'

Meanwhile, the murders continued unabated. By the beginning of 1981, the death toll – including children missing, presumed dead – had risen to 26.

Forensic investigators had found identical fibres on the clothing of many of the child victims, confirmation that this was the work of one serial killer. The fibres were examined at Georgia State Crime Laboratory and found to be of two types: a yellowish-green nylon that looked as if it came from a carpet, and a violet-hued acetate. News of this evidence appeared in a local newspaper in February 1981, and the killer at once changed his tactics. He turned his attention to young adults, several of them homosexual ex-convicts, dumping their bodies in local rivers after stripping them of most of their clothing.

On April 27, the asphyxiated body of 21-year-old ex-convict Jimmy Payne was recovered from the Chattahoochee River, six days after he had been reported missing. He was naked except for his shorts – but they carried a single matching fibre. For some weeks the police staked out local waterways, and on May 22 an officer heard a loud splash in the Chattahoochee. Alerted, police and local FBI agents stopped a station wagon and the driver identified himself as Wayne Williams, 23, 'music biz talent scout'. He said he had just thrown some garbage in the river, and was allowed to leave.

The body of Nathaniel Cater, a 27-year-old ex-convict, was dragged from the river two days later, and a yellowish-green carpet fibre was found in his hair. On June 2 a warrant was obtained for a search of Williams's home, which was found to be carpeted throughout with yellowish-green nylon. Williams seemed an unlikely suspect: the only child of two respectable schoolteachers, he lived at home with his parents. The detailed examination of the fibres was turned over to the FBI laboratory.

Wayne Williams was arrested on June 21, and charged with the murder of Nathaniel Cater. On July 17 he was indicted for the killing of Cater and Payne.

Given the statistical facts presented by the FBI of forensic evidence, the jury found Williams guilty on both counts on February 27, 1982; and he was sentenced to two terms of life imprisonment.

There were no more child murders in Atlanta following Williams's conviction.

JOHN FRANCIS DUFFY

RAILWAY RAPIST

The British police were slow to follow the American example of seeking the advice of psychologists in analyzing the behaviour of violent criminals. It was not until the 1980s that they began to employ the technique. One of the first examples of the successful application of psychological profiling came in 1986, with the apprehension of the 'Railway Rapist', who had turned to murder.

The rape attacks began on June 10, 1982, when a 23-year-old woman was sexually assaulted by two men near a railway station in north London. Over the next twelve months, the two carried out a further 18 rapes, all close to railway stations and most within a five-mile radius. In late 1983 the attacks ceased and the police remained hopeful that there would be no more.

However, beginning early in 1984, there came more rapes, this time by a man acting alone. The first was in a different area in southwest London and it was followed by many more, mostly in northwest London, although there were three further attacks close to the scene of the first. All took place near railway stations served by, or connected to, the North London Line.

On July 14, 1985, there were three violent attacks in a single night. The police, who had made little progress in their investigations, now set up a task force – 'Operation Hart' – which was soon to involve officers from four forces – the Metropolitan Police from Scotland Yard, British Transport Police and the police of the counties of Surrey and Hertfordshire.

In August, a man named John Francis Duffy appeared at Acton Town Court charged with a violent assault on his estranged wife and her boyfriend, and was granted bail. By now, the Hart

A PSYCHOLOGIST'S THOUGHTS

In November 1985 David Canter, Professor of Applied Psychology at the University of Surrey, was invited to lunch at Scotland Yard and asked whether behavioural science could be of value in criminal investigations. He later wrote:

> At that time I had never heard of 'profiling', but the whole idea of reading a criminal's life from the details of how he carries out his crimes was enormously appealing.

team had assembled a list of 4,874 possible suspects for the rape attacks, whittling it down to 1,593. Because of Mrs Duffy's allegations of her husband's sadistic sex behaviour, his name was added to the list of 'possibles'.

There was another rape attack on September 22, and a further two in October. Duffy was called for an identification parade but the 20-year-old victim was still in a state of shock, and could not pick him out.

Two months later, Canter (see box) read a newspaper report concerning the 'Railway Rapist' and made notes on the 24 sexual assaults described. Then he wrote a letter to Scotland Yard: 'I have no evidence that the one individual is the same person but, if it were, then one could see something about the relationship between the two men as a possible clue to the whole series. For example, a scenario that had one of them working near the railways . . . and only meeting up with the other under certain circumstances, possibly related to work, could lead to exploring the evidence . . .'

Several months later, Canter was surprised to be summoned to a high-level police meeting to discuss Operation Hart. He was told that the investigation had been on the verge of closing down when forensic evidence from two recent killings indicated that the rapes and murders had been committed by the same man. Both the rape and the murder victims had their thumbs tied together with a particular type of twine and a specific blood group had been found in the rapes and on the body of one of the murder victims.

Canter agreed to do what he could. As he said, he had no previous experience in criminal cases; his previous investigation had been market research into people's biscuit preferences – but, at least, the fee he had received had paid for a specialized piece of software. He was given a small room at police headquarters in Guildford, near the university, where he installed his desktop computer, and was joined by two police officers as assistants.

The descriptions of their assailant provided by the victims, under intense emotional stress, were far from consistent, so the team began to analyze behavioural characteristics. They entered every known detail about each crime on the computer, looking for patterns to establish that the same man was responsible for all the rapes and killings.

On December 29, 1985, 19-year-old Alison Day disappeared after leaving a train at Hackney Wick station on the eastern section of the North London Line. It was not until 17 days later that her body was found, dumped in the murky water of the River Lee, less than half a mile away. Her hands and thumbs had been tied behind her, her underwear was missing and she had been raped. The killer had then torn a strip from her shirt to strangle her. Afterwards, apparently, he had dressed the body again. The pockets of her sheepskin coat were filled with heavy stones so that her body sank in the water.

Because Alison's corpse had been so long in the river, there was little physical evidence, but what was eventually to prove of vital importance was the discovery of a number of 'foreign' fibres on her clothes and body. They had almost certainly come from the killer's clothing.

Just over three months later, on April 17, 1986, 15-year-old schoolgirl Maartje Tamboezer was raped, beaten and strangled, 40 miles away to the south in a Surrey woodland. One of her socks had also been thrust into her throat – probably to stifle her screams. Born in the Netherlands, Maartje had come to England several years previously with her family. She had been riding her bicycle along a path beside the railway near East Horsley station, and investigators found a length of fishing line tied across the path at chest height to cause her to stop. There were no eyewitnesses, but several people recalled seeing a smallish man rushing on to the station to catch a train to London. Laboratory tests on Maartje's clothes revealed semen stains with the same blood characteristics as in the previous many cases.

On May 18, the killer claimed his third victim. Newly-married Anne Lock, 29, left the station at Brookman's Park, Hertfordshire – nearly as distant north from central London as East Horsley was to the south – to cycle home. Her bicycle was found not far away by a police search team, but it was two months before Anne's badly decomposed corpse was discovered on an overgrown railway embankment. Given the condition of the body, it was difficult to be certain; but it appeared probable that she had been beaten and raped, with her hands tied behind her in the typical way, before being strangled.

It turned out that, three weeks earlier, two officers from the Hart team had by chance spotted John Duffy near North Weald station, on the northeast fringes of London. What was he doing, 25 miles from his known home in Kilburn, northwest London, and near a remote railway line? He was taken to the nearest police station and questioned, but there was no evidence to hold him. Following the discovery of Anne Lock's body, Duffy was again questioned and was now a prime suspect; but there was still no possibility of charging him.

By July, when Anne Lock's murder was confirmed, Professor Canter was under pressure from the Hart team to produce at least a preliminary profile. He announced that the killer was a casual worker in a job that seldom brought him into contact with the general public. Although he had little social contact with women, he had one or two close male friends. He also had an extensive knowledge of the railway system of the London suburbs. Putting the most consistent of the victims' accounts together with some of the forensic findings, Canter provided a working description of the man. He also suggested that the rapist-killer had been arrested for violence at some time – possibly in the period when the rapes had temporarily ceased.

But it was not what the computer revealed that was to prove the most important revelation and to provide Canter with a subject for many years work. He and one of his assistants had drawn up a series of maps on acetate overlays, marking the sites of the crimes: 'Casually I pointed to an area of north London circumscribed by the first three offences and said, with a questioning smile, "He lives there doesn't he?"'

So Canter informed the police that the killer lived in the Kilburn area.

After this, Canter heard no news of the progress of the investigation until he received a telephone call from the senior officer on the Hart team: 'I don't know how you did it . . . But that profile you gave us was very accurate . . .'

Following the information he had provided, Duffy's name had risen to the top of the suspects' list. But, realizing that he was under close surveillance, Duffy had persuaded a friend to assault him with a knife, and then staggered into a police station claiming to have suffered a vicious mugging and to have lost his memory. He was admitted to a psychiatric hospital, but contrived to slip out on October 21, 1986, and rape a 14-year-old girl.

The police were at last able to obtain a warrant to search Duffy's home, but at first could find nothing to link him to any of the crimes. However, at his mother's house they found a large ball of the unusual string that Duffy had used to restrain his victims. It was of a brand named Somyarn and manufacture had ceased in 1982; but a major quantity had been sold to British Rail. Finally, laboratory analysis established that the fibres obtained from Alison Day's body matched those from one of Duffy's sweaters.

At his trial in early 1988, Duffy offered an unconvincing defence of 'amnesia', and on February 26, the judge, describing him as 'little more than a predatory animal who behaved in a beastly, degrading and disgusting way', sentenced him to a minimum of 30 years for four rapes and two murders. The evidence against him in the case of Anne Lock was considered insufficient and he was acquitted on this charge.

Years later, in prison, Duffy 'recovered' his memory and named his boyhood friend David Mulcahy as his accomplice in the first series of rapes. Mulcahy is now also serving time.

CLIFFORD RAYMOND OLSON

BEAST OF BRITISH COLUMBIA

Few serial killers have profited much, if at all, from their murders, but on his arrest Clifford Olson made an extraordinary deal with the prosecution. He asked for, and received, 10,000 Canadian dollars per victim – paid to his wife and child in return for confessing to the four murders with which he was first charged, and leading police to a further six missing bodies.

Olson was born in Vancouver, British Columbia, on January 1, 1940, and spent most of his early adult life in trouble. A bully at school, he began his criminal career at the age of 16 – and between 1957 and 1980 he was arrested 94 times on such charges as armed robbery, sexual assault and even fraud. He became a police informer, and it is alleged that, during one of his many spells in prison, he forced a fellow inmate to write a confession to rape, murder and mutilation of a nine-year-old girl, and then appeared successfully as a prosecution witness at the man's trial. Out of prison, he lived with his girlfriend and their illegitimate son.

His first killing occurred in November 1980, when he was freed on bail on firearms and sex charges. He abducted 12-year-old Christine Weller from her home in a Vancouver suburb and her mutilated body was found in woodland on Christmas Day. Then, on April 16, 1981, Colleen Daignault, 13, vanished from the same suburb; and a few days later, Darren Johnsrud, 16, was abducted from a Vancouver shopping mall. His body, the skull bludgeoned and brutally fractured, was discovered in woodland on May 2. The police were now sure that a serial killer was at work, but had no clues to his identity.

The killing frenzy was accelerating. On May 19, Sandra Wolfsteiner, 16, disappeared while hitch-hiking on the outskirts of Vancouver; and, on June 21, 13-year-old Ada Court vanished while she was returning home from baby-sitting. In the same month 9-year-old Susan Partington disappeared after she was seen talking to a man in a shopping mall. Judy Kozma, 14, disappeared on July 9 and her mutilated body was found two weeks later in Lake Weaver, in a mountain valley 40 miles east of the city and close to Agassiz prison.

By now, the police were suspicious of Olson and he was under surveillance. However, he hired a car to take a 3,500-mile 'holiday' trip across the border. On his return, he was able to commit four more murders in Canada, within one week and without detection.

On July 23, Raymond King, 15, disappeared, his body being found on the shore of Lake Weaver after two weeks. Two days later, 18-year-old German tourist Sigrun Arnd was abducted while hitch-hiking near Vancouver. When Olson later told police where her remains could be found, she was identified by her dental records. Terri Carson was abducted soon after, and her corpse was recovered from Lake Weaver. Another hitch-hiker, 17-year old Louise Chartrand, disappeared on July 30.

Police officers covertly following Olson finally arrested him when he picked up two girl hitch-hikers. In his van they found an address book belonging to Judy Kozma. In custody, he made his outrageous deal and, despite the opposition of the police – and furious public protest – the BC Attorney General agreed to his demands.

Glorying in his description as the 'Beast of BC', Olson pleaded guilty to eleven counts of murder on January 11, 1982, and was sentenced to eleven terms of life imprisonment.

In 1996, Olson applied for a judicial review of his case and in August 1997 asked for parole at his hearing on August 23, at the same time claiming that he had been responsible for a total of 143 killings in Canada and the United States. It took the jury 15 minutes to reject his appeal for parole.

GARY RIDGWAY

GREEN RIVER MAN

Between 1982 and 1984, an unknown man committed at least 48 murders around Seattle, Washington State and nearby Tacoma. All his victims were female, many of them prostitutes, but also young girls who were abducted. For close on 20 years, the cases remained unsolved, although the files were never closed. It was only with the development of new methods of DNA analysis that the perpetrator was finally identified and caught.

The first two killings were not recognized as part of a series for some time. On January 21, 1982, the strangled body of 16-year-old Leann Wilcox was found in a field near Tacoma. And then on July 7, 1982, Amina Agisheff, 36, disappeared – her skeletal remains not found and identified until April 1984.

It was July 15, 1982, when the body of 16-year-old Wendy Coffield, reported missing a week earlier, was dragged from the Green River, east of Seattle. On August 12, the corpse of Deborah Bonner, 23, was pulled from the same river, about half-a-mile upstream from where Wendy's body had been dumped. Three days later, three more victims were recovered from the water: Marcia Chapman, 31, Cynthia Hinds, 17, and Opal Mills, 16.

The list of missing young women began to swell in the months that followed. Two 17-year-olds, Karen Lee and Terri Milligan, disappeared in late August; Debra Estes, 15, on September 14; and Mary Meehan, 19, the following day. Most of the identified victims were known to police as prostitutes – but the killer also targeted hitch-hikers and runaways. Shawndra Summers, 17, disappeared on October 7; Becky Marrero, 20 – a friend of Debra Estes – on December 2; Alma Smith, 19, on March 3, 1983; Carrie Rois, 16, on March 17; and Kimi Pitsor, 16, on April 28.

Although he was named the 'Green River Man', the killer picked at least four different sites to dispose of his victims' bodies. The remains of many were not discovered for some years, and one as late as 1988. Often they were dumped in isolated spots, covered with loose brush and branches.

Between May and October 1983, the killer added a further 13 names to his total; and then he took a break. The murders did not begin again until January 1984.

By April of that year, the Green River task force had listed 24 known dead and 13 missing, having recovered twelve new skeletons in the previous three months. By January 1986, with the discovery of more remains, the total had increased to 34; and it topped 40 by spring 1988, with eight women still missing.

There was one name that kept appearing in police reports: that of Gary Ridgway.

In 1980, he was questioned after a prostitute accused him of trying to throttle her. His explanation was that the woman had bitten him, so he choked her to make her stop. In 1982, the Green River task force picked him up with prostitute Kelly McGuinness. She disappeared a year later and her body was never found.

Following the disappearance of 19-year-old prostitute Maria Malvar in 1983, Ridgway was a leading suspect. The police questioned him and he denied all knowledge of her, even though a friend of Maria had seen her get into a truck that was thought to be Ridgway's. In May 1984 he took a polygraph (lie detector) test and was cleared.

Detectives from the task force continued their inquiries doggedly for years after the killings ceased, concentrating their attention on the deaths of the early victims, Opal Mills, Marcia Chapman and Cynthia Hinds

Ridgway remained 'a person of interest'. So, in 1988, they obtained a warrant to search his house, but found nothing incriminating. However, they were also given permission to take a saliva sample to determine his blood group.

Miraculously, the sample was preserved as evidence; and in November 2001 it was subjected to DNA analysis. When this technique was first introduced by forensic laboratories in the late

1980s, it required a relatively large sample to be taken. However, more recent developments had made it possible to work on very small samples – and Ridgway's DNA matched that of semen recovered from the bodies of the three women.

Ridgway was arrested, and charged with seven murders. At first, he maintained that he was not guilty, However, just before his trial, he entered into a plea bargain in order to avoid the death penalty. He confessed to 48 killings – although he said the total might be more than 60: 'I killed so many, I have a hard time keeping them straight.'

On November 5, 2003, Ridgway admitted that he had a deep hatred for prostitutes: 'I wanted to kill as many women as I thought were prostitutes as I possibly could . . . I thought I could kill as many of them as I wanted without getting caught.'

needle marks in the rubber sealing. She fired Genene on the spot and informed the Texas Rangers.

After two long grand jury hearings, Kathleen Holland was cleared of any involvement, but Genene was indicted on May 28, 1983, on two counts of murder in Kerrville.

On January 15, 1984, she stood trial in Georgetown, Texas. A month later she was sentenced to 99 years. She then faced a further charge of deliberately injuring one-month-old Rolando Santos in January 1982 by injecting him with an anticoagulant drug. October 24, she was found guilty and sentenced to a concurrent term of 60 years.

The psychological condition from which Genene suffered has been given a name by a British pediatric consultant – 'Munchausen's syndrome by proxy'.

Genene Jones gained such excitement and personal satisfaction from resuscitating babies who suffered sudden seizures that she began injecting them with near-lethal drugs in order to experience the thrill of restoring them to life. But sometimes things went very, very wrong.

In recent years, several cases similar to that of Genene Jones have been recorded. In 1989, American male nurse Richard Angelo was found guilty of injecting four patients at the Good Samaritan Hospital, West Islip, NY, with muscle-relaxing drugs. In a videotaped confession he said: 'I felt inadequate . . . I felt I had to prove myself.'

Later, in 1991, in England, Nurse Beverley Allitt was found guilty of four murders and three charges of attempted murder on children in her care. She had injected them with massive doses of insulin.

ANDREI CHIKATILO

ROSTOV RIPPER

At the time, few people outside the Russian police knew of the horrific series of rape-murders that occurred during the 1980s in the area around Rostov-on-Don in the Ukraine, part of the then-USSR. State censorship suppressed all news of child-rape and serial killing, crimes that were regarded as common only in 'decadent capitalist nations', and the police were hampered in their investigations, forbidden to broadcast descriptions of the murders and any suspects. Over a period of twelve years the killings continued, reaching a total of at least 56, before the murderer was finally apprehended.

As a youngster, Andrei Chikatilo had to share a bed with his mother; he frequently wet it, and was cruelly beaten. At school he did well, but failed the entrance examination for Moscow State University. Drafted into national service, he was discharged in 1960, taking a job as a telephone engineer, and married in 1963. Early experiences had led him to equate sex with violent aggression. However, although he was effectively impotent, he managed to father two children. He obtained a qualification in Russian literature in 1971 and found work as an assistant schoolteacher, but was forced to move from school to school after complaints of molestation by his pupils. Taking a job as factory supply clerk in Rostov in 1981, he was able to travel widely and commit his terrible crimes.

The first death had occurred on December 22, 1978, when Andrei Chikatilo was living in the town of Sachty, some 50 miles from Rostov. He had lured a nine-year-old girl into a shed and attempted to rape her. She struggled and he stabbed her to death. From that time on, Chikatilo could get arousal only while slashing young women and children. Although he was a suspect in this murder, another man, Aleksandr Kravchenko, was arrested and 'confessed' (Russian police methods of interrogation were notoriously brutal). He was tried, found guilty and executed by firing squad.

Travelling by bus or train in the course of his work, Chikatilo began to pick up runaways of both sexes, or prostitutes, at distant depots, leaving their terribly mutilated bodies in nearby woodland areas. Some victims were found with their tongues bitten off; others were disembowelled, with some of their organs missing. But all had suffered many stab wounds, particularly to the face.

During 1982, seven women and children fell victim to the Ripper. In 1983, he killed eight, four between June and September. At this time only six bodies from his total of victims had been discovered. Nevertheless, as news of the killings began to leak out, wild rumours spread. A credulous public whispered of werewolves, or even of 'foreigners' who were killing Russian boys before invading the country.

THE SHADOW OF CANNIBALISM

Andrei Romanovich Chikatilo was born in the village of Yablochnoye, in the Ukraine, on October 16, 1936. He claimed that his family had suffered greatly during the troubles of the 1930s under Stalin's despotic rule. His elder brother, he said, had been killed and eaten by neighbours during the terrible famine that had claimed so many Russian lives. And the condition of the Ukrainian people was no better during the German occupation of their country in 1941–43. It was his childhood, Chikatilo said, that led him to violence. He often imagined enticing Germans into the woods and executing them – fantasies that found a fatal fulfilment later in his life.

A special forensic team was sent from Moscow to Rostov under the command of Major Mikhail Fetisov, and a forensic specialist, Victor Burakov, undertook inquiries in the area of Sachty. All known sex offenders and mentally ill were investigated. As always in an inquiry of this kind, a number of men confessed to the killings but all were cleared – although at least one suspect hanged himself in his cell while under arrest.

As the number of boys murdered increased, the investigation turned its attention to homosexuals. Altogether, more than 150,000 people were interrogated before this line of inquiry was abandoned. Frustrated, the police mounted extra patrols and placed plain-clothes men at bus and railway station depots.

But the killing frenzy continued. In 1984, Chikatilo murdered 15 people, eight in the month of August alone. He was seen behaving suspiciously at a bus station in Rostov in September and arrested, but analysts were unable to match his blood type to samples of semen taken from the victims because he was a 'non-secretor'. However, he was found to be wanted for other minor crimes, and sentenced to a year in prison – but released after three months when local Communist officials protested that he was a decent Party member.

SECRETORS AND NON-SECRETORS

All human beings have blood of one of four types: A, B, AB, or O, due to the presence of specific substances. In 80 percent of the population, the same distinctive substances are secreted in their other body fluids – saliva, sweat, semen and urine. Before the development of DNA analysis, this proved particularly valuable in cases of rape, where semen could be matched to the blood of a suspect. However, some 20 percent of the population are 'non-secretors': their other body fluids do not contain the indicative substances.

After this, the murders became more infrequent. Two women were killed in August 1985 – one of them at Moscow airport. The case was taken over by Issa Kostoyev, and the pattern of the 'Rostov Ripper' killings was re-investigated. Once again known sex offenders were subjected to intense questioning, and in December the police resumed their patrols at railway stations close to Rostov. They also consulted a psychiatrist – said to be the first time that such a step had been taken in a serial killer investigation in the Soviet Union (Ukraine still being a part of the Soviet Union at the time).

Chikatilo was well aware of the police activity and managed to keep his murderous instincts under a degree of control, although he later confessed to the killing of a little girl and a 15-year-old boy in May 1987. However, in 1988 came another wave of killings. Chikatilo had now extended his area of operation, frequently far from Rostov. However, in April he murdered a woman in Krasny-Sulin, only 100 miles away, and of his other seven victims two were in Sachty. He is known to have killed only once during 1989, but totalled seven boys and two women during 1990.

In view of the proximity of the crimes to the main railway line out of Rostov, the police decided to drive the killer into a trap with 'Operation Forest Strip'. More than 300 uniformed police were placed in prominent positions in all the stations along the line – except for three, which were covered by plain-clothes officers. On November 6, 1990, Chikatilo killed and butchered his last victim. He was stopped and questioned as he left the scene of the crime but allowed to leave. However, his name re-emerged as a suspect and on November 20, when the body of this latest victim had been discovered, he was again observed behaving suspiciously in Rostov and arrested.

Between November 30 and December 5, he confessed to 56 cases of sadistic killing – 20 more than the police had on their files. Some of the murders had not been linked to the investigation because they had occurred far from Rostov and others were not revealed until Chikatilo led the police to the shallow graves in which he had buried the corpses. As three bodies remained undiscovered, he was charged with 53 killings.

Chikatilo stood trial on April 14, 1992, spectacularly confined in a cage in the middle of the courtroom. After three months of hearings he was found guilty and sentenced to death on October 15. President Boris Yeltsin rejected an appeal for clemency and Andrei Chikatilo was executed by gunshot on February 14, 1994. Alexandr Kravchenko, who had been found guilty of his first murder, was posthumously pardoned.

LEONARD LAKE & CHARLES NG

SNUFF TAPERS

It seemed, at first, like a common case of shoplifting. On the afternoon of June 2, 1985, a young Asian man was spotted stealing a bench vice from a San Francisco hardware store and putting it in the trunk of a car on the parking lot. As a police officer approached he ran off, but there was another man standing by the car. He was asked to open the boot: the vice was there, as well as a bag containing a .22 pistol fitted with a silencer. It was to set in motion a long trail of investigation that uncovered an unbelievably gruesome case of serial killings.

Silenced weapons are illegal in California, so the man was taken to the police station where he produced a driver's licence in the name of Robin Scott Stapley. He said he hardly knew the Asian, who had done some garden work for him. While a computer check was run on his car, 'Stapley' asked for a glass of water, some paper and a pencil. After scrawling a few lines, he put a capsule in his mouth, drank some of the water, and almost immediately collapsed unconscious.

It was assumed that 'Stapley' had suffered a heart attack and he was rushed to hospital. He was put on life support, but died four days later. At the autopsy, it became very evident that he had committed suicide with a massive dose of cyanide.

Meanwhile, the police had established that Robin Stapley had been reported missing five months earlier, but his description did not match that of the suicide. Who was he? And what had he done that made suicide so necessary? And who was 'Cricket', to whom he had hurriedly scribbled the suicide note? 'I love you. Please forgive me. I forgive you. Please tell Mama, Fern and Patty I'm sorry.'

A second computer check revealed that the man's car was registered to another missing man: Paul Cosner. In the car were letters addressed to Charles Gunnar, of Wilseyville, a small rural community northeast of San Francisco.

A call to the local sheriff, Claude Ballard, produced some interesting information. He said he suspected Gunnar and his Asian room-mate of dealing in stolen goods. Furthermore, the fingerprints of the man dying in hospital were found to be those of Leonard Lake, 39, who had a record for burglary and grand larceny.

A MISERABLE MAN

Leonard Lake was born in San Francisco in 1946. Both of his parents were alcoholics, and he was brought up by his grandmother. As an adult, he began to make amateur pornographic movies with girlfriends, and then with his wife – who, it turned out, was the 'Cricket' to whom he had addressed his final words.

Joining the Marines after leaving school, Lake served a term in Vietnam, although he was never in action. He was discharged on psychiatric grounds and, leaving his wife, drifted around communes and survivalist camps. Gradually, convincing himself that World War III was imminent, he sank into a depression in which the infliction of his pain and misery upon others seemed of secondary significance.

Inspector Tom Eisenmann, who was in charge of the investigation, drove out to Wilseyville to meet Sheriff Ballard, who had by now obtained a search warrant. The home where 'Gunnar' had lived was a seemingly ordinary ranch-style house, set in a spread of woodland. However, inside it was very different from what the two men expected. The bedroom was equipped with hooks in the walls and ceiling, with an assortment of chains and shackles. The closet was filled with sexy underwear, and in the corner was a set-up of expensive video equipment. They assumed that they had found a studio for the production of pornographic material.

Then one of a team of deputies searching the grounds reported that he had found some partially-burned bones and teeth that looked human. Leaving the house, Eisenmann spotted another building cut into the hillside behind. Ballard suggested that it was probably a self-made fall-out shelter. But he was wrong.

OPERATION MIRANDA

In his diaries, Lake outlined his 'master plan', Operation Miranda. Having built his bunker, he would stockpile food and weapons. He then planned to abduct women and turn them into 'sex slaves'. He described in detail how he had lured victims to his home, in some cases identifying them: Brenda O'Connor, her boyfriend Lonnie and their two-year-old child; Harvey and Deborah Dubbs and their child; Kathy Allen and her boyfriend Mike Carrol. Others were identified only by their first names.

The bunker was also fitted with hooks and shackles and the walls were covered with pornographic photographs. A filing cabinet proved to be full of videotapes. Eisenmann picked one out at random, labelled 'M Ladies Kathy/Brenda', and inserted it in a conveniently nearby player.

A young white woman was sitting in a chair in the main house, her hands cuffed behind her. A voice off camera said: 'Mike owes us and unfortunately he can't pay. We're going to give you a choice, Kathy . . . If you don't cooperate with us, we'll probably put a round through your head and take you out and bury you some place . . .'

At this, the balding, bearded head of Leonard Lake came into the picture. He locked a set of leg irons round the girl's ankles, undid the handcuffs, and ordered her to strip, which she did with obviously great reluctance. The video then cut to a shower, where Kathy was seen washing the genitals of a young Asian, whom Ballard immediately identified as Charles Ng, Lake's room-mate.

The next scene was one of Lake sodomizing Kathy, who was chained to a bed, and this was followed by a shot of him telling her that Mike had been killed. The tape then cut to another young woman, enduring similar treatment, whom Ballard recognized as Brenda O'Connor, a local girl who had been missing for four months.

This first video was, in retrospect, the least horrifying. Others showed women being raped, tortured, and finally killed. A further search produced Lake's two-volume diary. They detailed a history of brutality and killing, and it was apparent that Lake had begun his career of murder at least two years before arriving in Wilseyville. At that time, he wrote that he had killed his younger brother Donald and his friend Charles Gunnar.

The police were faced with the difficulty of determining how many people Lake had tortured and killed. In the bunker were photographs of at least 20 women between the ages of 18 and 25; these were published in newspapers, but remained unidentified.

Deputies combing the grounds of the house found a shallow grave with the remains of four bodies. Other graves produced more than 50 pounds of charred bones, which had been cut up with a chainsaw. Buried under a dog kennel was the naked body of a man, identified as that of Randy Jacobson; but the identity of many of the victims could not be established.

With Lake dead, the hunt was on for Charles Ng. On July 6, 1985, he was apprehended by two store detectives in a supermarket in Calgary, Canada, after he had shot another in the hand.

For this, he was sentenced to four and a half years in prison – but he was wanted for complicity in murder in San Francisco. The U.S. authorities applied for extradition, but Canadian law forbids extradition for anyone who might face death in another country. Legal experts argued the case for three years. Eventually – on the grounds that releasing Ng would make it seem that Canada was a safe haven for killers – extradition was granted and he was returned to California on November 26, 1991, to face 14 counts of murder in the first degree.

After numerous successful attempts at postponement, Ng finally went to trial, and was formally condemned to death on June 30, 1999. He remains on death row at San Quentin State Prison.

RICHARD RAMIREZ

NIGHT STALKER

It is not for nothing that Los Angeles has been named the serial killer capital of the world. During 1984, no less than five random murderers were at large in the city and its neighbouring communities, and the reaction of most Angelenos was simply to make sure that windows and doors were locked at night, and to console themselves with the thought that, among the city's millions, they were unlikely to be the one to die. Yet, nearly every day, a new name was added to the list of innocent victims.

I n the LA suburb of Rosemead shortly before midnight on March 17, 1985, Maria Hernandez parked her car in the garage of the condominium where she shared an apartment with her friend, Dayle Okazaki. As she left the garage she heard a sound; turning, she saw a man dressed all in black and pointing a gun at her. Raising her hand, she begged him: 'Don't shoot!'

Nevertheless, he fired – but the bullet was deflected by the bunch of keys that Maria was holding. Hurled to the ground by the impact, she was kicked savagely by her assailant before he ran into the apartment's rear entrance. Shaking, she staggered toward the front of the building as a second shot rang out. The gunman reappeared and she pleaded with him: 'Please don't shoot me again.' He disappeared into the night – but in the kitchen of the apartment, Dayle Okazaki lay dead with a bullet in her head.

Fortunately, Maria was able to provide a partial description of the killer. She said that he had dark curly hair, staring eyes, wide-spaced, rotting teeth and a strong body odour.

In fact, the spate of killings had begun nine months earlier, when 79-year-old Jennie Vincow was raped and murdered at her home in the suburb of Glassell Park in June 1984 – her throat slashed so deeply that she was almost decapitated. At that time, the police had no reason to suspect that this was the first in a horrific series. By mid-March 1985, however, they began to suspect a connection with two very different crimes: the abduction and sexual abuse of a 6-year-old girl in Montebello on February 25, and of a 9-year-old girl in Monterey Park on March 11. But they did not make their suspicions public for some weeks.

All changed on the night of March 17. Shortly after shooting Dayle Okazaki, the killer dragged law student Tsai Lian Yu, 30, from her car in nearby Monterey Park and shot her several times. She died in hospital the following day and ballistics examiners confirmed that the same .22 pistol had been used in both incidents. Also, on March 20, a man very much like the one described by Maria Hernandez abducted a young girl from her Eagle Rock home. He assaulted her sexually and then – surprisingly – let her go.

Police were sure that yet another serial killer was on the loose when the bodies of pizza-outlet owner Vincent Zazzara, 66, and his 44-year-old wife Maxine were discovered at their home in Whittier on March 28. They had been dead two days. Vincent had been shot and Maxine had been shot three times then brutally slashed and mutilated. And finally, the killer had gouged out her eyeballs and taken them with him.

It was no longer possible for the police to keep their developing investigation under wraps and they were forced to issue a public announcement. Newspapers quickly dubbed the killer the 'Night Stalker' and fear began to spread throughout Los Angeles.

For six weeks, there were no more related murders in the suburbs. It was later theorized that this coincided with one of the killer's regular trips north to the home of an unsuspecting woman friend in San Pablo, near San Francisco, to have his stained clothing laundered.

Back in the Los Angeles area, on May 14, 65-year-old William Doi was shot in the head with a .22 gun at his home in Monterey Park. While the 'Night Stalker' savagely beat Doi's wife Lillie – demanding that she tell him where the valuables were kept – Doi himself managed to stagger to the 'phone and call an emergency number before he died. Lillie survived and was able to add to the description of the killer. Then, two weeks later, even more details were provided.

On May 30, Carol Kyle was woken in her bedroom in Burbank by a torch shone in her eyes. She saw a man in dark clothing pointing a gun and was ordered out of bed into the adjoining bedroom, where her terrified 12-year-old son was handcuffed and locked in the closet. Carol offered the intruder her diamond necklace, which he pocketed before raping her and then – uncharacteristically – allowing her to live.

It was June 2 when two very elderly widows, Mabel Bell, 83, and her sister Nettie Lang, 81, were found near death in the home they shared in Monrovia, in the San Gabriel valley. The Night Stalker had struck on May 29, smashing Mabel's skull with a hammer and then using the wire from her bedside clock to electrocute her – finally drawing a pentagram on her room wall and another on her thigh. Then he raped and sodomized Nettie – who was an invalid and unable to come to her sister's aid – helped himself to a soda and a banana and left with a pillowslip packed with what valuables he could find. Nettie survived the attack but Mabel died on July 15.

Beginning at the end of June, the killer embarked on an accelerating orgy of carnage. On June 27, Patty Elaine Higgins, 32, was found with her throat slashed at her home in Arcadia. On July 2, 77-year-old Mary Cannon was slain in the same way, also in Arcadia. Three days later, in the same suburb, 16-year-old Whitney Bennett was beaten unmercifully with a crowbar, but she survived. On July 7 Joyce Nelson, 61, was battered to death at her home in Monterey Park, and that same night 63-year-old Sophie Dickman was raped and robbed at home nearby.

So the carnage continued. On July 20, the Night Stalker shot

TRYING TO ESTABLISH A PROFILE

The problem faced by the police was that the available details of the Night Stalker's appearance could describe any one of hundreds of local low-lifes. The Los Angeles County Sheriff's office received reports that a man was following young girls in East Los Angeles: he wore dark clothes, had stained and gapped teeth and a strong musky odour.

Detective Gil Carillo, one of the investigators on the case, was hopeful that the perpetrator had been spotted and obtained a search warrant on his house and a court order for an identification line-up.

> He wasn't picked up at the line-up . . . He did have some bizarre things at home, but he just wasn't my suspect. He was eventually arrested later on for other things, but not my guy.

To complicate matters, the 'Night Stalker' had no obvious pattern to his murders – apart from the violence of his attacks and the fact that nearly all occurred around midnight, when most of his victims were likely in bed. His choice of lethal weapon varied: a gun, a knife, a hammer – even an iron bar. His primary frenzied drive seemed to be sadistically sexual, but robbery also appeared to be a dominant motive.

Equally puzzling was his choice and age of target; both male and females who ranged in age from very young to very old. Furthermore, there was no similarity in their appearance – not the case in the choice made by other known serial killers – the only relatively consistent factor being that many were ethnic, first-generation Americans.

Police theorized that the killer was a drug addict and that the intervals between his crimes was related to how much money he could raise from robbery to feed his habit – and his frequent references to Satan suggested that he was obsessed with the occult.

elderly Max Kneiding and his wife Lela in Glendale, then went on to Sun Valley where he shot Chainarong Khovanath in his bed. He beat and raped the dead man's wife Somkid, forcing her to swear 'by Satan' that she would not cry out, and beat and violated her eight-year-old son before escaping with $30,000-worth of cash and jewellery.

It was only now that the various county and city forces agreed to co-operate, putting together a task force that rapidly grew to 200 strong. The manhunt was announced on August 8, two days after Christopher Peterson, 38, and his wife Virginia, 27, were seriously wounded by gunshot in Northridge. And, on the night of the announcement, the Stalker struck again, shooting 35-year-old Elyas Abowath dead in his Diamond Bar home and viciously beating his wife.

Around this time, the killer made one of his regular trips north to San Francisco, where he broke into the Lake Merced home of Peter Pan and his wife Barbara on August 17, and shot them both through the head. Barbara survived and was able to fit artist's sketches to her recollection of the Stalker's appearance. Police also found small calibre bullets that matched those from two of the LA murders.

Returning to Los Angeles, the killer invaded the home of 29-year-old William Carns in Mission Viejo, 50 miles south of the city, just after midnight on August 25. He shot him three times through the head (Carns survived, but suffered permanent brain damage) and raped his fiancée Inex Erickson twice, saying: 'You know who I am, don't you? I'm the one they're writing about in the newspapers and on TV.' Giggling, he ordered her to say: 'I love Satan', then he left. Through her tears, Inex was able to see that he drove away in a battered orange Toyota.

The car had also been spotted earlier that day by teenager James Romero, who was able to give the police three digits of its licence plate. It was found abandoned on August 28; it had been carefully wiped clean of fingerprints but, using a laser scanner on the interior, detectives found a single print left on the rear-view mirror. By great good luck, the State computer in Sacramento had been updated only days before, and within minutes it produced

THE SATANIC CONNECTION

Richard Ramirez, born February 28, 1960, was the youngest of seven children in a typical Mexican immigrant family, crowded into a tiny house in El Paso. He was raised in the strictly-held Catholic faith, but by the age of 9 he had already begun to withdraw from his family, haunting video arcades and experimenting with drugs. He broke into homes to steal and was a truant for most of his time at high school, dropping out at age 17.

On December 7, 1977, Ramirez was arrested on suspicion of drug possession. Even though he had in his possession a ski mask and a toy pistol, no charges were preferred. Further arrests followed until, in 1982, he was convicted, receiving a suspended sentence and a $115 fine, and was placed on parole for three years.

When he moved to Los Angeles in 1983, the Satanist movement in California had been in existence for nearly 15 years. Anton LaVey, a former 'carnie' and a persuasive charlatan, published his *Satanic Bible* in 1969, and the terrifying killings of Charles Manson's 'family' occurred in the same year. Although publicity decreased after this, the sinister activities of the Circe Order of Dog Blood, the Four Pi, and the Process Church of Final Judgment, continued. Although there is no evidence that Ramirez was connected with any of such movements, his beliefs were clearly influenced by their teachings.

a match. The print belonged to a petty thief and known drug-abuser from El Paso, Richard Leyva Ramirez. Photographs and a detailed description of the wanted man made the front pages of every newspaper in the state of California.

Ramirez, meanwhile, had been in Phoenix, Arizona, to score cocaine and had not seen any of the Californian papers. On the morning of August 31, dressed as usual all in black, he arrived by bus at the Los Angeles depot. Fifteen minutes later, he strolled casually into a liquor store and saw his own face staring up at him from the front page of the Spanish language paper, *La Opinion*. As customers began to shout, he raced from the store. Frantically running for nearly two miles, beating on doors and shouting 'Ayudame!' (Help me!), desperately trying to hi-jack a car, he was at last overpowered and beaten by a crowd of neighbours – just as a patrol car screeched to a halt beside them. 'Save me, please! Thank God you came! Save me before they kill me!' he gasped. He was wearing a pair of Avias, model 440.

By September 29, 1985, Ramirez was facing a stunning total of 68 felony charges, including 14 counts of murder and 22 of sexual assaults. In December, eight more felonies, including two further rapes and one attempted murder, were added. It looked like an open-and-shut case but it was not until January 29, 1989, that he stood trial. His attorneys entered a plea of not guilty, but he showed no sign of repentance. With a pentagram drawn on his left had, Ramirez had waved to photographers during his preliminary hearing shouting loudly: 'Hail Satan!'

Back in his cell, he told a fellow prisoner: 'I've killed 20 people, man. I love all that blood.'

The trial lasted eight months, the jury having to be reconvened twice. Finally, on September 20, 1989, Ramirez was found guilty of 13 murders and 30 related felonies.

On October 4 he was recommended for execution, and was formally sentenced to death on November 7, when he told the court: 'You maggots make me sick. Hypocrites one and all! You don't understand me. You are not expected to. I am beyond good and evil. I will be avenged. Lucifer dwells in us all.'

Outside the court he told the waiting newsmen: 'Big deal. Death always went with the territory. I'll see you at Disneyland.'

Ramirez was finally removed to death row in San Quentin in September 1993, where he died at the age of 53 from complications secondary to B-cell lymphoma, having been on death row for 23 years. On October 3, 1996, he was married to a magazine writer, Doreen Loiy, with whom he had corresponded for many years.

DAVID & CATHERINE BIRNIE

FOLIE À DEUX

The case of Fred and Rosemary West (see pages 167–70) in the UK is an unusual example of a series of killings in which a husband and wife are equally guilty. Nevertheless, a not dissimilar case occurred in Australia at a time when the Wests' murder of at least nine young women had not yet been discovered. This new killing spree ended after only a month; but within that time, four young women died; and it might have continued much longer if a fifth potential victim had not escaped from the killers' clutches to raise the alarm.

On the afternoon of November 10, 1986, a teenage girl, half-naked and sobbing desperately, suddenly burst into a supermarket in Fremantle, Western Australia. Between gasps, she managed to blurt out that she had been raped.

Taken to the police station, she said she was 17-years-old and came from an affluent suburb of the nearby city of Perth. There, the previous evening, she had been dragged into a car by a man and a woman. They had driven the short distance from Perth to Fremantle, taken her into a small bungalow and chained her to a bed. The man then raped her twice. In the morning he had left the house, apparently going off to work, leaving the woman on guard. Making a plausible excuse, the girl persuaded the woman to unchain her and managed to escape through a small window. One police officer later described her as a 'very alert, intelligent and brave female'. Following the directions given by the victim, officers went to the bungalow in nearby Willagee, where they immediately arrested the occupants, David and Catherine Birnie.

The couple did not resist, and within hours they had confessed to four rape-murders and were leading officers of the Perth Major Crimes Squad to the graves. Three bodies – all of strangled young women – were buried in Glen Eagle State Forest, a remote area some 30 miles southeast of Perth. The fourth, stabbed and axed, was in a pine plantation some 20 miles north of the city.

THE KILLING COUPLE

David Birnie, born in 1950, was a scrawny, insignificant-looking young man, who had been in and out of institutional care as a youngster. However, he was described as having an 'almost insatiable sexual appetite', demanding sex six times a day. Catherine, born in 1953, was a small, hard-faced woman with a tight mouth – an indication of her controlling nature.

David and his partner-in-crime had been lovers as teenagers; but, after they had served terms of juvenile detention for joint burglary, each married other people. Catherine at first took a job as a domestic help, but soon married the son of the house and had five children. David's marriage failed; and in 1985 he renewed his relationship with Catherine, who left her husband and children for him. It was then that they began to discuss the idea of jointly abducting and raping girls.

Like the Wests, the couple had 'a combined depravity – a husband and wife whose energy bounces off each other' (see pages 167–70). In August 1986, David's younger brother James was given a twenty-first 'birthday present': sex with Catherine, to which she readily agreed.

On October 6, 1986, 22-year-old student Mary Neilson called at the Birnie's house to buy some car tyres. Without a second thought, David immediately forced her into the bedroom at knifepoint and raped her while Catherine watched. The couple then carried her off to the forest, where Birnie raped her again before strangling her with a cord. He and Catherine then mutilated the body and buried it in a shallow grave.

The ease with which the crime had been carried out encouraged the couple to try again, They placed an advertisement in a local newspaper for 'a lonely young person, prefer 18–24 years . . . '.

It was not this advertisement, however, that attracted the second victim. She was 15-year-old Susannah Candy, a hitch-hiker whom the couple picked up. She was kept captive for several days, during which time David enthusiastically and repeatedly raped her. Indeed, it was suggested later that it was his very enthusiasm that caused Catherine to strangle the girl, who was buried close to the body of Mary Neilson.

The next victim – 31-year-old airline hostess Noelene Patterson – was actually acquainted with the Birnies. When the pair came upon her, stranded with her car, they helped push it to a filling station. They then forced her into their own car and took her to their home. For three days she suffered a series of rapes, until Catherine demanded that David kill her. He fed Noelene a large dose of sleeping tablets and then strangled her when she fell uncon-scious. When, two weeks later, Catherine led police to her grave, she spat upon it.

On November 4, Denise Brown, 21, was abducted close to her home in Perth. After two days of rape, she was driven to the pine plantation, where David raped her again, at the same time stab-bing her with a knife. When he did not succeed in killing Denise, Catherine handed him a bigger knife with which he stabbed Denise to death in the neck.

Following their confessions, both Birnies agreed to plead guilty to all charges. David claimed that this was to spare the families of the victims the pain of having the cases described in detail in court, but it may have been a bid for leniency. The trial was held in Perth on March 3, 1987 and lasted only a half-hour. Both culprits were sentenced to life imprisonment: a minimum of 20 years before consideration for parole, but the judge suggested that David 'should not be let out of prison – ever'.

David Birnie was committed to the maximum security Casuarina prison, Perth, and Catherine to Bandyup women's prison, northeast of Perth. For some years the couple exchanged letters every other day, but more recently Catherine refused to reply to her former lover's letters. There was a minor sensation in February 2005 when a man was awarded $A72,000 in compensation after claiming that he had been raped by Birnie while on remand in Casuarina. The man's lawyer said: 'We've got other material to suggest that there's been a lot of bad behaviour at Casuarina and people have been targeted, and that the prison authorities know . . .'

The Justice Department protested against the compensation judgment and there were demands for Birnie to be brought to court, but on October 7 he hanged himself in his prison cell. There were rumours that he had been allowed a pet cat in the cell and that this had also been found dead.

For over a month Birnie's body lay in the prison morgue because no next of kin would come forward to claim it. In the end, he was given a secret pauper's funeral on November 21, 2005.

PAUL BERNARDO

FINALLY BROUGHT TO BOOK

Between May 1987 and December 1992, an unidentified man raped or sexually assaulted at least 18 women in the suburbs of Toronto, Ontario and across the lake in St Catharine's; and he murdered three more. The living victims were able to give descriptions of their assailant to the Royal Canadian Mounted Police, who also had his DNA samples. Even the name of the perpetrator was on the police files – and yet it was five years before he was apprehended.

The name of a suspect emerged after the fifth rape in the suburb of Scarborough. A woman told a friend in the police that she was having trouble with a man named Paul Bernardo. He owed her money, and she described his behaviour: '. . . [it] progressed from gesturing to slap her in a joking manner to threatening to do so, to giving her light taps, which became harder and harder.'

In his car, he held a knife to her throat and demanded sex, which she refused. In November 1987, after driving to an isolated factory area, Bernardo had frenziedly begun searching for his knife, yelling: 'Why do I do this, why?'

She managed to escape and hid. The policeman's report, naming Bernardo, described him as: 'A violent, knife-wielding, sexual sadist with a pattern of frenzied sexual assaults.'

The report was submitted on January 22, 1988. However, most unfortunately, it was not brought to the attention of the team investigating the Scarborough rapes.

A composite description of the rapist was later published in the newspapers and another woman contacted the Sexual Assault Squad with a report that Bernardo fitted this description. She said he carried a knife in his car and spoke of picking up girls and raping them – and she said he was about to move to St Catharine's. Eventually, two detectives came across the earlier report in the files; they interviewed Bernardo and obtained samples of his hair, saliva and blood. They classified him as a possible suspect, but no higher, because the rapes had ceased in Scarborough in May 1990.

A CATALOGUE OF VIOLENCE

The official report on the rapes, published in 1996, described the offender's *modus operandi* in graphic detail:

> Stalking, then attacking from behind, dragging the victim into a driveway or bushes, punching and beating, raping . . . taking trophies such as jewelry or an article from the victim's purse, sometimes personal identification. Some of the rapes were accompanied by death threats . . . tightening a ligature or electrical cord around the victim's neck . . . biting, threat of further violence, gagging, cutting clothes and underwear with a knife, smashing the victim's head on the ground, forcing the victim to say she loved the attacker, forcing the victim to utter words of self-deprecation, threatening to return later to the victim's house and rape and kill her, and cutting the victim with a knife.

In St Catharine's, Bernardo was living with Karla Homolka. On 23 December 1990, Karla agreed to make him a 'Christmas present' of her younger sister Tammy.

It was only years later that Karla described how the couple gave Tammy drinks heavily laced with the proprietary sedative Halcion. Then Karla held a cloth soaked in anaesthetic over her sister's face, while she and Bernardo took turns in committing sexual acts on the girl's unconscious body – and videotaped them.

In her drugged state, Tammy vomited, inhaled the vomit and, unable to breathe, expired.

Early next morning, the two reported that Tammy had died in her sleep; and the death was recorded formally as being 'from natural causes'.

Beginning some four months later, a series of rapes occurred in St Catharine's. The first was of a 14-year-old, who was dragged into a woodland thicket and assaulted. She was able to provide a detailed description of the attack – and an investigator later pointed out that the assailant was undoubtedly the 'Scarborough rapist'.

In June 1991, Leslie Mahaffy was abducted at knifepoint by Bernardo from outside her house. He took her home, raped her and then told Karla to do the same while he videotaped everything.

He then killed Leslie, cutting her corpse into pieces that he set in concrete and dumped in a lake near Burlington. The remains were discovered on June 29, 1991.

Bernardo murdered Kristen French in April 1992, after he and Karla had forced her to their home. There, they sexually assaulted her and Bernardo strangled her. He dumped her body in Burlington because, as Karla later confessed: 'He wanted to confuse the cops, like then they wouldn't know if the guy was from Burlington or from St Catharine's.'

The final test results on Bernardo's DNA samples, taken in 1990, were not available until 1993. Before then he had married Karla, but she soon sickened of his sadistic sexual tastes and was persuaded by her parents to live with her other sister, who was married to a Toronto police officer.

It was not long before Karla confessed and, in exchange for a light sentence and committal to a psychiatric ward, pleaded guilty to her involvement in the murders, and stood witness against her husband. The police found overwhelmingly incriminating evidence in Bernardo's videotapes, and the journal he had kept of his crimes, but it was Karla's testimony that clinched the case. He was sentenced to life imprisonment.

However, the story continued. On July 4, 2005, Karla Homolka was released after serving her agreed 12-year sentence. The following day Bernardo, through his lawyer, alleged that it had been his original intention to release Leslie Mahaffy after her ordeal but that Karla had herself attempted to murder Leslie to prevent her from identifying the couple. However, the Quebec Justice Department announced that she would not face any further charges and restrictions that had been imposed upon her for a year after her release were lifted on November 30, 2005.

In January 2006, the movie *Karla*, based upon the crimes of the couple, was released in Canada. On February 21, 2006, Paul Bernardo's lawyer revealed that his client had confessed four months earlier to at least ten sexual assaults. Claiming that he did not know why Bernardo was admitting these crimes so many years after the event, the lawyer speculated that it might be attributed to 'the resurgence of interest with *Karla*'s release'.

HAROLD SHIPMAN

DR DEATH

When 81-year-old widow Kathleen Grundy was discovered dead on the morning of June 24, 1998, her attendant physician, Dr Harold Shipman, signed the death certificate, giving the cause as 'old age'. Nevertheless, her daughter found the circumstances of her mother's death oddly inconsistent. She was even more troubled when, some three weeks later, she learned that Mrs Grundy had recently made a will leaving all her money, and her house, to the doctor. It was the start of a chain of events that was to lead to the unveiling of the most prolific serial killer in criminal history.

D r Harold Shipman was a respected local physician in Hyde, Cheshire, on the outskirts of the major city of Manchester in northwestern England. Many of his patients were elderly ladies, in a doubtful state of health, and it did not seem remarkable when they died – their death certificates, as was normal, being signed by their doctor. Indeed, even after Shipman was charged with murder, many of his patients continued to express confidence in his caring treatment.

Shipman's obsession with death and the effects of morphine appears to date from the age of 17, when he sat by his mother's bedside in 1963, watching her die, slowly and agonizingly, from lung cancer.

Perhaps it was this that caused him to pick upon the medical profession as a career. He entered Leeds University to study medicine in September 1965, and it was there, at the end of his first year, that he made his one-and-only girlfriend, plain and plump 17-year-old Primrose Oxtoby, pregnant. They were married, in an almost surreptitious civil wedding, on November 5, 1966, and their daughter was born three months later. Three more children followed over the years.

Graduating in 1968, the new Dr Shipman completed his qualifications working as a 'houseman' at Pontefract General Hospital in Yorkshire, and on March 1, 1974, joined a group practice in the town of Todmorden, close to the Yorkshire-Lancashire border. Said one of his partners: 'He was young, enthusiastic, full of energy and anxious to do more than he was paid for. He taught the rest of us a lot, because he was last out of medical school and knew all the latest methods . . . He liked to do everything himself. If he could do it he would – he didn't use a nurse as much as other doctors would . . .'

However, Shipman's time with the practice came to an abrupt end in July 1975, when a pharmacy assistant revealed that he had been withdrawing large quantities of pethidine, a synthetic opiate similar to morphine. His partners ordered him to admit himself to a clinic for drug addiction.

Then, in February 1976 he entered a guilty plea in court to the forgery of eight prescriptions and asked for 67 more to be taken into consideration. He was fined a substantial amount; but the British General Medical Council did not strike his name off the register of doctors, and he found work with a local health authority in Durham, over 100 miles away, supervising children's care.

After eighteen months, Shipman once more joined a group practice, this time in Hyde. He freely admitted to his partners that he had been addicted to pethidine, but swore that he was cured. As a doctor he was liked, although the staff at the practice found him bad-tempered and arrogant. However, he was renowned as a hard worker, and it was now that he began to take on the home visits to elderly women patients that his partners found time-consuming and unrewarding.

Almost as soon as he joined the practice, Shipman began to accumulate stocks of diamorphine, filling out prescriptions for cancer sufferers in his care, but administering only a part of the quantity.

In 1981, 14 of Shipman's patients died; the following year

another 12; and in 1983 a further 11. Many of these deaths were expected and attracted little attention. However, with hindsight, he has been suspected of hastening – at the very least – the death of eight or more; and a further seven between 1984 and 1987.

In July 1992, Shipman parted company acrimoniously with his partners and set up alone only a few hundred yards away. From this time on, the number of his elderly patients who died began to accelerate.

At the height of his activities, he is believed to have committed several unsuspected murders every month – seven in February 1998 and six the following month.

Unlike other serial killers, however, he could not be accused of cruelty to his victims. They died peacefully, without pain, and trusting in the skill of their respected physician. Yet, like so many other killers, he did keep items of inexpensive jewellery from his victims – and sometimes small amounts of cash. It was only when the queried Grundy will was examined in 1998, and compared with the typewriter in Shipman's office, that it was declared to be a blatant forgery – and suspicions about Mrs Grundy's death were aroused.

Her body was exhumed on August 1; and on the same day police searched Shipman's premises and home. He was his usual arrogant self, remaining calm as the police took away bags and boxes of medical records. A month later, the police were informed that a lethal dose of diamorphine had been found in Mrs Grundy's body.

Shipman was arrested and other exhumations followed, with discoveries of further incriminating evidence.

Shipman's trial began on October 5, 1999. Apart from the charge of forgery, he faced 15 charges of murder. Although the police now had evidence of many more cases, it was decided that 15 would be difficult enough for the jury to consider.

The hearing lasted more than three months, during which Shipman spoke in his own defence, appearing to regard himself as superior to everybody else in the courtroom, and above the law.

However, on January 31, 2000, he was declared guilty on all counts and sentenced to life imprisonment.

At dawn on January 13, 2004, he hanged himself in his prison cell.

JEFFREY DAHMER

MILWAUKEE CANNIBAL

Near midnight on Monday, July 22, 1991, two police officers were sitting in their patrol car on North 25th Street, Milwaukee. Suddenly, a short, dark man rushed up to the car, with handcuffs dangling from his left wrist, and gasped out an incoherent tale of a 'weird dude' in the nearby Oxford Apartments. He gave his name as Tracy Edwards and went on to say how he had 'been with the devil' and described how the man had been about to stab him 'with a big knife' – and so the killing career of Jeffrey Dahmer came to an end.

Reluctantly, on that Monday night, the officers accompanied Edwards to the apartment he had escaped from and asked the man who answered the door for the key to the handcuffs. Told that it was in the bedroom, one officer walked into the room, and glanced idly into an open dresser drawer. To his horror, he saw Polaroid photographs of dismembered corpses, skulls and a skeleton hanging from a showerhead. Moments later, opening a refrigerator, his companion discovered a severed human head. Jeffrey Dahmer, who lived alone in the apartment, had come finally to the end of his slaughter.

The foul smell of rotting flesh filled the rooms. A cursory investigation uncovered another head in the refrigerator and seven more with the flesh partly boiled from the skull. A large barrel of acid contained four male torsos, slowly dissolving, and there were scraps of male genitalia in a pot. It was clearly no longer simply a matter of assault on Tracy Edwards. Dahmer was immediately arrested and detailed examination of the apartment was carried out, to reveal even more gruesome evidence of his activities. Very soon, his confession filled 179 pages of report, detailing the murder of 17 male victims.

Jeffrey Dahmer was born in Milwaukee in 1960. His parents argued bitterly and frequently, and he seemed to have developed strong feelings of neglect. The family relocated to rural Ohio when he was aged 6, and he deeply resented at this time the birth of his younger brother David. In 1968 he was sexually molested by an older boy, which may have been the incident that triggered his subsequent treatment of homosexuals.

By the age of 10, Dahmer was 'experimenting' with small animals – decapitating rats, treating chicken bones with acid and mounting a dog's head on a stick. In grade school, he would laugh when other children were hurt at play. A former classmate described his behaviour at high school: 'He was lost. He seemed to cry out for help, but nobody paid any attention to him at all. He would come into class with a cup of Scotch whiskey. If a 16-year-old drinking in an 8.00 a.m. class isn't calling out for help, I don't know what is.'

Dahmer's parents finally divorced in 1978 and he stayed on living alone in the family home. On June 18, 1978, 19-year-old Steven Hicks was hitch-hiking back from a rock concert near Cleveland to his home in Massillon when he was picked up by Dahmer, who suggested a drink of beer at his parents' home nearby. After some time, Steven said that he had to leave; after a brief argument, Dahmer picked up a barbell and smashed it onto Steven's head before strangling him. Dragging the body into the crawl-space under the house, he dismembered it with a knife. Then he stuffed the pieces into garbage bags and drove out into country. He was stopped by the police on suspicion of drunk driving but, when they asked about the bags in the back of the car, he told them he was taking them to the local dump.

Disturbed by this incident, Dahmer returned home and buried the bags in a shallow trench in the backyard. Two weeks later, when the stench of decomposition was very noticeable, he dug them up again, smashed the bones with a sledgehammer and threw the fragments over a rocky ledge back of his home. Years later, police investigators were able to recover bone fragments from the crawl-space.

Dahmer entered Ohio State University in the fall of 1978, but he spent most of his first term drinking, and at term's end enlisted in the U.S. Army. He trained as a medical specialist and was posted to Germany. But his drinking continued and after 18 months he was discharged for substance abuse and aggressive behaviour.

In 1982, Dahmer moved into a self-contained basement apartment in his grandmother's house in a suburb of Milwaukee, where he gained employment, first in a blood plasma company and later in a chocolate factory. But he was already revealing perverted sexual behaviour. As early as August 1982 he was arrested for exposing himself at the Wisconsin State Fair and fined $50. Soon he began haunting gay bath houses, experimenting by administering sleeping pills to the young men he picked up there.

In summer 1986, Dahmer was arrested again for exposure. He claimed that, having been drinking, he needed to urinate. The charge was reduced to one of 'disorderly conduct', and he was ordered a year's probation and counselling. Following the end of his probation, a man accused Dahmer of having drugged and robbed him. He was questioned once again, but the evidence was considered insufficient for any charge.

However, the police did not know that in the previous two years and whilst still on probation, Dahmer had already killed three more young men: Steven Tuomi, James Doxtator and Richard Guerrero. He had invited them to his basement apartment in his grandmother's house and, once there, he offered to photograph them in the nude and have sex with them before strangling them and sometimes having sex with their corpse. He kept the bodies for some time before disposing of them in garbage bags. The stench of what he claimed were his 'experiments' caused his grandmother to insist on his leaving. So he found a sleazy apartment in the city at 808 North 24th Street.

On September 26, 1988, the day he moved, he offered money to a 13-year-old Laotian boy to come into his new apartment. He attempted to seduce the boy, and laced his drink with sleeping pills. However, the boy left before he collapsed, and passed out when back at home. His parents informed the police and Dahmer was arrested the next day. In January 1989, his plea was one of guilty to second-degree sexual assault. As a result, he was due for sentence in May.

On bail and awaiting sentencing, Dahmer moved back into his grandmother's home. On March 25, 1989, he killed would-be photographer's model Anthony Sears. He kept the head, boiling it until only the bare skull remained, which he then painted. When he came up for sentencing on the sexual assault charge, the prosecution pressed for a prison sentence of five to six years, but Dahmer's attorney argued for psychological counselling and treatment for alcoholism. The judge agreed, sentencing Dahmer to a year in prison under a work-release program, and five years probation. He was released in March 1990, and in May moved into an apartment at 924 North 25th Street.

Within weeks, Dahmer had picked up Raymond Smith at a gay club and enticed him to the apartment to be photographed. Once more he kept his victim's head and added his skull to his collection of trophies. Soon after, he found his seventh victim, Edward Smith. And, on September 24, he lured his eighth, Ernest Miller, took photographs and then cut Miller's throat with a hunting knife. He flayed the flesh from the corpse and hung the skeleton in his bathroom. He kept pieces of the flesh in his freezer and later claimed that he had eaten some, after seasoning it with salt, pepper and A1 sauce. The same day, David Thomas was reported missing and was to become Dahmer's ninth victim.

Some months passed before the killer struck again – or, at least, four months before another murder to which Dahmer confessed.

In February 1991, Curtis Straughter was strangled and dismembered after having sex and his skull was kept as another gruesome trophy. Errol Lindsey joined the list on April 7. All that was found was his skull and photos of his corpse. Then, on May 24, Dahmer unusually picked on an older man, 31-year-old deaf mute Tony Hughes, communicating with him in writing. His skull, too, joined the collection.

On May 27, 1991, Jeffrey Dahmer picked up a young Laotian boy, Konerak Sinthasomphone – by coincidence, the brother of the boy for whose abduction he had been sentenced two years before – and offered him money to take photographs. After taking several Polaroid shots, he slipped some sleeping pills into Konerak's drink and the boy passed out.

Realizing that he was fresh out of beer, and thinking he had time to go to the store while the boy slept, Dahmer left the apartment. But, while he was gone, Konerak woke and, dazed, naked and bleeding from head wounds, stumbled out into the street. Neighbours summoned the police and Dahmer returned to find them trying to question the boy, who spoke no English. He quickly explained that Konerak was his 19-year-old live-in boyfriend who had had too much to drink, and the patrolmen escorted both back to the apartment – where Dahmer strangled the boy, had sex with the corpse and took more photographs.

After slaughtering Konerak Sinthasomphone, Dahmer changed his hunting ground, travelling to Chicago on June 30 to pick up Matt Turner at the bus station, and persuading him to return to Milwaukee and pose in the nude. His head was stored in the freezer and his torso was dropped into the vat of acid. Five days later, the pattern was repeated with Puerto Rican Jeremiah Weinberger, who suffered an identical fate.

Dahmer found his sixteenth victim just around the corner from his apartment on July 15. Oliver Lacy's head ended up in the refrigerator and his disembowelled body, together with his heart, in the freezer. Four days later, on July 19, Joseph Bradehoft became Dahmer's last victim, his head joining that of Lacy in the refrigerator. Just two days later, Dahmer's homicidal career came to an end when the police entered his apartment.

By August 22, 1991, Dahmer had been charged with 15 counts of homicide – although he confessed to 17. His trial opened on January 30, 1992, and he filed a plea of guilty but insane. For the defence, Dr Fred Berlin of Johns Hopkins University testified: '. . . [that the accused was] out of control . . . The power of what was driving him basically took over . . . I don't think the normal man could even force himself to walk around thinking of having sexual contact with dead bodies.'

For the prosecution, Dr Park Dietz disagreed – although Dahmer suffered from a variety of sexual disorders, he was capable of distinguishing right from wrong, and stopping himself from killing. And Dr Frederick Fosdal concurred, testifying that Dahmer suffered from necrophilia but: '. . . he was able to refrain and had some control as to when he followed through on his sexual desires.'

The prosecutor begged the jury: 'Please, please, don't let this murderous killer fool you with this special defence.'

On February 15, they found Dahmer sane and guilty. The court imposed 15 consecutive life sentences – totalling a minimum 936 years – plus 150 years for habitual criminality.

In prison, after an initial attempt on his life – from which he emerged almost unscathed – he was murdered on November 28, 1994, by fellow inmate Jesse Anderson. His killer was judged insane: he believed himself to be the Son of God and carrying out the wishes of 'his father'.

COLIN IRELAND

WANNABE SERIAL SLAYER

The announcement came in a telephone call to the London newsroom of the *Sun* newspaper on March 9, 1993. In a gruff voice, and giving an address in a southwest area of the city, the caller said:

I've murdered a man. I'm calling you because I'm worried about his dogs. I want them to be let out. It would be cruel for them to be stuck there . . . I tied him up and I killed him and I cleaned up the flat afterwards. I did it. It was my New Year resolution to kill a human being. Is that of any interest to you? He was a homosexual and into kinky sex.

The police were at once alerted and they went to the address given. Forcing open the door, they found the two dogs – and their owner, 45-year-old Peter Walker, lying naked and spreadeagled on his four-poster bed, his wrists and ankles tightly knotted to each post. A plastic bag was tied securely over his head.

Walker, a theatre director, had been openly gay for some twenty years, and the first question was to decide whether this was truly a case of murder or the outcome of an auto-sadomachistic sex session. Reasoning that the victim could not have put the bag over his own head after tying his hands, detectives decided that another person must have been present. The death could still have been accidental, but not if the anonymous caller was to be believed.

On May 28, 1993, the body of 37-year-old librarian Christopher Dunn was discovered in similar circumstances at his home in a northwest London suburb. Dunn was found tied and gagged, naked except for a leather bondage harness, and with a plastic bag over his head. But local detectives decided that the death was accidental.

There was one strange injury: his testicles appeared to have been scorched. It was some time later before it was discovered that £200 had been taken from Dunn's bank account; clearly, he had been tortured before death to reveal the PIN number of his ATM card.

It was only after two more murders, however, that police realized that there were common factors in all four deaths. On June 4, 35-year-old HIV-positive American executive Perry Bradley was found at his home in west London, gagged, bound and strangled – with £100 missing from his billfold and £200 taken from his bank account. Three days later, 33-year-old residential home supervisor Andrew Collier was found similarly killed in northeast London, with the body of his strangled cat laid obscenely on his naked body.

The linking of the killings was provisionally confirmed by a series of telephone calls received by the police from the presumed perpetrator. In the first, before Andrew Collier's corpse had been discovered, he said that he had read the FBI Crime Classification Manual, and had decided to become a serial killer: 'I know what it takes to become one. You have to kill one over four to qualify, don't you? I have already killed three. It started as an exercise, I wanted to see if it could be done, to see if I could really get away with it . . . Have you found Christopher Dunn yet? I killed him too. I haven't seen anything in the papers.'

A second call came a few days later. The caller explained – despite his apparent concern for Peter Walker's dogs – why he had killed Collier's cat: 'I don't want anybody to get any wrong ideas about me. I am not an animal lover.'

Of Perry Bradley, he said: 'I did the American. You've got some good leads on my identity from clues at the scene.'

Police inquiries had established that at least three of the victims were habitués of the Coleherne, a famously gay pub a few minutes walk from Earls Court underground railway station – and close to the apartment of Perry Bradley. Police surveillance was mounted in the surrounding area. Yet, despite the wave of fear that swept the gay community, the establishment remained as crowded as ever.

Emmanuel Spiteri, a 43-year-old Maltese-born chef, was at the Coleherne on the night of June 12. His body was discovered three days later, after police received another telephone call: 'Have you found the body in southeast London yet, and the fire?' Forcing open the door of Spiteri's apartment, they found him naked, bound and strangled. An attempt had been made to set fire to a pile of furniture, but the flames had quickly died out.

Armed with a photograph of Spiteri, the police set out to trace his movements. After leaving the Coleherne, he had most likely taken a train from Charing Cross station to his home in the southeastern suburbs. Taking possession of the video surveillance tapes from the station's cameras, the police quickly spotted Spiteri several times – and close behind him a half-view of a heavily built man, over 6 feet tall, apparently in his thirties.

COLIN IRELAND – 'SOLDIER'

Born in 1954, Ireland embarked on a life of petty crime as a youngster, and was committed to a correctional institution in his teens. Police records listed his arrest some 30 times, and 19 convictions. He served a short spell in the army, then was imprisoned for two years in 1981 for robbery. After a brief marriage – his second – he became a drifter, claming to be a former French Foreign Legionnaire.

He was said to be proud of his reputation as a self-sufficient loner, claiming to have learnt survival techniques in the army, and would often spend nights alone in the southeastern marshes, snaring rabbits and birds for food.

The pictures, together with a computerized photofit and an artist's impression, were widely circulated, but no one came forward to say they knew the man. By 21 July the police were no further forward in their investigation. But, on the same day, a tall, burly man walked into a lawyer's office in Southend-on-Sea,

30 miles from London, and said he needed legal representation. His name was Colin Ireland, and he was the man whom the press had dubbed the 'Fairy Liquidator' (Fairy Liquid being a popular brand of kitchen detergent).

He travelled quietly back to London with the lawyer, and together they went to the police. However, Ireland then withdrew his initial confession. He had been with Spiteri, he said, but had left when another man arrived. The police, however, were able to match his fingerprints to one found in Andrew Collier's home and, confronting Ireland with this evidence, they expected a full confession. However, Ireland remained obstinately silent and they soon realized the kind of personality they were up against.

Without being told that a suspect was in custody, British psychologist Paul Britton – who had already assisted police on a number of occasions – was asked to draw up a profile of the killer. He described the offender as sexually ambivalent: 'The victims must have seen something in him. Unless they were convinced he was homosexual, they wouldn't have invited him home or allowed themselves to be tied up . . . He won't like the fact that they regard him as one of their own.'

Britton felt that the precision and economy of the killings, and the 'command and control' style of communication with the police and media, suggested some military training. He said that the killer had created a 'tableau' at each scene: 'One, it gave him pleasure; and, two, it set you a puzzle.'

Next day, informed of Ireland's identification, Britton drew up a plan for the police interrogation: 'Every soldier knows to give nothing away under interrogation. However, he isn't truly a trained soldier. He doesn't have the personal resources to sustain himself indefinitely. It is extremely difficult to maintain a silence, and he doesn't yet know how difficult. He's going to learn.'

But, after two days of intensive interrogation, Ireland still admitted nothing and was remanded in prison. Said Britton: 'He will still be hearing the questions you ask him . . . He has to set the record straight. That's when he'll confess.'

Three weeks later, Ireland asked to speak to the police: '. . . but not those bastards who interviewed me. They really got under my skin.'

In a detailed statement that took two days to record, he admitted all five murders, and gave a wealth of detail. He was tried at London's Old Bailey in December 1993, and sentenced to five life sentences, with a recommendation that he should never be released. He died of lung disease in 2012.

MOSES SITHOLE

ABC MURDERER

The Republic of South Africa, after the United States, has the second highest rate of serial killing in the world. The causes are various: the climate of unrest and violence that persisted during and after apartheid, and in an often loose domestic structure and ongoing tribal differences among the indigenous population, among others. Notorious in particular are the deprived 'townships' – and probably none more so than Atteridgeville, on the outskirts of Pretoria.

Atteridgeville has a bloody history of serial murder, so it came as no great surprise when the badly decomposed body of a woman, her dress pulled up over her breasts, was found there on January 4, 1995.

Just over a month later, on February 9, a second woman's decomposed body was discovered. She was naked, but her clothes had been piled on top of her, weighted down with stones. On March 6 a third victim was found naked in a ditch, partially covered with earth. And, on April 12, another was discovered out in the nearby veldt. She was fully clothed, but had been strangled with her bra, while another was tied around her wrists. Eight days later the body of her young son, a bloody bruise to his head, was found not far away.

Victim number six was discovered on May 13, strangled with her own clothing. Then the seventh, a few miles north of Atteridgeville on May 25. She was naked. On June 13 yet another woman's body was found, sitting against a tree, still wearing her dress, but her panties and the strap of her handbag tied around her neck. And, on June 26 a badly decomposed woman's body was discovered in the nearby veldt, her hands and ankles tied together.

Pretoria's Murder and Robbery Unit formed a task force on July 17. It included South Africa's first woman profiler, forensic psychologist Micki Pistorius. She drew up a provisional profile of the Atteridgeville Strangler: '. . . [but] the feeling was vague, and I was confused . . . I predicted that he would be in his late 20s. I said he would be a flashy dresser and a sophisticated ladies' man. The murdered women were not prostitutes. They were career women who would not have gone with a derelict, but be more inclined to accompany someone who resembled a businessman. He needed charm to lure them away.'

The day after the task force was formed, another decomposed body was found, fully clothed but strangled with a piece of clothing; and a woman's decomposing corpse was discovered every week for some time after.

During the ensuing investigation, a man was arrested for assaulting a woman in her Atteridgeville home. He claimed to be the 'Strangler' and seemed to know something of the crime scenes. But Pistorius was sure he was not the murderer. Taken to court after two days of interrogation, he confessed that he knew only what he had read in the newspapers.

On September 18, the bodies of eight women were reported near Boksburg prison, in the veldt an hour's drive to the southwest of Pretoria. Most of the bodies were in an advanced state of decomposition; but one was still fresh, and dogs detected two more. This was obviously a dumpsite used by the killer. None appeared to be prostitutes and all were between 20 and 30 years of age, with their hands tied to their necks.

Robert Ressler, the renowned FBI profiler, arrived by invitation on September 23, and spent a long time in conference with Micki Pistorius. He concurred with her profile, and concluded that an earlier series of killings in Cleveland was linked. This gave the press the lead to dub them the 'ABC murders' – 'A' for Atteridgeville, 'B' for Boksburg, and 'C' for Cleveland.

Meanwhile, the police had traced one of the victims to her place of work and obtained from a colleague a description of the man she had last been seen with. Then, in early October, a

Cape Town newspaper, *The Star*, received an anonymous telephone call from 'the man that is so highly wanted'.

He said he had been arrested in 1978 for a crime he did not commit, and had spent 14 years in prison – during which time his parents and a sister had died without him: 'Hurt has been my daily bread, hurt has been my prayer, hurt has been my feelings all the time, hurt has been there every hour, every minute, every second, every day, every week, every month and every year . . . [so] I force a woman to go where I want, and I go there I tell them, "Do you know what? I was hurt, so I'm doing it now." Then I kill them.'

Alerted by a relative, the police found Moses Sithole, a 31-year-old ex-convict and founder of 'Youth Against Human Abuse Organisation', hiding out in Johannesburg on October 18. He wounded an officer with an axe, but was then shot and disarmed.

On October 21, 1996, Sithole appeared in court in Pretoria, charged with 38 murders, 40 rapes and six robberies. His trial finally opened in February 1997, and on December 5 he was found guilty on all counts and sentenced to 2410 years.

Even before Moses Sithole had been traced and apprehended, Micki Pistorius and Robert Ressler had considered that an earlier series of killings in Cleveland showed distinct similarities. In the first years of the 1990s, the strangled bodies of a number of women had been found at a mine dump in Cleveland, south of Johannesburg. In 1994, police arrested David Selepe and charged him with 11 murders. He took them to one of the crime scenes, but was shot and killed when – as police alleged – he attacked a detective with a stick while trying to escape.

Selepe's wife maintained that her husband had been framed, and even threatened to sue the government for his death. She protested: 'They killed the truth when they killed my husband . . . David was not a killer.'

It is now believed, however, that both men collaborated in the Cleveland killings.

IVAN MILAT

BACKPACKER KILLER

On September 19, 1992, expert orienteer Ken Seily took Keith Caldwell for a training course in Belanglo State Forest, which lies between Sydney and Canberra in New South Wales, Australia. It was springtime in the southern hemisphere and the forest, which covers some 40,000 acres, was looking its best. The two men had enjoyed a stimulating hike with map and compass, when they paused for a brief rest at a prominent landmark known as Executioner's Drop. It was then that they were struck by a pervading odour of rotting flesh.

Alerted, the hikers began to look around and, behind a boulder, spotted an unusual pile of forest litter, heaped together as if by hand, with bone and hair protruding. Then they noticed a T-shirt and shoes among the sticks and leaves. Abandoning their orienteering, Ken and Keith made their way as quickly as possible to the forest edge, and called the police by cell phone.

It was dusk by the time the first police officers arrived at the scene, but Seily was able to lead them by torchlight to the site of the discovery, while they had marked the way with reflective tape. Soon they were joined by detectives from nearby Bowral, followed by a scene-of-crime unit and by officers from the regional homicide squad. There was no doubt that a murder had been committed, and calls were immediately made to the Sydney police and the Missing Persons Bureau.

The scene-of-crime officers carefully removed the layers of sticks, and uncovered the almost intact body of a girl, still fully clothed, lying on her stomach. The corpse was delivered to forensic pathologist Peter Bradhurst and he worked through the night on the autopsy. In the cold of the preceding winter, the body had become partially mummified and he was able to observe multiple stab wounds, mostly to the back, and determine that they had been made with a single-bladed knife. Then, the following morning, as he was making out his report, he learnt that investigators searching the murder site in daylight had discovered another body, only 30 yards from the first.

Records of missing persons had by now turned up the names of two British backpackers, Joanne Lesley Walters and Caroline Clarke, both aged 22, who had disappeared five months previously. There were other backpackers reported missing, but by late afternoon the two girls had been positively identified. Caroline had also been stabbed and then shot ten times from three different angles, as if the killer had used her body for target practice. Police were also convinced that Joanne had been sexually assaulted.

Dr Rod Milton, a forensic psychiatrist, was asked for an assessment of the first two murders discovered. He was struck with the way in which Caroline Clarke had been shot so many times: '. . . [it was a] deliberate cold action, with considerable enjoyment on the part of the person who did it . . . Why would someone continue to fire shots into the cranium of a dead person? It suggests an absorption with weapons – weapons for their own sake.'

Finally, Dr Milton came to the conclusion that two people were involved: 'It's very hard to imagine one person carrying out two totally different sets of behaviours (the ferocious stabbing of one victim and the clinical shooting of the other) . . . the deliberate, cold kind of person who seeks power on the one hand, and the explosive, aggressive person on the other.'

A detective from the Forensic Ballistics Unit recovered the bullet shells from the scene and recognized that the gun used was the American-made Ruger 10-22 rifle. Unfortunately, tracing ownership was to prove a mammoth task, as 40,000 of the rifles had been imported into Australia.

After a year, no further clues had been found and the investigation began to wind down. Then, on October 3, 1993, a local man scavenging for firewood in Belanglo Forest discovered a thighbone and a human skull. When detectives arrived, they found, close by, a pile of brush with two shoes sticking from it and a concealed skeleton. The police realized that they likely had a case of serial killing on their hands and mounted a massive search of the woodland. Two days later, two more corpses were found – and within weeks, three others. Pathologist Bradhurst, working with the reports of missing persons, began his long task of identification.

The two years that had elapsed since the killings meant that much physical evidence had rotted away in each case.

FIVE BACKPACKERS IDENTIFIED

Deborah Everist 19: missing from Victoria since 1989, skeleton discovered October 3, 1993. Her bones showed marks of several stabbings and her skull and jaw were fractured. Identified by dental chart and personal jewellery.

James Gibson 19; her companion, skeleton discovered October 3. Violently stabbed in the thorax and upper back, some of his skeletal bones being cut clean in half. His black hat was found nearby but his backpack and camera were picked up by police on the roadside 80 miles away. Positively identified by dental chart.

Simone Schidl 20; German; missing since January 1991, discovered November 1, 1993. Multiple stab wounds to her back, one of which had severed her spinal cord.

Gabor Neugebaue 21; German; missing since December 26, 1991, remains found propped against a tree on November 4, 1993. Gagged and strangled, then shot six times: three shots to the left side of the skull and three to the rear base.

Anja Habschied 20; German; his companion, found in the same sitting position on the same day. Decapitated with a single violent blow and head not found. Lower half of clothing missing suggesting possible sexual assault. Some clothing believed to belong to Anja and Gabor found later the same day, but in the two intervening years it had decayed and could not be positively identified.

The investigators now had eight related murders on the books. Frustrated by the failure of nationwide enquiries into the owners of a Ruger 10-22 rifle, they turned to the local gun club. Members' weapons were examined, without success, but one member told investigators of something odd that had been related to him by a friend.

The friend was named Alex Milat, one of a family of fourteen, their father being a Croatian immigrant married to an Australian woman. Interviewed, Alex said that, a year or two before, he had seen two vehicles driving into the forest. One had two men in the back seat and between them a woman with a cloth tied around her head. The other had one man in the back, beside another woman who also appeared to be restrained. He did not explain why he had not reported the incident.

The police held a press conference and appealed for tip-offs from the public. One woman caller reported that she knew a man who lived near the forest and had a number of guns. His name was Ivan Milat. Another spoke of a man, 'Paul Miller', who had shown unusual knowledge of where the bodies were found. His real name, it turned out, was Richard Milat. It was clearly time to look into the backgrounds of the Milat family.

Ivan Milat seemed a prime suspect, but there was no evidence directly linking him to the seven killings. Then, out of the piles of paperwork that the police had amassed, a report eventually came to light.

Way back on January 25, 1990, a British backpacker named Paul Onions was offered a lift in a silver off-roader by a heavily-built man with a distinctive moustache, who said his name was 'Bill'. Close to Bowral, on the edge of Belanglo Forest, the man braked, pulled out a gun and a length of rope, and announced that this was a hold-up. Onions leapt from the vehicle, ran up the road and managed to persuade the driver of an oncoming car to take him to the police. A statement was taken but he had left his backpack and passport behind, and he was sent at once to Sydney, where he was repatriated by the British High Commission.

THE PRIME SUSPECT

Among the Milat family, the fourth child and one of ten sons, was Ivan Robert Marko, born on December 27, 1944. He was found to have a revealing criminal record. He had left school at the age of 15 and found work with road and construction gangs. However, at 17, in 1962, he had been convicted of theft. Later charges included burglary, car theft and armed robbery. In 1971 he had been charged with rape, picking up two girl hitch-hikers on the highway, driving off-road and threatening to kill them with a knife if they refused to have sex with him. One girl finally agreed, on condition he let them go – so the charge was reluctantly dismissed as she had consented.

Ivan married in the late 1970s and found a house in a western suburb of Sydney. The couple divorced some years later and, in 1992, after receiving a large redundancy payment, Ivan built a house which he shared with his sister. In his neighbourhood he was known as a neat and friendly man, a great favourite with the local children. Little did anyone know of his violent secrets.

It was not until November 13, 1993, that Paul Onions, having read reports of the backpacker murders in the British papers, wondered whether any action had been taken following his complaint. He got through to the hotline in Sydney, was thanked for his call – and heard no more. Five months later, a note of his call surfaced, together with a report filed from the woman who had picked him up on that fateful day. Immediately, a detective telephoned London and arranged for Onions to be flown to Australia.

Taken down the highway from Sydney to Canberra, he was able to point out landmarks on the way and even identify the spot where his horrifying experience had occurred. Next day, back in Sydney, Onions was shown 13 photographs of people who resembled his description of 'Bill'. After some hesitation, he pointed to No. 4: it was Ivan Milat.

Meanwhile, the police had obtained valuable evidence. Ivan Milat had owned a silver off-roader, but had sold it. Cleaning out the car, the new owner had found a bullet – from a Ruger 10-22 – and the wife of Alex Milat had handed over a backpack that she said Ivan had given her. It belonged to Simone Schmidl.

It was time for the investigators to exercise the search warrants they had quietly obtained for every home of the Milat family. In Ivan's house they found a mass of belongings that he had taken from his victims, and they found more in the homes of other members of the family – items that been given to them by Ivan. But the most important find, hidden in a wall cavity, was part of a Ruger 10-22. The barrel was missing, so that rifling marks could not be identified, but the breech-bolt and firing pin were there. Next day, test firings matched these to markings on the shells that had been found by Caroline Clarke's body.

Milat was arrested on May 22, 1994, but his trial, at which he was charged with the seven known murders and the attempted murder of Paul Onions, was not held until the following year. It was Australia's biggest murder hearing, lasting three months and involving around 145 prosecution witnesses and more than 350 gruesome exhibits.

Milat pleaded not guilty and his lawyers suggested further that one or more of his brothers had carried out the killings, and then attempted to frame him. Nevertheless, the jury took only three days to find him guilty on all eight counts.

He was sentenced to life imprisonment on each count, plus six years for the attempt on Paul Onions. The judge ordered that he should never be released.

Some disturbing questions remain. Did Ivan Milat act alone or, as Dr Milton suggested, was he accompanied by someone – even one of his brothers? The detective in charge of the case was sure that some members of his family had at least an inkling that he was 'up to no good'.

The Sydney police have continued efforts to link Milat with other unsolved murders along Australia's eastern coast, but so far without success. Are there more bodies undiscovered out in the bush? Police suspect that there are at least four. Ivan's brother

Boris remarked: 'Everywhere he's worked, people have disappeared. If Ivan's done these murders, I reckon he's done a hell of a lot more.'

Asked how many, Boris suggested: Twenty-eight? While serving his life sentence, he cut off his little finger and otherwise self-mutilated. In 2012, his great-nephew Matthew Milat and his friend Cohen Klein were convicted of a copy-cat killing.

ROBERT PICKTON

THE PIG FARMER

Convicted of the second-degree murder of six women – with another twenty on the books – Robert William 'Willie' Pickton was caught on video in his cell boasting that he had killed 49 and kicking himself that he had not killed one more to make 50. He also bragged that he had disposed of the bodies in the filthy rendering plant on his run-down pig farm near Vancouver.

I n the late 1990s, the police began to notice that women were going missing from Vancouver's notorious Downtown East-side, known as 'Low Track', where prostitutes as young as eleven plied their trade alongside drug addicts and down-and-outs. The inhabits of the so-called 'Low Track' were transients, changing their names and addresses regularly, or simply moving on elsewhere, so for years there was no reason for police suspicions to be raised.

But early in 2008 officers began in earnest to compile a list of missing people as it became apparent that as many as 24 women may have been murdered in the area between 1983 and 1997. Soon, the list was so vast that the authorities set up a cold-case task force to investigate and despite the reluctance of prostitutes, pimps, drugs dealers and users to talk to the police, the list continued to swell.

Then, in July 1998, the task force finally got the break they needed. Bill Hiscox – who worked for a salvage firm owned by brothers Robert 'Willie' and David Pickton and occasionally went to the Pickton brothers' pig farm in Port Coquitlam, just outside Vancouver – came forward to police after reading a newspaper report on Vancouver's missing women. The woman who cleaned Robert Pickton's trailer had recently told Hiscox that she had noticed bags of bloody clothing and women's identification there. The cleaner's disclosure and the report about the Low Track disappearances confirmed Hiscox's longstanding suspicions, raised a year earlier after a stabbing on the farm.

On the 24th March 1997, a couple driving past the pig farm at 1.45 in the morning found a woman partially clothed and covered in blood by the roadside – she had been stabbed several times. This woman, Wendy Lynn Eistetter, a Low Track drug addict and prostitute, had been picked up by Robert 'Willie' Pickton the previous evening. He drove her to the pig farm, handcuffed her and began to stab her repeatedly with a brown-handled kitchen knife. Despite being handcuffed, she managed to grab the knife, stab Pickton and escape. Robert Pickton was charged with attempted murder and a trial date was set. But after Wendy Lynn Eistetter failed to show up in court, the charges were stayed as the attorney-general's office decided 'there was no likelihood of conviction'. Pickton walked free.

Bill Hiscox told the police that Pickton 'frequents the downtown area all the time, for girls' and informed them that: 'All the purses and IDs are out there in his trailer.' However, when the police searched the pig farm – three times according to press reports – they found nothing. Meanwhile the list of missing women continued to grow and four years passed until the police got another break.

On 7 February 2002, Robert 'Willie' Pickton was again arrested, this time for the possession of unregistered firearms after another employee had contacted the police. The task force seized the opportunity to scour the pig farm once again, successfully finding clothing and property belonging to some of the missing women. Pickton was released on bail, but was arrested again on 22 February – this time on two counts of first-degree murder. The victims were identified as Sereena Abotsway and Mona Lee Wilson. Both names were on the Low Track missing list. Partial remains and an asthma inhaler had been found on the farm and on the 8 March, these were conclusively identified through DNA tests as belonging to Sereena. Mona's head, feet and hands were also found. Both had gone missing after Bill Hiscox first reported his suspicions to the police in 1998.

THE PICKTON BROTHERS

The brothers were shunned at school because they were filthy and smelled of pig manure. Willie was said to be 'weird' and 'slow'. When they inherited the farm, they converted an outhouse into the 'Piggy Palace', as a drinking club for local bikers, with 'entertainment' provided by prostitutes from the Low Track – though some were afraid to go there because they had heard stories about a scary guy living in a beaten up truck. A sign outside warned: 'This property is protected by pit bull with Aids.'

The Pickton brothers were already known to the police. As well as Robert's stabbing, David Pickton had been convicted of sexual assault in 1992, fined $1,000 and given thirty days' probation. He had attacked his victim in his trailer at the pig farm, but she managed to escape.

A month later, as more evidence was uncovered, Pickton was charged with three more counts of murder – those of Jacqueline McDonnell, Heather Bottomley and Diane Rock. At the time the police would not say what kind of evidence had been found, but admitted that forensic DNA was part of the investigation. Only six days later, Robert Pickton was also charged with the murder of Angela Josebury. Then on 22 May, a seventh first-degree murder charge was filed against Pickton when the remains of Brenda Wolfe were found on his farm. Again, all these women had gone missing after Hiscox first fingered Pickton. In all, Pickton was charged with 27 counts of first-degree murder.

When his trial began at the British Columbia Supreme Court on 30 January 2006, Pickton pleaded not guilty on all counts. Reviewing the evidence, the judge threw out one of the counts, ruling that Pickton could not be charged with the murder of a woman whose remains had been found, but not been identified.

BUNGLED INVESTIGATION

The question had to be asked, if Pickton was responsible for the abduction and murder of women from the Low Track, why had the searches of the farm in 1997 and 1998 not unearthed any evidence? And how could he have continued to abduct and murder victims afterwards, when he should have been under police surveillance? The authorities were adamant that the evidence had been hard to come by as Pickton went to great lengths to dispose of the bodies. Some had been left out in the open to decompose or be eaten by insects. Others were fed to the pigs on the farm. Forensic anthropologists spent two years and $70 million shifting through the soil on the farm in an attempt to find traces of remains. In March 2004, the authorities said that the victims' flesh may have been ground up and mixed with pork from the farm. This pork was never sold commercially, but fed to visitors to the farm – perhaps even the victims themselves. One witness even said she saw a woman's body hanging from a meat hook while Pickton stripped the flesh from it, but said nothing for fear of her life.

The indictment was then trimmed to just six counts on the grounds that trying all twenty-six charges would put an unreasonable burden on the jury.

During the trial, the jury heard that a victim's jawbone and teeth were trampled into the ground beside the pig-farm's slaughterhouse, skulls cut in half and hands and feet were found in the freezer. The remains of one victim were stuffed in a garbage bag in a dustbin. Her blood-stained clothes were discovered in Pickton's trailer, along with night-vision goggles, two pairs of faux fur-lined handcuffs, the aphrodisiac 'Spanish Fly', a syringe with three millilitres of blue liquid inside, boxes of .357 Magnum handgun ammunition and a loaded .22 revolver with one round fired and a dildo placed, bizarrely, over the barrel. In a videotape played to the jury, Pickton claimed to have used the dildo as a makeshift silencer.

One witness said Pickton had told him a good way to kill a heroin addict was to fill her syringe with anti-freeze. Another testified that Pickton had talked about killing prostitutes by handcuffing and strangling them, then bleeding and gutting them before feeding them to pigs. However, no eyewitness to the murders came forward, so the jury could not find Pickton guilty of first-degree murder. But they did find him guilty of second-degree murder on all six counts presented to them. He was sentenced to life and the judge ruled out any possibility of parole for twenty-five years. This was the maximum sentence allowed under Canadian law. There would be no further prosecutions on the other outstanding charges as further convictions would not increase his sentence.

To the outrage of victims' families, while in jail Pickton wrote his memoirs claiming he was 'the fall guy' for a bungled investigation. These were smuggled out of jail and published. A petition that amassed 50,000 in a matter of hours got the book withdrawn by Amazon and dropped by the publisher.

THE SUFFOLK STRANGLER

Also known as the Ipswich Ripper, Steve Wright was a long-term user of prostitutes, even when he was living with his partner, Pam, who intended to marry him. Then on 30 October 2006, he began murdering them, killing five before he was arrested on 19 December. Pam recalled watching a television news report of the murders with Steve at the height of the killing. She asked: 'What sort of a monster is capable of such crimes', and Wright merely shrugged. After watching *Eastenders*, he dropped her off for her nightshift at a local call centre, then went on to kill again.

On 2 December 2006, the body of a woman was found in a brook at Thorpe's Hill in Suffolk, less than two miles outside Ipswich. The victim was identified as Gemma Adams, a 25-year-old prostitute who had disappeared from Ipswich's red-light district in the early hours of 15 November. The police announced that her friend, 19-year-old prostitute Tania Nicol, had been missing since 30 October. Six days after Gemma's corpse was discovered, Tania's body was found in the same stream, nearby at Copdock Mill. Both were naked, but there was no evidence that they had been sexually assaulted.

The police had already warned Ipswich's sex workers to look out for one another and began checking similar cases in East Anglia to see whether a serial killer was at large. Their fears were confirmed on 10 December when the body of a third victim was found in woodland. It was identified as that of 24-year-old Anneli Alderton from Colchester, Essex who, like the other victims, had worked as a prostitute in Ipswich. Enquiries revealed that her last traceable movement was catching the 5.53 pm train from Harwich to Colchester on 3 December. A passing motorist came forward to the police as he believed he had seen the body beside the road on 7 December, but at the time had thought it was a discarded mannequin and so had not reported. A post-mortem found that she had been asphyxiated and was three months pregnant when she died.

Two days later the police expressed their grave concerns for the safety of another two women – 24-year-old Paula Clennell and Annette Nicholls, aged 29, who had not been seen since the 10th December. The police continued to urge prostitutes to stay off the streets, having already upped their patrols of Ipswich's red light district. Shortly before she went missing, Paula had been interviewed by ITN – she said the killings had made her a bit wary about getting into a punter's car, but she was prepared to face the perils of working on the street.

The police appealed to the killer to give himself up: 'Make contact with Suffolk Police. Clearly you have a significant problem. Give me a call and we can deal with this.' They also appealed to Ipswich's sex workers for information about their clients – and they duly cooperated – as well as to the clients themselves – who were less forthcoming.

On 12 December the bodies of Paula and Annette were found in woodland near the village of Levington, five miles south of Ipswich. Paula had been strangled, while the cause of Annette's death remained unclear.

Six days later, a 37-year-old man, known to girls in the red-light district, was arrested on suspicion of the murder of all five women, and was released without charge. The following morning, the police arrested another man known as a regular by Ipswich's prostitutes: forklift-truck driver Steve Wright was arrested. On further investigation, forensic evidence was found linking Wright and his Ford Mondeo to the murders: seven flecks of blood on the backseat partially matched the DNA profile of Paula Clennell, along with hairs from Annette Nicholls.

Wright refused to respond to questioning by the police – and in court, he pleaded not guilty to the murders, although he admitted having sex with all five victims. At the trial, the jury were shown harrowing pictures of the dead women. After strangling or

WEIRD BEHAVIOUR

Described as 'the most boring bloke in the world' by fellow members of Seckford golf club, Wright masked a tormented private life, including attempted suicide and domestic violence. As well as an addiction to prostitutes, he had a penchant for compulsive gambling, bankruptcy, petty theft and heavy drinking. He was well known to local sex workers, most of whom were afraid to have sex with him because of his weird behaviour and cross-dressing. Some knew him as 'the soldier' because he wore camouflage trousers. Others described how he would cruise the streets dressed in high heels, PVC skirts and a wig. One Norwich prostitute said: 'If you didn't get in the car he would get naked and just sit there with the headlights on. He freaked me out.' However, at home with Pam and her son Jamie, he could not have appeared more normal.

smothering them, Wright had stripped them before dumping their bodies. Two of the women had been posed in the shape of a crucifix. The jury also heard that Wright had been stopped by the police halfway through his killing spree, while driving through the red-light district. He had been released when he told officers that he was just out for a drive and was unaware that he had strayed into the area. They let him go. Two nights later Anneli Alderton vanished and three more women lost their lives.

Summing up after the six-week trial, the judge said: 'You may view with some distaste the lifestyles of those involved . . . whatever the drugs they took, whatever the work they did, no-one is entitled to do these women any harm, let alone kill them.' It took the jury eight hours to find Wright guilty of all five murders and he was sentenced to life imprisonment with a whole-life tariff. Later, he dropped his appeal and ever since he has refused to talk of his motives. His father has since come forward urging him to confess – when confronted by his father, Wright said: 'I can't remember'.

THE VICTIMS

Tania Nicol, 19, worked as a prostitute to fund her addiction to cocaine and heroin. Previously, she had worked in massage parlours, but was sacked for taking drugs. Her mother, a care-home assistant, did not know she was a sex worker. Working under the name Chantelle, Tania was taking up to £50 worth of heroin a night.

Gemma Adams, 25, was from a wealthy middle-class family, but she lost her job at an insurance company for using heroin. Her partner, a fellow addict, knew she was a prostitute; her family did not.

Anneli Alderton, 24, dreamt of becoming a model, but became addicted to drugs at the age of 16 after her father died. She ran away on the day of his funeral. Over the following years she spent four spells in prison for theft and became a mother. Her stepsister said that before going off the rails: 'She was very bright, very intelligent and she made us laugh.'

Annette Nicholls, 29, quit college, where she had been training to become a beautician, when she became addicted to heroin. Her family did not know she was a prostitute until one of them saw her touting for business. She was the mother of one.

Paula Clennell, 24, was the mother of three daughters who had been taken into care. Shortly before she died, she wrote: 'Xmas will never be the same for me again without the girls. For me instead of it being a happy day of joy and togetherness it's only a dark, lonely and depressing day.' Her family said she took to drugs to 'block out the pain'. She told friends that she would be dead before the age of 25.